Level Design for Games

Creating Compelling Game Experiences

D0882275

New Riders Games
New Riders
1249 Eighth Street · Berkeley, CA 94710

Level Design for Games: Creating Compelling Game Experiences

Phil Co

New Riders • 1249 Eighth Street • Berkeley, CA 94710 • 510/524-2178 • 800/283-9444 • 510/524-2221 (fax)

Find us on the Web at: www.newriders.com
To report errors, please send a note to errata@peachpit.com

New Riders is an imprint of Peachpit, a division of Pearson Education

Copyright © 2006 by Phil Co

Project Editor: Kristin Kalning

Compositor: Specialized Composition, Inc.

Production Coordinator: Andrei Pasternak

Indexer: FireCrystal Communications

Copyeditor: Liz Welch

Cover design: Mimi Heft

Tech Editor: Christine Miller

Interior design: Mimi Heft

Proofreader: Liz Welch

Media Producer: Eric Geoffroy

This book is dedicated to my wife, Jocel, and my son, Addison.
Thank you for giving me inspiration every day.

I would also like to dedicate this book to my parents, Victoriano and Silvina,
as well as my siblings, Chris and Gail.
Thank you for all of your support and encouragement throughout my life.

Acknowledgements

To me, this book was a development project, and I was just part of the team. I would like to give a very special thanks to Kristin Kalning, who is mostly responsible for the creation of this book. Thanks also to rest of the book team, especially Christine Miller, Liz Welch, Andrei Pasternak, Marjorie Baer, and Eric Geoffroy.

This book would have been quite empty if not for the many people who contributed materials to it, especially Justin Chin, Tim Schafer, and Erik Robson. Special thanks to id Software, Double Fine Productions, Lucasarts, Electronic Arts, Flagship Studios, and Valve Software for permitting me to use materials from their products in this book. And finally, we thank Mark Rein of Epic Games for allowing us to use the Unreal Editor.

I've had the pleasure of working with some of the greatest artists in the industry. Thanks to all of these artists who have created pieces for this book, including Cory Allemeier; Peter Chan; Steve Chen; Oscar Cuesta; Ron Kee; Mike Khoury; Yujin Kiem; and Alex Munn.

Many different people have helped and taught me over the years. I owe everything to my friends and co-workers at:

Cyclone Studios: Jennifer Hubbart, Yujin Kiem, Maarten Kraaijvanger, Brian Lippert, Ron Little, Owen Lockett, Kerry Moffit, Erik Robson, Greg Savoia, Fred Selker, and Daryl Tung.

Infinite Machine: Cory Allemeier, Justin Chin, Stephen Hwang, Steve Kalning, Japeth Pieper, Matt Tateishi, and Trey Turner.

Knowwonder: Ed Byrne, Ben Coleman, Crista Forest, Elijah Emerson, Greg MacMartin, and Christopher Vuchetich.

Blizzard North: Oscar Cuesta, Colin Day, Jeff Gates, Jeff Kang, Charlie Lapp, Victor Lee, Steve Librande, Julian Love, Alex Munn, Jason Regier, Cory Rogers, Tod Semple, Marc Tattersal, and Grant Wilson.

Valve: Dario Casali, Steve Desilets, Bill Fletcher, Brian Jacobson, Gabe Newell, Dave Sawyer, David Speyrer, Robin Walker, and Josh Weier.

And elsewhere: Rachael Bristol, Steve Chen, Lloyd Kinoshita, Joe McCloud, Rob Pardo, and Han Yi.

Table of Contents

Introduction

This Is Work?

When you were growing up, were Lego, Lincoln Logs, and building blocks your favorite toys? Did you ever drape a huge blanket across the furniture in your bedroom so you could make a tent? Did you look forward to going to the beach so you could make a sand castle big enough for you to crawl inside? Was there a tree house or a clubhouse in your backyard that you either built yourself or helped build? Did your family members have to weave around obstacles in your living room that you fashioned out of cushions and chairs? If you have answered "yes" to any of these questions, you're not alone. Plenty of other people like to design and build things straight from their imaginations. Plenty of people do it for a living. I should know—I'm one of them.

Only 15 years ago, people like us did not have many career choices. I chose to study architecture, since it involved planning and designing structures that real people would move in, around, and through. Still, architecture didn't offer me the same satisfaction I'd experienced as a kid, building my forts and playing with Lego. The focus in architecture is to design solid, structurally sound, and functional buildings, not challenging playgrounds. I graduated with my degree, but I was still waiting for something else to come along.

Around the same time, the video game industry started to grow. Many games featured more than just simple mazes and flat landscapes as a form of game progression. Games became much more complex as graphics, technology, and design evolved. Game companies needed people to design and build *levels*, which are the spaces and environments in video games. I could become one of those people, I realized. My Lego days were not over; I could become a level designer.

The Level Designer

So, what is a *level designer*, exactly? Level designers create the spaces and environments that you move through and experience as you play video games. And while the volume, complexity, and style of levels vary from project to project, most level designers model and arrange architectural elements as well as create various forms of obstacles.

Level designers are an integral part of every stage in the game development cycle, and they work closely with the entire team. Level designers work with artists to make the spaces and experiences look as compelling as possible for the player. Together, the programmers and level designers push the limits of the technology in pursuit of more efficient, more believable, and more distinguished environments. Level designers also work closely with the game designers—the people responsible for the game's difficulty and balance—to fill the levels with challenges while ensuring that the players feel a sense of progression and accomplishment.

Designing a level also involves thinking from a player's point of view. You don't have to be a hard-core gamer, spending hours and hours in front of your computer or console. But it's important to have played video games, and have an appreciation of what's enjoyable and what's not. Keep in mind, though, that fun is a subjective term. It's also important for you to be interested in hearing feedback from gamers who play your levels. You won't know how fun a level truly is until you let others play it and listen to their comments.

It's important to have patience, both with other people and with yourself. Things might not work out the way you envision, but you'll need to continue despite difficulties and setbacks. For instance, a programmer might tell you that a feature is technically impossible after you had planned for it as a major portion of your level. A designer might tell you that the level is too long and you have to cut out portions of it. Or a tester might tell you that the level is too difficult to complete. Like all members of the team, and like people in other creative fields, level designers need patience to understand what the issues are and how to fix them. Also, nowadays levels take a lot of time to complete. You may have days in which you stare at your screen trying to figure out a solution—and the only one that makes any sense is starting over again.

Level designers are not typically artists by training, but they should have an artistic eye to be able to determine what looks good and what fits in a certain location. And although most level designers don't have a technical background, they should have an appreciation for and basic knowledge of the technology available for game developers. But most important, level designers should have an open mind, an active imagination, determination to continue until the end, and a passion for games.

How Do I Get This Job?

The video game industry is growing, but it is also relatively young. Most people are completely in the dark about how a game is developed and who is involved in the process. So if you're interested in getting into games professionally, or even if you've been in the business for a while, you'll find this book valuable because it describes the game development process through the eyes of a level designer.

Level design is a good place to start in the video game industry. It's a position that people can train for without a lot of investment. You can even get into level design as a hobby. Level editors, which are programs used to create levels, are sometimes bundled with commercial games, or you can download one from the Internet. Anyone can make a level and submit it to a game company for consideration. This book helps you gain the experience you need to put your best foot forward.

What's Inside This Book?

A room or a space in a game can start out as an empty box, but empty boxes are boring. Level designers are responsible for making them interesting. Visually, you must imagine how an area might look before you actually build it. Artists can give you a sketch to help you along, but they can't sketch out the entire game. Designers or writers can provide you with a verbal description of an event, but they might need you to envision how that event takes place in the game.

Level designers use various tools in their work, typically starting with pencil and paper. But once you move beyond the initial conceptual stage, you'll need software to plot out and build your levels. This software is called the *level editor*. Level editors vary in function and method. Some are a complete 3D modeling package that allows you to create intricate pieces and details, while others take pieces and details from other programs and simply arrange them to put levels together. UnrealEd, Epic Games' level editor for the Unreal game series, is somewhere in between. You can use UnrealEd to model simple geometry, apply textures and lighting, and place objects and details.

In this book, you'll be using a runtime demo version of UnrealEd, which is included on the accompanying CD. You'll also find sample maps that demonstrate some of the building practices used in UnrealEd, sample textures in different themes, and sample static meshes you can place in your level.

Sometimes, it's very difficult to start creating something when you're given a completely blank slate. The CD also contains concept art created by industry artists that you can use to inspire your creations.

Over the course of the next ten chapters, you will be able to create a level that fits into a realistic project. Before we start, though, let's establish a context for the level inside the game, the game as a project, and your role within that project. On to Chapter 1!

CHAPTER 1
How Do You Make a Game?

THE LEVEL DESIGNER PLAYS a key role in the overall process of game development. But what is the overall process? How does an idea move from paper, and to development, and finally, to store shelves?

In this chapter, I'll describe a typical game-development process, but keep in mind that the specifics will vary, depending on the company, the team, and the game.

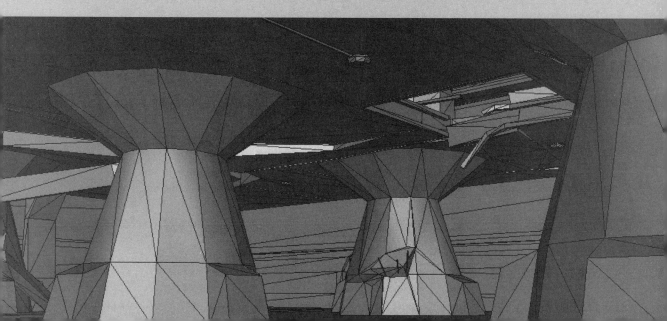

Every game-development project is unique. The length of the project, the structure of the team, and the process of development all depend on aspects of the game itself. For example, if a game is based on a popular movie license, it's best if the game is on store shelves when the movie is released in theaters. That way, the marketing machine can promote the license as a package instead of trying to sell the movie and the game as separate products. This can often limit the development cycle to a shorter period of time and the game itself may be limited to the story and characters of the movie.

On the other hand, some other games, like Bungie Software's Halo, are completely original. Bungie hoped to establish the first Halo game as a franchise, with enough consumer interest to support at least one sequel. In these cases, the team is wise to take more time to develop something unique and different.

How Long Does It Take to Make a Game?

A project can take anywhere from six months to six years from concept to completion. These time periods are probably extreme, but they are certainly not uncommon. Some companies simply have different philosophies (and budgets). An existing game, particularly one that still has its team, structure, technology, and art in place, could be an example of a shorter project. On the other hand, a project that lacks a full team for the crucial initial development phase might find its ship date pushing out further and further.

To add even more variation to the process, development teams at game companies change from project to project. During the brief period of time when a game ships and the next one is started, some team members move on to other teams, other companies, or other careers. Some team members may shift into other positions either horizontally or vertically. In addition, games constantly need new content, new technology, and new gameplay. Even sequels of the same franchise must focus on improvements and variations to sell more units. The dynamic of the game-development process is what makes every project special.

Typically, the game-development process consists of two main parts: preproduction and production. During the preproduction phase, the project moves from an idea in someone's head to an organized plan to make that idea a game that will appear on store shelves. The plan undoubtedly changes and grows as the project moves into the production phase, but having an initial plan can save time and money later. During the production phase, the development team puts the plan into action by creating content and technology. At the end of production, the game is complete and ready for the public. **Figure 1.1** gives an overview of the entire game-development process.

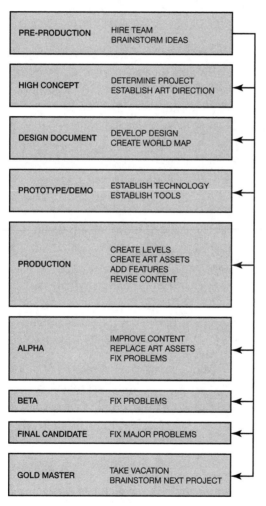

FIGURE 1.1 As you'll notice in this diagram, the production phase represents a much larger percentage of the total process. What happens in preproduction, however, is just as important.

Preproduction: Getting Ready

During preproduction, members of the team prepare all of the elements that are involved in the game-development process. At the beginning, the only element available may be the initial idea for the game. This idea gets fleshed out into detailed descriptions that are then collected into a single document. The team uses this document throughout the development process as an outline for the entire game.

Game-development projects require a vast amount of resources. Some of these resources are assets that need to be built, including the geometry, textures, and animations for both backgrounds and characters. It is important to establish the workflow, or the "asset pipeline," to have a consistent and efficient process for content creation. Another resource, and by far the most important resource of game-development, is the development team, and having the right team is critical to creating a quality game.

Go team!

For any given game, the team will most likely consist of the following departments: programming, art, and design. The programming team typically consists of programmers and scripters, and these are the people responsible for the game's technology. The art team, which is in charge of the game's visuals, may consist of character artists, background artists, animators, technical artists, and concept artists. And finally, the design team (which includes the game designers and level designers) is tasked with figuring out how the game will be played.

Most of the positions are filled during the beginning of the preproduction phase, and *leads* are put into place to manage their groups. Leads are just that—the "leaders" of the project. Usually, every department on the team has a lead, and the project itself has a project leader. You can see a sample structure of a development team in **Figure 1.2**.

Similar to a film director, the project leader is usually the person responsible for the overall vision of the project. This vision starts with the high concept.

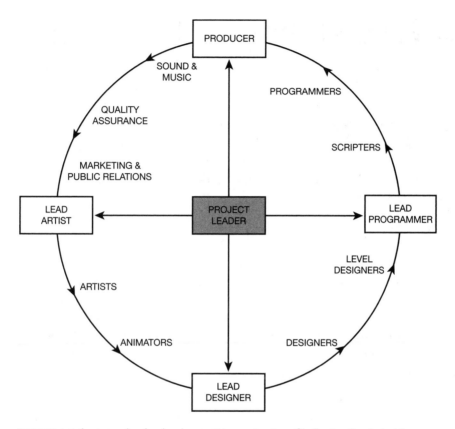

FIGURE 1.2 An example of a development team structure. Similar to other industries, managers are responsible for the members of their groups. Developers are individual contributors who perform the tasks on their schedules and report to their managers. Some positions aren't necessarily above or below others. For example, producers can work parallel to project leads to help with certain tasks.

The high concept

Before any work can begin on the game, the team must understand some elements of the overall vision. During preproduction, several very important questions are raised about the project. What kind of game is it? What's the game about? How is the game played? Who is this game for? How many copies do we want to sell? The high concept is essentially a broad description of the game that answers these questions.

Actual High Concept Example from Requiem: Avenging Angel

Requiem: Avenging Angel is a real-time, first-person action game combining hot-blooded combat with sophisticated problem solving. The visceral thrill or combat that comes from playing first-person shooters is undeniably addictive. But, in most first-person shooters, this thrill is offset by the fact that in a single-player game, the constantly twitchy action and the simple artificial intelligence (or AI) becomes repetitive and boring. Requiem: Avenging Angel is an intelligent shooter combining that visceral thrill with stronger AI, interaction with realistic nonenemy characters, and an engaging story.

Determining the high concept may be up to the project leads. In other cases, a publisher has initiated the high concept and has shopped around to find a developer capable of bringing the idea to fruition. In either case, the project lead is responsible for the articulation of the high concept and must ensure that this vision is carried through in every facet of the game. On a daily basis, this usually involves playing through versions of the game (once the game is in a playable state) and approving content and design.

Of course, at this early stage, much of the high concept is not set in stone. However, these early decisions provide a necessary framework for the entire project. Once the high concept has been defined, the project and department leaders start to outline and document the ideas for the game.

The design document

The design document is the blueprint for the game. It describes in specific terms how the game will be played and what the game should contain when it is completed. The design document includes the high concept, but it also dissects the high concept down to individual pieces: What is the scope of the game and how many levels will it have? What is the overall look and feel of the game? What sort of technology best suits the game?

As you might imagine, a document of this scope requires input from the entire team. At some small companies, every member of the team can submit ideas for a game. But in most cases, members of the team communicate through the lead designer and the producer. The lead designer heads up the design team and usually maintains the design document, although he or she can certainly assign parts of the document to other designers on the team. The producer is basically the person who helps everyone do their job as efficiently as possible. In most companies, the producer also handles the schedule, quality assurance, hiring, and personnel issues. A producer can help collect and organize ideas from the team and pass them along to the lead designer. They regularly meet with individual team members to discuss thoughts or concerns about the project.

As the design document becomes more complete, the producer schedules meetings with team members who are directly involved with each part of the design to go over the individual tasks and assets that need to be implemented. **Figure 1.3**, on the next page, shows how a player might navigate through a game's menus. A producer would take this diagram to a programmer to make sure it's reasonable, and get time estimates for all of the steps involved. The producer can take this same diagram to an artist for their input. If any issues crop up with either the programmer or artist, the producer can communicate with the lead designer what changes need to be made. Once the design is agreed upon, a schedule can be created, and work can begin.

No matter how well you plan, some game aspects can be changed, rethought, or thrown out once the game starts production. This is to be expected. But this document serves as a stake in the ground—a detailed, thought-out starting point for the team.

Game Designers vs. Level Designers

Game designers are sometimes level designers, and vice versa. Some teams have designated game designers who are responsible for the game's balance, flow, and even story and dialogue. They can work with level designers to help place enemies and set up events that are supposed to take place in certain areas.

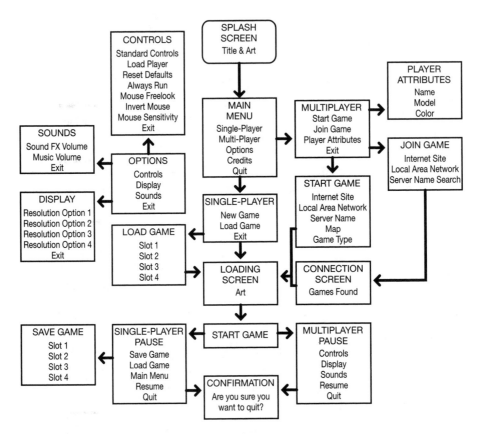

FIGURE 1.3 This diagram shows all of the menus a player might encounter in a game, from the first splash screen to the save game screen. A menu diagram is just a small piece of the design document.

Creating the game world

One key component of the design document is the world diagram. Also known as a mission flow chart, the world diagram (**Figure 1.4**) maps out all of the levels in the game, as well as the general order of these levels.

During preproduction, level designers frequently meet with the lead designer to come up with the world diagram. Because the world diagram contains all the levels in the game, level designers can use it to determine the scale of each level. If a game only has 10 levels as opposed to 20, those 10 levels will be noticeably larger in scale and will need to contain more content.

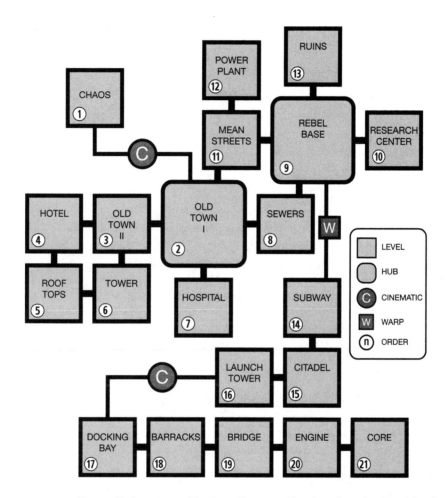

FIGURE 1.4 The world diagram used for the action game Requiem: Avenging Angel developed by Cyclone Studios and The 3DO Company. The world diagram shows a simple, abstract representation for each level. The levels themselves could be larger or smaller, depending on the objectives.

World diagrams usually start out as a list of locations and objectives. Changes of scenery during a game add variety and a sense of progression for the player. Since these scenery changes will involve development down the line, the game designers start listing these potential locations very early on. Players also like to experience slight changes in gameplay as they advance forward in a game. In game designer terms, these slight changes amount to a set of objectives for the player. For example, the first level could require the player to rescue a hostage, and the next level could ask the player to escort that hostage to a safe location. By determining which locations match certain objectives, the designers can seam the entire game together through a world diagram.

For some projects, the levels in the world diagram need to act in parallel to the game's story. Certain plot points are essential to the story's development and may require levels to be constructed around them. Games based on movie licenses operate in this way.

Levels: The meat of the game

After the world diagram has been developed, the levels get assigned to individual level designers. Typically, the level designers divide up the levels equally. At this point, the level designers can start putting those creative wheels in motion, brainstorming ideas for their respective levels.

> **NOTE** Although level designers take ownership of certain levels, they may rotate the levels to bring a fresh perspective. On Requiem: Avenging Angel, our level design team rotated levels halfway through the production process. One designer concentrated on lighting, one designer added more puzzle elements, and another took more time to place enemies and balance gameplay. This also helped make the levels more consistent.

Level designers use the design document as a guide to create a level diagram for each level in the game. A level diagram is a drawing that shows the areas the player will progress through; it may also describe events that take place in each area. Depending on the project, level diagrams can be extremely detailed and thorough, or they can be vague and abstract. Simple diagrams, like the one in **Figure 1.5**, give a basic understanding of the level progression and outline the major areas and level objectives.

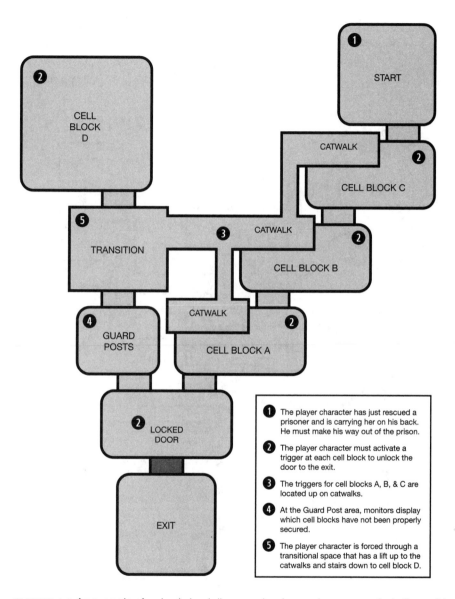

FIGURE 1.5 An example of a simple level diagram, showing a prison rescue. As in the world diagram, spaces are represented by abstract shapes that may or may not be properly scaled.

More detailed level diagrams can dissect the level even further to zoom in on the geometry of spaces and the elements of puzzles (**Figure 1.6**). These kinds of level diagrams may allow the development team to analyze the levels more closely— and identify potential problems—before the level designers start to build them.

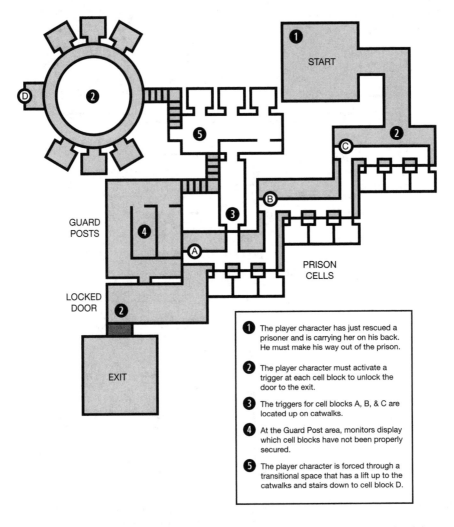

FIGURE 1.6 In this detailed level diagram, the shapes of the spaces are more defined than those in Figure 1.5, and the diagram appears almost like an architectural drawing of the level. In this figure, the shapes and scale of the cell blocks represent the geometry that the level designer plans on creating.

Level designers tend to work on their level diagrams separately, but they frequently meet to go over them with the lead designer and other members of their team. Together, they can compare notes, share ideas, and make sure the levels are consistent with the high concept, the design document, and other level diagrams.

The Lead Level Designer

Some development teams are large enough to merit having a lead level designer. The lead level designer will not only manage the rest of the level designers, but also set the pace, workflow, and style for the level design team. He or she might create the first level diagram that others can use as a model for the remaining levels. Some lead level designers also build a "sandbox" level, or a simple test area, to help establish measurements like door widths and jump heights. The sandbox level can also help to identify potential problems before the level designers start their work.

Defining the look and feel

While the design work is going on, the art team is busy working out the concepts and reference materials for the visuals of the game. For example, if you're planning a fantasy adventure game (more on themes and genres in Chapter 2), your artist will want to collect reference materials from books and movies to make sure the visuals are accurate. After poring over this material, concept artists will work closely with the art director or lead artist to define the vision of the game. The end result is concept art, as seen in **Figure 1.7**, on the next page.

Although not all of the art assets in a game require that concepts be created for them, the concepts can help make the visuals consistent and may save time later on.

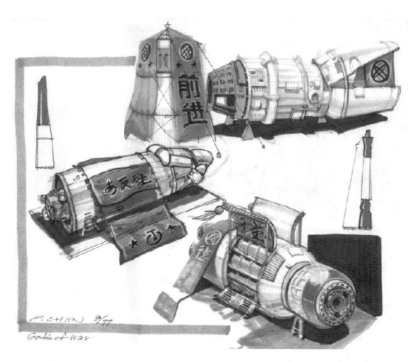

FIGURE 1.7 Concept art for the rocket train level in New Legends, an action game developed by Infinite Machine and THQ. Although a drawing like this one concentrates on specific objects in the level, the overall style for an area can still be carried across.

The Lead Artist

The lead artist manages the overall art team. The lead artist works with the concept artist to get verbal and graphical descriptions of the characters and backgrounds of the game. The lead artist also collaborates closely with the lead designer and level designers to get a sense of the overall game world and levels.

Some projects divide the art team into smaller, more specific teams, which could include a character art team, a background art team, and an animation team. In most cases, each group would have its own lead, so an art director would likely take responsibility over the entire art department.

Developing technology

As the artists are defining the look and feel of the game, and the designers are determining gameplay and game mechanics, the programming team is busy figuring how to make the vision a reality. At this stage, the lead programmer works with graphics programmers to create the "engine," which is the program that runs the game and displays the visuals.

> **NOTE** Many developers license technology from other developers. Buying a ready-made engine from a developer saves time, but the programming team will need to learn how to plug that third-party technology into their own.

The game's engine grows as the project gets further into development. Design and graphical features are added as the overall design and vision for the game is more clearly defined. For example, if the art team wants to add fog to an area, the programming team will need to implement fog as a feature.

The design document should outline a list of design and graphical features, and based on this list, the lead programmer will begin to assign various tasks to the programming team. Of course, all of the features in a game may not be present in the design document. Some of the best game features are often ideas from the team that pop up when the game is already in production.

Near the end of preproduction, the programming team may put together a demonstration to show the engine in its early stages. This demonstration can be as simple as a character running around a room or landscape, or as complex as two players competing against each other in an arena.

Developing the engine for the game is just one part of the technology side of preproduction. The development tools are another part. They allow the rest of the team to start creating content for the game.

The asset pipeline

Every game contains content or *assets*, which are general terms that describe art, animation, levels, and effects in a game. There are many different ways to create content for a game. For example, artists and animators might use any number of three-dimensional (3D) programs to create models and animations, and these assets must be imported into the game's engine. That's where development tools come into play.

Just as there are many ways to create content, there are lots of ways to bring that content into the game. Tools programmers are responsible for content creation tools such as *level editors* for level designers and *exporters* and *importers* for artists to transfer content from other programs to the game.

The rules and standards by which all content is created and brought into the game are referred to collectively as the *pipeline*. In order for the workflow to be its most efficient, it's ideal for all artists, designers, and programmers to have a consistent set of tools and a standard process.

> **NOTE** Assets should not flow through just one team member, or he runs the risk of becoming a bottleneck. Instead, all members of the art team should understand the pipeline process, and one team member may be designated as the point person for the pipeline. For example, if the levels are created in a 3D modeling program and imported into the game engine, any of the level designers or background artists should be able to perform the process.

Establishing the pipeline should take place early on in the development cycle so that the team can start creating content. Because this pipeline impacts both artists and programmers, the lead programmer and the lead artist typically work together to come up with a workflow.

Presentation

These days, many commercial games are developed by one company, but published by another. For example, Double Fine Productions, a small studio in San Francisco, developed the game Psychonauts, but the game was published and distributed by Majesco Entertainment. Publishers provide financing, marketing, and distribution for the development studios. In return, the publishers require the developers to meet certain deadlines known as *milestones*. One of the first milestones in the lifetime of a project may include a full presentation of the game's design document and the level diagrams, as well as a demonstration of the game's technology and a description of the asset pipeline.

Self-publishing developers also tend to call for a formal presentation before moving forward. And since commercial games require a significant investment of time, money, and human resources, it makes sense for the team to have a very solid plan for the game's production before getting started.

Production: The Main Course

Once the high concept, the design document, the art direction, the technology, and the tools have been established, the production phase can begin. Teams can begin to use the design document as a companion guide to create content and features throughout production. Of course, the design document is a living document that can (and often will) change over the course of production.

Although the art, programming, and design teams will proceed along different paths, they should all receive constant direction from the leads and the producers. Production is the longest phase of the development process, but if the project has been planned out thoroughly during the previous phases, everything should fall into place fairly easily. From the design document and level diagrams, the design team will start building the levels. The early versions of the levels will be created quickly so that the design elements can be evaluated. Most or all of the technical features will be in place to test the level accurately. Once approved, the levels will go through an art pass to integrate the visual styles defined by the art team. Other elements will be added to the levels to make them complete.

Sampling the core gameplay

Gameplay is the general term used for how the game is played. Does the player control an army of soldiers to defeat another army? Does the player control a character that walks around and collects items? Can players control opposing fighting characters? Every game has its own unique gameplay, and most production phases start with a simplistic version of that gameplay to build upon. This simplistic version is sometimes called the *core* gameplay.

The first objective during production is to build one prototype level that shows examples of the core gameplay. The team focuses on developing that one level to a near-complete state. This level becomes a kind of prototype for the rest of the game and can be used to demonstrate the game's technology, visual style, and innovative design. The core gameplay tends to grow with the game, and the prototype level can even show a taste of how that will happen.

> **NOTE** Level designers don't always build levels in the order they are supposed to be played. The first level of a game is often the most difficult to design because it needs to gradually introduce several elements of the game to players.

The project leads and the producers will go over the design document and the level diagrams, and then decide which level should be the prototype. They also determine a list of tasks that will have to be completed and a schedule for those tasks. Creating a prototype level usually involves the entire team. The art team starts with the art pieces in the level, modeling, texturing, and animating them. The programming team starts implementing the gameplay features necessary to play the level. The design team begins building the level geometry.

Level Geometry

The level geometry is essentially the 3D model of the level. It can be built in a 3D modeling package or with a level editor. The level geometry defines the spaces in a level—where the character can walk, jump, fall, or climb.

The level designer responsible for the prototype level uses the level diagram as a base to make a template, or "block mesh," of the level. This is essentially a rough draft. Someone can play through the level from beginning to end to get a feel for what the level will be like. The geometry is simple, with no extraneous details (**Figure 1.8**).

At this point, the art can be *placeholder*, which means it will be replaced later down the line. Some functionality, like a puzzle, a special feature, or a scripted event, may be missing at this stage, but the level designer should make room for this functionality to be added later.

> **NOTE** For this first prototype level, it is not uncommon for the level design team to work together on pieces of the same level. Many aspects of the process hinge on this prototype and the schedule should be aggressive to solidify many issues.

FIGURE 1.8 A simple ramp created in Maya. During the template phase of building a level, stairs can be represented with ramps. This saves time and gets the ideas across without wasted effort.

As a level designer, you can enlist other members of the larger team to help you develop the prototype level. Scripters, which are a type of programmer, often help level designers and designers create scripted sequences, which are special events based on specific areas. For example, in the action game Half-Life 2, developed by Valve Software and Sierra, the player controls a character named Gordon Freeman. The game contains scripted sequences where Gordon's friends speak directly to him when he enters a room to describe his next mission or objective. At other points in the game, enemy soldiers drop down on wires when Gordon passes through certain sections of a level. Scripters and level designers set up these sequences to achieve the desired effect.

> **NOTE** Occasionally, level designers and designers must script their own events. Scripters can develop a scripting language that simplifies the process. A scripting language typically creates a user-friendly interface to edit programming commands.

Once the prototype level is in a completed template form, it is ready for initial testing and feedback. In most cases, the entire team will put together a *build*, a version of the most current game code and assets, for play testing. Initial play testing usually happens within the team or within the company, although it is fairly common to bring in external testers at this stage. Most of the time, the team will play the template version of the level and submit comments, usually into a database. The level designer can choose to be a spectator and watch players go through the level in person, or wait to read the submitted comments without physically witnessing the play test session.

After the level designers have received feedback and has played through the template enough to know problems or issues, they can start to change elements of the level for improvement. This modification can include *balancing*, or adjusting the game's difficulty.

When the team is satisfied with the gameplay in the prototype level, they can turn their attention to making it look and feel more like a finished product. The level can be passed on to the artists, who will give it final textures, models, and lighting.

Integrating the visuals

A game's visual appeal is a huge selling point. As any game developer will tell you, the "art style" of a game is a hugely important decision, since art makes up most of the content in a game. All game art—character art, background art, and user interface elements (such as the heads-up display, maps, loading screens and menus)—must be consistent with this overall art style. Usually, these different art assets are created by different people or teams, but on smaller teams, artists may be more cross-functional. The overall art team creates character and background assets, animations, and effects that can enhance the prototype level to something the entire team is proud of.

Character artists focus on the characters in the game—the actors who move and who the player may control. Character artists start by building a character model from a concept art piece in a 3D modeling program; some character artists also paint and texture their models to add depth. Artists "paint" their models by applying a 2D image on parts of the model—almost like cutting out sheets of wallpaper and pasting them to flat pieces of the character. They use software like Adobe Photoshop and Corel Painter to create the images.

Once a character has been modeled and textured, it needs to be set up, or "rigged," for animation. Rigging a model is like forming a skeleton inside the character and assigning joints that an animator can work with. Most teams have a technical artist who can rig all the models. This frees up the artists, and also ensures that the models are set up consistently for the animators.

Technical Artists

Technical artists are relatively new to the game-development pipeline, but they have become increasingly more important. In fact, many teams have more than one technical artist, particularly if the project is ambitious or the schedule is intense. Technical artists work closely with the tools programmers to make the asset pipeline as smooth as possible. They can also implement scripts for external modeling packages specific for the project.

Like character artists, background artists also use concept art to craft environments. Background artists also work with level designers to make the levels visually complete, and are therefore usually assigned to a level. The roles of the background artist and level designer vary. Sometimes, the level designer will provide a template to the background artist who will assume ownership of the level until completion. Most of the time, however, the background artist will take a pass at the level, integrating models, textures, lighting, and other details before returning it to the level designer. **Figure 1.9**, on the next page, shows what the ramp from Figure 1.8 might look like after a pass from a background artist.

The background artists, like character artists, create background models in a 3D modeling program like Maya, 3ds Max, or Softimage XSI. Background artists can also paint textures for both the level geometry and the background models. Of course, the lead artist will need to give his or her approval to the background art to ensure it is consistent with the overall art style.

FIGURE 1.9 The ramp from Figure 1.8 has been converted to stairs. Some of the level geometry can be rebuilt by the background artist to add complexity and detail, but most of the level should stay within the restrictions set by the template and revisions. Level designers and background artists often build and revise levels over several passes until completion.

Characters and backgrounds can look stale and lifeless without animation. Animators literally give life to characters and background pieces. Usually, the producer will work with both the lead artist and the lead designer to come up with a list of animations for every character. From there, the animators will take one character and create a base set of animations for it. For most action games, a base set of animations for an enemy includes an idle (standing and waiting) animation, a walk/run animation, an attack animation, a "take damage" (get hurt) animation, and a death animation.

Once this base set is complete, the animator will add some variations and special animations to make the characters seem more realistic. For example, when a player character punches an enemy soldier, the standard "take damage" animation might have the enemy soldier being knocked back by the blow. The game can seem plastic if the player sees the same animations over and over, so the animator might create a special animation that shows the enemy solider bending forward after a second punch. These little touches add a lot of depth to a game.

Level Textures

Texturing levels presents a unique set of challenges for the background artist. Given unlimited time and computer processing power, every piece of geometry in a level would have a unique texture. However, due to time and hardware constraints, every level has a preset texture "budget," which is how much memory is allowed to be taken up by level textures. As a result, the background artist needs to be very smart about how he balances this texture budget versus visual quality.

In order to texture a level more efficiently, artists create tiled textures, like a brick wall or a city street, that repeat across many surfaces. Occasionally, a level designer will break up the repetition with a variation of the tiled textures. For example, a tile of grass might have patches of dirt for variation.

Integrating the audio

Much like watching a film, playing a game would feel incomplete without sounds and music. A strategically placed sound effect can cause a player to jump out of his seat or laugh out loud. For example, in Capcom's horror game, Resident Evil 4, zombies yell out a specific cry when they are near. When the players hear this cry, they know that they need to get ready to defend themselves. The musical score in a game can also get adrenaline pumping at key moments or signal that something is about to happen.

The sound designer will often work with the artists and designers to develop sounds and music for the prototype level. As the level nears completion, the level designers and game designers will compile the list of sounds that will be needed for the level. Special objects, like a clock tower, might require a unique sound while more common pieces, like doors, can share the same sound. The sound designer might provide the design team with a batch of preliminary sounds to use until the level geometry has been finalized. This early work helps to establish the audio standard for the rest of the game.

Characters require sounds for everything from the footsteps on the different surfaces of ground to the dialogue they speak. Backgrounds require two kinds of sounds: ambient and triggered. An *ambient* sound is a sound that plays in the background, such as wind blowing or water running. A *triggered* sound is something that the player causes to start, such as a floorboard creaking or a door opening.

The music is added on top for the final touch. These days, the music score is typically outsourced to a third party. There are a few in-house composers and musicians who create music for select titles, but they are quite rare. Usually, the producer handles the communication between the team and the music department or outside composer.

> **NOTE** Music is not necessary for the prototype level but it can make a huge difference. Developers often use existing music to give an idea or base for the musical direction in the prototype level.

Rinse and repeat

The prototype level should put all the facets of the game together into one neat container. Of course, the level is by no means complete. It will need some revisions later on in the process, but it provides a much-needed example for the team to work against in the coming months (or years!).

Once the prototype level is complete, small groups of levels proceed through the same route until all of the levels meet this standard. Depending on the time remaining in the schedule, the team can go back and look at content that needs improving.

> **NOTE** At any point during production, content can be cut from the game. Even after creating just the first level, development times can be calculated for the remaining levels, and the leads and producers may decide that the project is too ambitious.

Alpha

You've probably heard the term *alpha* to describe a phase of software development. In game development, alpha means that the game is feature-complete and can be played from beginning to end. This doesn't mean that the game or all the levels are complete. In fact, the alpha stage implies that there is still a lot of work to do: Some art assets and sounds will be placeholders, and there can still be a lot of bugs affecting the gameplay or visuals. It's at this critical point that the testers, or the quality assurance (QA) department, steps into the process.

Once the game is in alpha, it's ready to test. The lead tester, who manages the QA team, establishes a test plan for the game. This test plan breaks down the game levels into small, manageable areas for testers to play through and verify that they're bug-free. Testers submit errors through a bug database, and the development team will fix the bugs that relate to their specific tasks. Once a critical mass of errors has been fixed, the programmers create another build of the game, and QA retests the latest build.

My First Job in the Game Industry

The build-and-fix phase starts in alpha and continues until the game ships. It is important to keep the bug database under control at all times to allow for further testing and feedback. Testers are usually assigned specific areas to test during the alpha phase and, in effect, become masters of these areas. Testers can also submit design suggestions and improvements early in the alpha stage, and they can give feedback to the level designers on specific levels and balancing issues.

QA can be a great place to start in the game industry. I worked as a tester for two different companies before I became a level designer. Most of the testers I worked with went on to become producers, but some went into other areas of development.

Level designers typically check the bug database every day. Some entries in the database reveal issues that require level designers to "optimize" parts of their levels, which will help them run more smoothly. Optimizing a scene can include rebuilding with simpler geometry, using fewer textures, or even removing some decoration that does not contribute to the gameplay. The Buddha statue in **Figure 1.10**, on the next page, had to be remodeled and textured several times for performance reasons.

FIGURE 1.10 This area in New Legends featured an enormous Buddha statue that the player character fought around. The statue had to be rebuilt several times before the game could progress out of alpha stage.

During alpha, the artists and level designers take a final pass on all of the levels and characters. Some levels may require more details and "eye candy" (the visual elements that really "pop" in a level). These additional elements make the game appear more polished, but the refinements could conceivably go on forever. So, the producers set a "lockout" date during the alpha phase, which means that no new art can be added to the game. Once the lockout date is reached, the artists can only fix bugs or issues with the art that already exists in the game—no new additions at this point. This also marks the movement of the game from the alpha phase to the beta phase.

Beta

As with most other types of software development, the *beta* stage is the "nearly done" stage. As mentioned earlier, the game assets (art, audio, and gameplay features) are locked down, and assets can only be replaced to fix a bug. At this point, developers exist solely to fix bugs. The game is essentially complete, but errors must be fixed before the game can be called final.

Not all bugs will delay the shipment of a product. In games, bugs are usually categorized into four types: A-bugs, B-bugs, C-bugs, and D-bugs. A-bugs, also known as "show-stopper" bugs, are the most important, and can prevent a game from shipping. Some examples of A-bugs include those that force the game to crash or stop functioning altogether, as well as those and that prevent the player from completing the game. Games can also get held up over legal issues, such as failing to gain permission for art used in the game.

Sample A-Bug: Extremely Serious

Frequently, in the snowy mountain level, at the end of the rope bridge, when the player character faces the post and swings his sword, the game resets.

Although not quite as serious as A-bugs, B-bugs may cause a lot of player frustration and should be fixed before the game ships. B-bugs include gameplay issues such as characters passing through geometry or running into invisible walls. B-bugs aren't the end of the world, but they can have a real impact on the player's experience. Most B-bugs are serious enough to hold up a game's shipment, but a few might make it through.

Lower still on the list are C-bugs, which are typically graphical errors that do not affect gameplay. These issues are relatively minor and can include mistakes such as textures mapped onto objects incorrectly or characters playing the wrong animations. Very few games get tied up because of C-bugs.

D-bugs are essentially comments that ask for improvements to the game. Have you ever played a game and thought that a particular enemy was a little too tough, or that a level could have benefited from just one more spot to save your game? Testers write these kind of suggestions into the bug database, where they are typically classified as D-bugs. Most D-bugs eventually get the lowest priority, and the development team usually does not get enough time to implement them.

> ### Sample D-Bug: Take It or Leave It
>
> In the refinery level, if the player character shoots down the helicopter with the assault rifle, the helicopter falls to the ground and explodes. The pilot of the helicopter should jump out of the cockpit as it falls.

In general, bugs are dealt with in a few different ways: Most bugs are fixed, and they no longer occur. Other entries in the bug database are not bugs at all, and are part of the player experience intended by the game designers. Some minor issues, classified as C-bugs or D-bugs, may be dismissed without fixing. Once most of the bugs have been addressed to the satisfaction of the producer, the lead tester, and the project lead, the game is almost complete.

Going for the Gold

Although the team has probably been working like crazy to get to this point, there's still one final push to get the game done: the "final candidate." As mentioned earlier, once the team leads have signed off on the bug fixes, the team will submit a build for final approval (the final candidate). If bugs are found during this phase, the fixes take place almost immediately so that a new version can be created and tested again. Each subsequent build requires a certain amount of bug-free testing hours before it can graduate from final candidate to "gold master." The gold master is the version of the game that will be shipped to stores—the end product, the finish line.

Once the game has "gone gold," the team can celebrate—but not for too long! Shipping one game means that another one can start up, and some members of the team will begin to brainstorm ideas for the next project.

In chapter 2, we'll take a step back, toward the beginning of the preproduction phase to the high concept. During this period, the game developers contemplate the important question: "What game should we make?" The decisions made about theme, genre, target audience, and platform will inform all of the art, design, and technology choices discussed in this chapter. The high concept phase is the creative part, but it's important to get it right. So, let's get to it!

CHAPTER 2
Defining the Game

WHEN YOU WALK INTO A STORE and see the box for a game, you can immediately tell whether you want to buy it. The cover artwork gives you an idea about the story of the game and maybe even its "genre," or what kind of game it is. For example, if the package shows an image of a warrior, you can expect to experience fighting of some kind. The warrior may be holding a medieval sword, a modern-day gun, or a weapon you've never seen before. From these clues, you may be able to figure out where and when the game takes place. This information describes the content in the game, which is sometimes called its "theme." From the title written on the box, you may be able to figure out even more, especially if the game is based on a popular license or franchise.

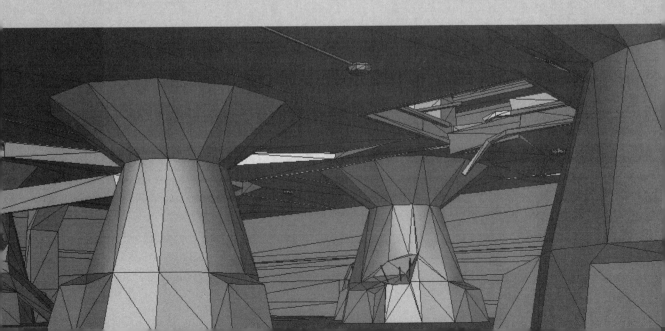

The game package also contains other clues. All box covers are legally required to feature a ratings stamp, assigned by the Entertainment Software Rating Board (ESRB). After assessing a game, the ESRB assigns it a rating symbol, based on the appropriate age, as well as content descriptions of objectionable material for potential consumers. In addition, the box cover should indicate the platform or system the game is designed for. For your first assignment (located at the end of this chapter), I'll ask you to try your hand at creating a back-of-box description, including genre, theme, target audience, and platform, for a fictional game.

The cover items encapsulate what's sometimes called the "high concept," or the "big picture," of the game. You've already seen how establishing the high concept is one of the first steps in the preproduction phase. That's because the high concept affects so much of the development process. The high concept determines the gameplay in general terms, which leads us to the specifics of the game's overall design. Only by understanding the game's overall design can we start designing the game's levels.

A Matter of Perspective: Character Point of View

Before we launch into game genre, we should touch briefly on the concept of character point of view. The point of view is closely tied in with genre; you've probably heard the term "first-person shooter" or "third-person action" as a description for a game.

Games are a form of entertainment, just like movies and books. And while the point of view of the character in a movie or a book may seem transparent, it impacts how you, the viewer, the reader, "see" the story and the action. If you see a book through the character's eyes, for example, you empathize with the character differently than if you were seeing all of the characters objectively. This is also true in games, which is why the point-of-view decision is so critical.

The two most common point-of-view options in games are first and third person. From a development standpoint, the player's point of view goes hand in hand with the game camera. The game camera determines how the game is viewed during gameplay. If the camera shows the player character from outside the character's body, the game has a third-person perspective. If the camera is placed inside the character's body, the game has a first-person perspective. The position of the game camera might be the most important decision made during the high-concept phase, since it can change the way the game is played.

> **NOTE** ▶ In a lot of games, the player can actually control the game camera. The camera can rotate, tilt up and down, and can even zoom in and out in some games. The position of the camera, though, represents more than just its location; the camera position is actually its relationship to the player character.

First-person perspective

First-person games place the game camera into the body of the player character. This type of camera, common in shooters (which I'll discuss in the genre section of this chapter), allows the player to control the character from their point of view. This type of perspective provides an "immersive" experience for the player, because the players gets to see exactly what the character sees and nothing more. Enemies attack your character, and you can witness the close combat as a participant. Other characters, who might engage the player character in conversation, seem to speak directly to you—as if they're looking into your eyes.

The main advantage in a first-person perspective game is the player's ability to aim accurately. Shooting a projectile—such as a bullet or a rocket—in first person is much easier than from third person because the player can line up a target in the middle of their monitor. Games that use the first-person perspective also tend to have a faster pace because players are so skilled at aiming and shooting. Of course, with this advantage comes a disadvantage: in first-person games, the player has no vision beyond their character's vision, so enemies can really catch the player by surprise.

Id Software's hugely popular DOOM was one of the first games to use the first-person perspective. The player took on the role of a space marine who had to battle countless enemies armed with an arsenal of projectile weapons and his own fists. The popularity of DOOM initiated a flood of first-person games that continues to this day. **Figure 2.1**, on the next page, shows a scene from DOOM 3, the third installment in the DOOM series.

FIGURE 2.1 A scene from DOOM 3 developed by Id Software. The player character is not shown except for the weapon he is carrying and the hands holding the weapon. DOOM 3 © 2004 Id software, Inc. All rights reserved.

First-person games are considered the most immersive because, in a sense, the player becomes the character. The other game character perspective, third person, allows you to develop a relationship with the character you control.

Third-person perspective

Third-person games show the player character on the screen and allow the player to control their character. So, if a player tells their character to jump by pressing the jump button on their controller or keyboard, they actually see their character jump. This point of view provides a buffer between the player and the character in the game: The character isn't you, the player, but rather a separate entity. **Figure 2.2** shows a scene from Flagship Studios' Hellgate: London, where players can see their character fighting monsters.

FIGURE 2.2 A scene from Hellgate: London by Flagship Studios and Namco. The player character is shown on the screen fighting monsters with a gun in one hand and a blade weapon in the other. The third-person perspective can properly show weapons that the player character swings around to attack enemies. © 2005 Flagship Studios, Inc. All rights reserved.

The third-person perspective shows the interaction between the player character and the environment around him. For instance, in a first-person game, the player can't really see the player character bump into a wall. If the character is facing the wall, the player sees the texture of the wall from a very close view and the character stops. If the character is facing away from the wall, and the player backs him up into the wall, the player just realizes something is blocking the character because he has stopped moving. In a third-person game, the player sees both the character and the wall in any circumstance. This perspective might make some gameplay experiences more intuitive, such as the player character climbing a ladder or bouncing on a trampoline.

Of course, in general, it's more difficult to aim in third-person games than in first-person games. Many third-person games have attempted to fix this problem in various ways, but in the third-person perspective the player has to draw a line from their character to a target instead of placing a point in the middle of the screen.

Third-person games have been around in various forms since the earliest video games. If you think about it, Pac-Man, the classic arcade game by Namco and Midway, was a third-person game. The player could see their character, Pac-Man, and control it as it ate up dots around a maze. The player could also see where the enemies, the ghosts, were. The camera in Pac-Man, however, always showed the same view of the game. In more recent years, the third-person game Tomb Raider, developed by Eidos Interactive, was one of the first games to use a third-person perspective in a three-dimensional world where the camera moved around with the character. The gameplay in Tomb Raider was suited for a third-person perspective because the player character, Lara Croft, performed actions like climbing ledges, pushing and pulling objects, and dodging traps. (It certainly didn't hurt that Lara Croft was a character that players enjoyed looking at either.)

Determining the point of view is a key decision in all kinds of storytelling. In games, the point of view affects the role of the player within the game and the level of interaction for the player. Once these facets are established, we can start to explore the game's genre.

Choosing the Game Genre

If someone asks you to describe a game, you're more than likely going to start by telling them what kind of game it is. In the game industry, the game type is called the genre. The game genre can say a lot about the game with a simple word. When you hear the phrase "racing game," for instance, you can immediately picture a vehicle traveling along a track. If you hear the phrase "survival horror," it's pretty clear that the game will be dark and gruesome. By creating a game within an established genre, development companies can appeal to large groups of game players. Just as fans of horror movies wait for the next slasher flick to hit the screens, someone who likes racing games will eagerly anticipate the next Gran Turismo installation.

There are dozens of different genres in video games, and even those genres can be broken down into different types, but not all game genres need levels. We're going to concentrate on a few popular game genres that make frequent use of levels.

The action genre

Action games have a lot of confrontational elements that pit the player against an enemy. Enemies can be anything menacing: armies of monsters, soldiers, robots, demons, or aliens. These enemies can act using artificial intelligence (AI) through the game program or they can be controlled by other human players who are playing the game as competitors. The pacing and intensity of action games are meant to keep the player alert and anxious.

Some of the more common types of action games include the shooter, the brawler, the combat simulation, and the survival horror.

The shooter

Probably the most popular action subgenre, the shooter typically features player characters running around environments, shooting projectiles at several enemies. and picking up items that they need, such as health, armor, weapons, ammunition, and keys. Level designers work with shooters frequently because they are so popular, and also because they are easily accessible for user-created levels. People who get together to create new content for games are commonly referred to as the "mod community" (see sidebar on page 37).

As I mentioned earlier, the shooter usually uses a first-person camera. The player only sees what the character sees. As such, the shooter is sometimes referred to as the "FPS," or first-person shooter. **Figure 2.3**, on the next page, shows a scene from Cyclone Studios' Requiem: Avenging Angel, an example of one of the many first-person shooters to come after DOOM.

The player does not always have to control a character in shooters: tanks, planes, ships, or robots may also take center stage in the game. Sometimes, as in Bungie Studios' popular Halo games, players can control a character for part of the game, and then control a vehicle that the character pilots for another portion of the game.

FIGURE 2.3 A scene from the hospital level in Requiem: Avenging Angel, a first-person shooter. In most first-person shooters, the player sees the environment and the weapon their character is holding.

In most shooters, two or more players can play with or against each other in the same levels. This is called multiplayer gameplay. Depending on the game, multiplayer gameplay can be as important, if not more so, than the single-player experience. Playing with friends is a social activity, and competing against them is often much more interesting than playing against artificial intelligence. "Deathmatch"-style multiplayer games allow players to battle with their characters in an arena to see who can get the most kills. Sometimes, as in ID Software's Quake III Arena, these games don't even have much of a story, and the levels are set up like a tournament or competition.

Many shooters contain several multiplayer modes, including deathmatch. Players can sometimes work with other players as a team and progress through the game's story in what is called cooperative gameplay. Still other shooters, like Valve Software's Counterstrike, allow teams of players to compete against other teams of players in what is called team play.

The Mod Community

In recent years, it's become common for game developers to release a game to the public and expect that some of the players will expand the content—or even create a new game. These user-created modifications are called "mods." To create a mod, a player will take an existing game and change it slightly, or add some new content. For example, a player might take a game, like id Software's Quake, and add models and textures to create their own characters. In some cases, the mod community will create an entirely new game, called a "total conversion." Counterstrike, based on Valve Software's Half-Life, is an example of a total conversion.

The shooter genre has spawned the largest number of these user-created mods. This is partly due to the genre's popularity, and also because of the support that developers provide to the mod community. In fact, many shooters will ship with level editor tools, or the developers will provide those tools for download. Players can use these tools to make their own user-created levels. Even if the developers don't release a game with a level editor, the game just might be popular enough for someone to create a level editor for it.

Shooters require a certain amount of skill from players. Reaction time, speed, aim, and even a little strategy all add up to make a good player. The skills themselves translate well from one shooter to the next, and this may be why shooters are so popular.

The brawler

The brawler has the same level of intensity as the shooter, but it usually focuses on close combat or "melee" weapons, such as swords, axes, staffs, and clubs. The player character gets attacked from all sides in brawlers, and players need to press buttons or keys in combinations to make the player character perform certain fighting moves. Some brawlers, like New Legends, have both projectile and melee weapons that the player can alternate between. Brawlers usually employ a third-person camera, so that players can see their characters move. Because of the level of intensity and the game's camera in brawlers, levels that contain large, open areas tend to work better than those with smaller, enclosed spaces.

Using Third-Person Game Cameras

Any game developer will tell you that third-person cameras are extremely difficult to establish. A camera that moves in an annoying way can make players feel sick. Cameras that show too much or too little can make players frustrated.

Some third-person cameras are fixed, stationed around the environment like security cameras. The perspective switches from one camera to the next as the player character moves to different areas. The fixed cameras are set by the game designers, and can't be modified by the player.

Scripted cameras are similar to fixed cameras, but they can actually move depending on the player character's movement. The scripted camera moves along a preset path, usually determined by the game's level designers.

Most third-person game cameras use a "follow" camera, which, as the name suggests, follows the player character around the environment. Most games allow players to control the follow camera in addition to controlling the player character. The spaces in the level should accommodate both the player character and the camera. **Figure 2.4** shows how the third-person camera might need more room.

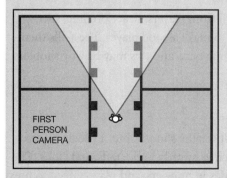
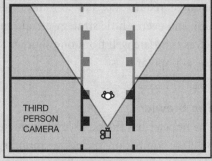

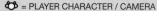

FIGURE 2.4 The camera in many third-person games can often collide with interior walls and architectural details as it follows the character. Some third-person games fade geometry that obstructs the camera's view of the character.

The combat simulation

The action portions of combat simulations are quite different from shooters and brawlers. For one thing, combat simulations put the player in realistic settings with realistic variations of gameplay. For example, players in Konami's Metal Gear Solid series use true-to-life techniques to avoid detection and combat. Players track enemy patterns to sneak around areas without confrontation, and triggering alarms will alert enemy soldiers. In other combat simulations, like Tom Clancy's Rainbow Six series of games (published by Ubisoft), players can control a team of soldiers to replicate squad-based combat. Using special sets of commands, players can send orders to their team to follow, scout ahead, or hold their positions.

Unlike many shooters and brawlers, combat simulations often feature virtual replicas of true-to-life weapons, and characters in the game get hurt in an accurate way. One bullet wound can often maim or even kill a character, whereas it might take dozens of bullets and a rocket to finish off a character in a shooter. All elements of the game maintain the same standards of realism. Environments sometimes match actual buildings and scenes so the level designers may need to do thorough research to ensure that the levels are accurate.

Combat simulations can be either first or third person, or they can even switch back and forth between the two depending on the situation. In Metal Gear Solid 3, the player character can hide from enemy soldiers by crawling among tall grass. The player can switch to third-person mode to make sure their character is totally hidden, and then go back to first person to get a closer view of the enemy.

The survival horror

Like the horror genre in film, the survival horror game has the primary goal of creating the most frightening experiences possible. These games sometimes let the player control the last survivor in an overrun city or village, as in Capcom's hugely popular Resident Evil games. Survival horror games are much slower-paced than shooters and brawlers, emphasizing combat with a small group of enemies.

The camera for survival horror games can be in either first or third person. The third-person camera allows players to see their characters react, while a first-person camera can promote more surprises along the way. In Resident Evil 4, the game camera rides closely behind one shoulder of the player character to combine the best of both scenarios.

Atmosphere is paramount in survival horror games, so level designers focus on making areas dark, foggy, and claustrophobic. In an attempt to keep players on their toes, designers insert special scripted sequences, such as monsters dropping from the ceiling or crashing through a window, throughout the game.

The adventure genre

Adventure games, pioneered by LucasArts with games like Full Throttle, tend to emphasize the story or the narrative throughout the game. Players use various tools like conversations with other characters, finding and combining items, and even combat, to progress through the game. At many points in the game, the player loses interactivity in cut-scenes or cinematic sequences that reveal more of the story. Most adventure games use a third-person camera to show the player's character interacting with the levels. Like the action genre, the adventure genre has several basic types, but the story adventure and the action adventure are most dependent on strong level design.

The Cinematic vs. the Cut-Scene

There are many ways to convey story in video games. The most popular way, and the most visually appealing, is a cinematic. Cinematic sequences are basically short pieces of a film that get interspersed within a game. They may contain dialogue between characters with a lot of special animations, or they may show epic landscapes that are impossible to show in the game's engine. A cinematic sequence can completely remove the player from the game's interaction.

In some cases, a cut-scene is used instead of cinematics to impart story elements. Cut-scenes are scripted so that the player is forced to see something happen during gameplay. For example, when I worked on Electronic Arts' Harry Potter™ and the Chamber of Secrets™, we used cut-scenes to show the effects of Harry's actions. If a door was locked and Harry had to cast a spell in another part of the room to open it, a cut-scene would play to show the door unlock.

The story adventure

In story adventures, players control a character in a story and interact with other characters through dialogue and item-exchange. Players explore environments, poking around until some kind of puzzle or gameplay element blocks their progression. The player must use found items, information that they hear, or systems that they learn to find a solution. In LucasArts' Grim Fandango, the player character is instructed to find pigeon eggs. Among the items that the player has access to are bread crumbs and balloon shapes, which he'll use for this puzzle. To scare the pigeons away, the player character combines items by placing an inflated balloon in a dish and covering it with bread crumbs. When the pigeons try to eat the bread crumbs, they break the balloon. The noise scares the birds, who fly off, leaving their eggs unattended.

Story adventure levels can be much more compact than levels in other genres. A single room or area can contain a puzzle that may involve a lot of gameplay. As you can see **Figure 2.5**, a player might spend several minutes exploring an area before finding the solution to the puzzle.

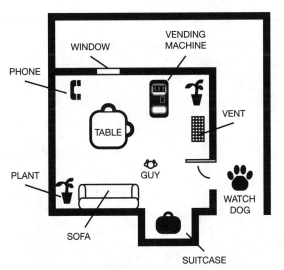

1. The "guy" must escape from the room and exit the building through the hallway.
2. A watchdog blocks the doorway.
3. In a vending machine, the guy sees packs of beef jerky.
4. Through a vent cover, the guy sees a coin.
5. The guy can break off branches of the plants to use as sticks.
6. In the suitcase, the guy finds some chewing gum.
7. If the guy combines the chewing gum with a stick, he can retrieve the coin from the vent.
8. With the coin, the guy can purchase the beef jerky.
9. The guy can drop the beek jerky out of the window.
10. In a cut-scene, the watchdog runs around to the window and the guy escapes.

FIGURE 2.5 In this example diagram, the player character has to escape from the room he is in.

Levels in story adventures drop plenty of hints to players, leading them to the objects and characters that will help them move forward in the game. In the previous example, an operational vending machine gives the clue that the player character can find a coin somewhere to get an item out of it. In this case, the item is a snack that can be used to distract a watchdog. Of course, these clues get progressively harder to find as the player advances through the game.

The action adventure

Games can combine different genres to make new ones. The action adventure takes some of the pacing and combat elements from the action genre and uses them as part of the learning process for the player. It's a lot different to solve a puzzle or problem when some enemy or monster is attacking your character. Action adventures are the most popular form of adventure game mainly because many of them, like Harry Potter and the Chamber of Secrets or Indiana Jones and the Infernal Machine (**Figure 2.6**), are based on some franchise or license. These days, many films that involve action or a popular character are translated into an action adventure video game. For example, Electronic Arts publishes several James Bond titles as well as the Lord of the Rings games.

FIGURE 2.6 A scene from Indiana Jones and the Infernal Machine © 2003 LucasArts and LucasFilm Ltd. The action adventure subgenre can encompass a broad range of characters and worlds. You can be Harry Potter and attend Hogwarts search for treasure as Indiana Jones, or you can play as Spider-Man and protect New York City in Activision's Spider-Man 2: The Game.

The role-playing genre

In role-playing games, or RPGs, players create a character and continue to modify and customize that character throughout the game.

Evolved from table-top games like Dungeons & Dragons, computer role-playing games are dominated by numbers and statistics. Player characters advance by finding or receiving items, learning skills, and gaining experience. Characters earn experience by killing enemies, completing missions or quests, and exploring new parts of the game's world. Enemies are classified by difficulty level, and the combat revolves around the amount of health or life characters and enemies have and how much they lose.

Some RPGs simulate combat as if the player were rolling dice and taking turns with an opponent attacking and defending; the outcome could be determined by who has the best weapon, the best armor, or the highest level of experience.

Creating random levels

A lot of the content in role-playing games is random, giving it a unique "replayability" factor that is appealing to fans of the genre. Level designers create random levels, with modular pieces that can be rearranged to create a completely different experience. The monsters that appear, items that are dropped, and even the level layouts can all change the next time the player encounters them. Modular pieces can be laid out by the game program in a procedure known as "random level generation." Level designers can also place modular pieces together in a special tool, and group the pieces into a "preset." A preset level is still a level made from modular pieces, but the level designer has complete control of the placement of those pieces.

Level Designer Lego

Modular pieces, sometimes called "tiles," can fit together in endless combinations like Lego pieces. Levels can be assembled with a room-based tile set or a component-based tile set. Room-based tile sets are basically rooms or spaces with doorways or openings that line up at each direction (**Figures 2.7 and 2.8**).

Component-based tile sets break the rooms down to their components, which are borders and the spaces created by the borders. Depending on the area, the borders and spaces can be walls and floors, trees and ground, or pits and walkways (**Figures 2.9 and 2.10**). Component-based tile sets are much more random than room-based tile sets because each room or space that the components create is random itself. However, because they are designed to fit together so closely, they can look repetitive.

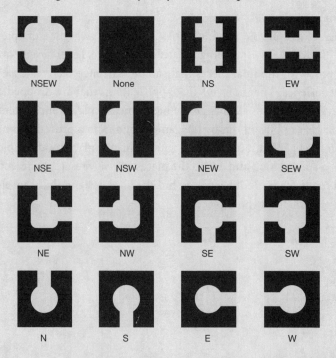

FIGURE 2.7 An example of a basic room-based tile set. The names of each tile are based on the directions of the doorways (N=North, S=South, E=East, W=West).

continues

Level Designer Lego   *continued*

FIGURE 2.8 A diagram showing the room-based tiles arranged in a random order.

continues

Level Designer Lego *continued*

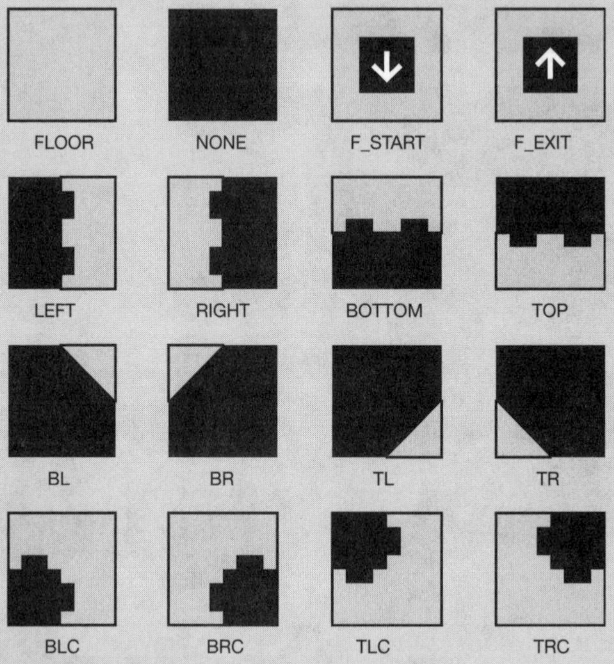

FIGURE 2.9 An example of a basic component-based tile set. The names of these tiles are based on the sides that the borders block (R=Right, L=Left, T=Top, B=Bottom). The tiles with no borders are labeled starting with "F" for floor. The F_Start tile can be used as the entrance piece and the F_Exit tile can be used as the exit piece.

continues

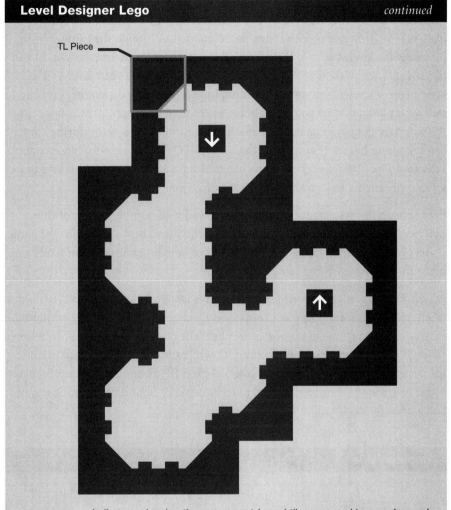

Level Designer Lego *continued*

TL Piece

FIGURE 2.10 A diagram showing the component-based tiles arranged in a random order.

The action RPG

The action RPG combines the feeling of character growth and customization from role-playing games with faster-paced combat. Although the game still measures the levels between the player's character and an enemy, the skill of the player can often make up for the difference. For example, if your level-10 character meets a level-12 enemy, you still might win the battle depending on your skills as a player, despite your level being lower than your opponent. Unlike other RPGs, where the player character has a limited number of actions during combat, the player has more control in the action RPG. You can control your character to dodge attacks, pick up items like health packs and potions, and circle around the enemy to attack from another direction.

Even though the systems for action RPGs use a lot of numbers, most of those numbers are hidden from the player so they don't interrupt the flow of the game. Players can move their characters in and out of combat easily and can battle many more enemies at the same time.

Action RPGs, such as Blizzard Entertainment's Diablo 2, have multiplayer modes where players can work together cooperatively to complete missions or "quests." Players can even compete against each other. The cooperative mode is sometimes called "PVE" (Player versus Environment), while the competitive mode is sometimes called "PVP" (Player versus Player). Action RPGs can use both random and preset levels for experienced players to feel a sense of familiarity in some areas and a need for exploration in other areas.

Replay Value

The beauty of role-playing games is the replay factor. Many RPG fans will play a game to the end, and then start all over again, this time as a different character. Successful RPGs allow players several different character and ability choices. For example, in Diablo 2, you can choose to play a Necromancer, which is endowed with the natural ability to resurrect slain enemies and use them for your own purposes. You could also choose to play a Barbarian, who fights alone. Some games offer the ability to play parts of the game in a different order. All of these choices add up to replay value, which changes a game's life span from a few hours of enjoyment to a few years.

The MMORPG

The Massively Multiplayer Online Role Playing Game (MMORPG) creates an enormous world populated by player characters, nonplayer characters (NPCs), and enemies. Players can form groups to complete missions or quests, meet other players to trade items, or even simply socialize by chatting. Some MMORPGs, like Blizzard Entertainment's World of Warcraft, ask players to pick characters aligned to one of two opposing armies. In World of Warcraft, players can join either the Alliance or the Horde. Player characters on the same side can battle against player characters on the opposing side.

Hundreds of different player characters may occupy the same area in an MMORPG. Level designers construct incredibly vast landscapes that might contain dozens of quests or missions so that players will have hours and even days of content to complete before moving on. Unlike other RPGs, the MMORPG must always keep its game world "open." At any given time, player characters occupy areas of the world. Therefore, most of the world in MMORPGs is static, not random.

Open Worlds

Although most games have levels or areas that the player progresses through, not all games push the player from one level to the next in a linear way. In some cases, designers create what is sometimes called an "open world" that the player character can travel through with many choices along the way. Missions or quests lead the player character in certain directions, so that they can complete certain areas before moving on to the next. Characters get funneled at junctions or "choke points" that might be blocked until players are ready, as shown in **Figure 2.11**, on the next page.

Certain missions or quests become available to players as they complete more of the game and gain more experience.

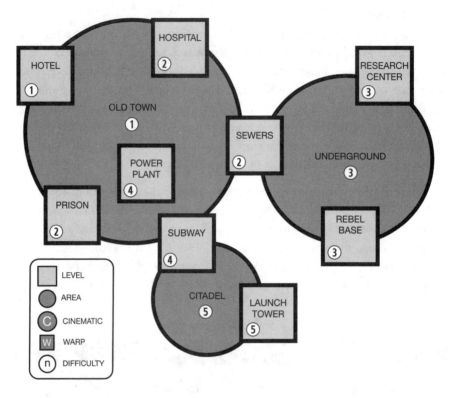

FIGURE 2.11 The mission flow diagram in Figure 1.4 (back in Chapter 1) showed how some games use levels as a basis for progression. This figure, from Cyclone Studios' Requiem: Avenging Angel, shows the same locations as Figure 1.4, but places them in an open map layout. You'll notice that the levels do not have an order; they have a difficulty setting. Players can access groups of levels that they can complete in any order.

The platformer genre

The "platformer" genre gets its name from the jumping and landing areas that these games use in their levels. These games grew from the two-dimensional "side scrolling" genre that dominated the video game market years ago with titles like Nintendo's Super Mario Bros and Sega's Sonic the Hedgehog. The side scrolling genre "scrolled" the screen to follow the player character as he moved through the levels. Movement remains the primary gameplay element in platformer games, and most levels test the player's reflexes and navigational skills as opposed to their deductive skills. Player characters have a set of abilities from running and jumping to climbing and sliding that help them move from one end of the level to the other.

Platformer games tend to appeal to a younger audience than other genres. The goals set up by the game, to move a character from one point to another, are easy to understand and accept. Also, since the gameplay revolves around movement, there isn't much need for violent actions like shooting guns and slashing enemies. Controlling a character to jump on a turtle and flip it over is an activity most parents would approve of.

Most platformer games, such as Naughty Dog's Jak & Daxter, use a third-person camera so that players can see their characters and their character's relation to the world. It's easier to see when a character is close enough to an edge to jump when both the character and the edge are in view.

The strategy genre

Strategy games, like Ensemble Studios' Age of Empire series, let players control an army as if they are a general or military leader. Players can gather materials, manage resources, build facilities, and send troops to attack enemies. Players compete against an opposing army controlled by artificial intelligence or by other players. In multiplayer games, players can also form teams and work together to defeat another team.

The levels for strategy games cover a large area to give each side room to grow without revealing plans to enemies. Level creation on strategy games involves the placement of materials that will be found and gathered, the clearing of areas that can be built on and explored, and the balancing of the paths in between. Multiplayer maps must be constructed so that no player has an advantage over another.

The Changing Face of Levels

A level can occasionally change considerably during the course of a game. In strategy games, such as the Warcraft series, the player's army can clear areas that were once impassable. In Warcraft 3, forests and sections of trees that block characters can be cut down for wood materials, and characters can then move through to a new area. The level becomes more open as paths and clearings grow. Some nonstrategy games, like THQ's Red Faction, also have *destructible* architecture—pieces of geometry that can be destroyed to create new passages.

The racing genre

Racing games, as the name suggests, allow the player to drive some sort of vehicle around a track, usually in competition with other drivers. Add in a time and speed element, and the resulting gameplay is quite fast-paced and exciting.

Depending on the game, players may use their characters to pick up items on the tracks and use them on competing characters. Nintendo's Mario Kart series allows players to foil other racers by shooting special projectiles or by leaving banana peels on the track. Level designers create the shapes for the tracks, place obstacles, and even change the surface materials. Racing levels are usually built on a much bigger scale than levels in other kinds of games because the character or vehicle is moving so fast that they must cover a greater distance. That also means that the levels typically do not contain as much detail as levels in other games. The faster the players progress, the lower the level of detail in environments.

A lot of racing games feature racecars on special racing tracks, but other racing games, like those in Sony's Wipeout series, allow players to control futuristic ships that travel on suspended roadways and through tube tunnels. The kinds of vehicles and the environments of the tracks depend on the game's theme, which we'll discuss next.

Selecting the Game Theme

While the game genre can convey a lot about the gameplay, the game theme tells you what the game is about. The game theme describes the content of the game, and can also impart what the game might look like visually, what story the game will tell, and what level of reality the game will have. Most games can be classified into a few major themes: fantasy, modern, science fiction, and alternate reality. Games can also have any combination of these themes.

The fantasy theme

If a game involves medieval weaponry and architecture, mythical creatures, and magic, there's a good chance it's a fantasy-themed game (see **Figure 2.12**). Levels can take place in dungeons, castles, churches, villages, temples, caves, and various forms of wilderness. Because the levels don't need to strictly imitate reality, fantasy-themed games offer more creative freedom for the level designer.

FIGURE 2.12 A concept piece for a dungeon area in a fantasy-themed game. Common detail elements for fantasy environments include statues, chains, candles, torches, and banners.

With the added element of magic, level designers can explore content that is not based on reality. In Sega's Beyond Oasis, an action RPG with a fantasy theme, the player character can summon a fire spirit from any flame found in the levels. The fire spirit can be used to break through ice barriers for the player character to continue through the game.

The modern theme

A game with a modern theme can be based in the not-so-distant past, the present day, or the near future. These games can revolve around realistic settings, figures, or events, and contain elements that people will find familiar. Unlike the fantasy theme, the modern theme relies heavily on realism. All gameplay elements must be believable, and it might be more challenging for level designers to come up with ideas. Rockstar Games' Grand Theft Auto series uses a modern theme to replicate actual vehicles, weapons, and even locations from the present day. Although some modern-themed games, such as Electronic Arts' Battlefield series, are set in the past, they are based on actual historic events and use a similar standard of realism.

The science fiction theme

The science fiction theme is probably the most popular theme in video games. This theme exists in all of the Star Wars titles from LucasArts, including the action game, Jedi Knight, and the racing game, Star Wars Episode I – Racer. This theme covers just about everything set in the far future or an alternate universe where space travel, aliens, high technology, and robots are all quite common. **Figure 2.13** is a piece of concept art that could be used for a science fiction game.

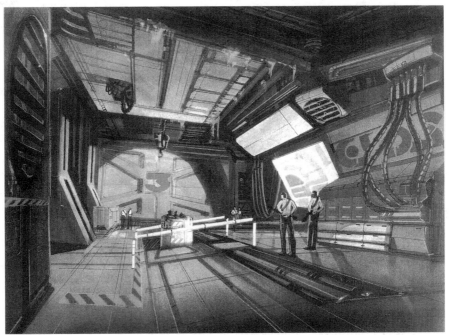

FIGURE 2.13 Concept art for a docking bay for a science fiction–themed game. Common detail elements for science fiction environments include pipes, generators, storage containers, and ventilation shafts.

Although most science fiction games still use a degree of reality, some elements can require the player to understand fictional systems. For example, in many science fiction games, like the Quake series by id Software, player characters might use a teleporter for characters to travel from one place to another. Players become familiar with teleporter in the very first area of the game, when setting their difficulty level.

The alternate reality theme

The alternate reality theme creates a completely different universe. This theme ranges from the cartoon-like and comical, like LucasArts' Monkey Island series of games, to the somber and surreal, like American McGee's Alice by Electronic Arts. Most of the elements will make sense within the specific game universe, but these elements will not necessarily make sense in real life. For example, in American McGee's Alice, level geometry like walkways and platforms often floated in mid-air. Setting up these elements in a consistent system should be one of the first tasks for the level design team. All of the levels can start out following the same sets of rules.

The Construction of Levels

Levels are often deconstructed into three parts: the level geometry, textures, and lighting. Level geometry consists of the brushes (more about brushes in Chapter 6) or the solid construction of the level. Pieces like walls, floors, platforms, stairs, ceilings and landscape are considered the level geometry, and images applied to the surfaces of the level geometry are textures. Lighting brightens or darkens the surfaces giving them depth.

Themes, like the alternate reality theme, are chosen for artistic and design reasons, but they are also chosen to appeal to certain groups of players. A younger audience might like the more colorful, exaggerated characters and backgrounds of an alternate reality whereas an older audience might prefer a more realistic theme.

Developing for an Audience

The ideal game would appeal to everyone in the entire world. You would sell over 6 billion copies and have men, women, and children of all ages writing rave reviews of your game on Amazon.com. Unfortunately, this probably isn't possible. People and tastes are just too individual, as the genre and theme descriptions illustrate, and you will need to focus on a target audience for your game. The target audience decision is critical in determining gameplay and level design, and as a developer, it forces you to answer squarely who the game is intended to reach. The categories for the audience include age, gender, nationality, and locale.

Level designers need to pay special attention to both age and locale. While gender may be important for product placement and even with establishing certain content decisions, males and females with similar game-playing experiences tend to play levels in similar ways. And, while nationality may be important for cultural differences and traditions, levels in games don't usually discriminate.

> **NOTE** There are a few issues concerning nationality that may apply. For example, some Asian cultures consider it bad luck to travel through architecture that resembles an animal's mouth. I don't know if this translates into video games, but it might be worth considering.

The age category for the target audience has the biggest effect on level design. Age can determine difficulty, level size, game content, and even how much gameplay is in a given area.

Age: Generations of gamers

Designing a level for an eight-year-old is much different than designing the same level for an 18-year-old. Younger children might not have the same coordination or patience as adults or even older children, and the challenges should reflect the skill level of the target audience.

The One-Handed Player

While developing the Harry Potter and the Chamber of Secrets game for the PC, our team watched children ages 8–12 (the target audience) play all of the levels. The control system for the PC version of the game uses keys on the keyboard to control Harry's movement and the mouse to control his spell-casting. While observing some of the younger kids, we discovered that a lot of them use only one hand to play the game. They would place their left hand in their lap while controlling all of Harry's actions with their right hand. Areas that required Harry to run, jump, and cast a spell at the same time were either saved for levels at the end of the game, when players would be more experienced, or used for optional gameplay.

Most people play video games to have fun, but they also like to feel challenged. Levels designed for adults and older children should demand more skill from the player. For example, if the player character must jump over a pit in a children's game (see **Figure 2.14**), the length of the pit should not force the player to perform the jump perfectly. The pit should be longer in a game for an older audience, so that the action of jumping over it isn't merely an annoyance.

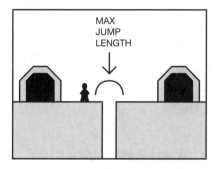

A. Easy: The player has a buffer on either side of the pit.

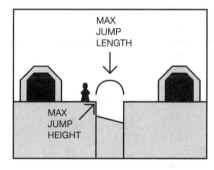

B. Normal: The player gets a second chance by going back and jumping up.

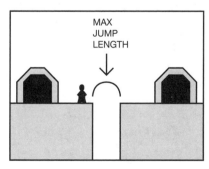

C. Difficult: The player only gets one chance and it has to be perfect.

FIGURE 2.14 An example of a pit designed for three different skill settings.

The "easy" jump in the above figure could be used throughout the children's game and even at the beginning of the teen or adult games. The "normal" and "difficult" jumps could be expected in a teen or adult game where the player has progressed to a more challenging level. The most frustrating situation for a player is to continuously fail a challenge, especially early in a game.

The age of the target audience can affect not only the difficulty of the challenges but also the density of the content. Children's titles tend to have shorter levels filled with constant interaction and obvious cues, whereas titles meant for an older audience have longer levels with more subtle visuals. In LucasArts' Lego Star Wars, which targets young children, levels are packed with collectible Lego pieces that player characters must use special abilities to get to. Players are encouraged to return to completed levels with different sets of characters to find all of the pieces.

The content of the game itself relies on the target audience. Games that contain more mature elements might not be appropriate for children. Development companies need to follow a ratings system to ensure younger players are not exposed to questionable material.

The ratings system for games

Like most entertainment products, video games have a ratings system. As I mentioned earlier in this chapter, the Entertainment Software Rating Board (ESRB) has divided ratings into six groups based on age and maturity:

- Early Childhood (EC)—Age 3 and older

- Everyone (E)—Age 6 and older

- Everyone 10+ (E10+)—Age 10 and older

- Teen (T)—Age 13 and older

- Mature (M)—Age 17 and older

- Adults Only (AO)—Age 18 and older

The ESRB assesses many factors when assigning a rating for the content in a game, including violence, sexual content, language, and substance abuse. Knowing the audience at the beginning of the project can help level designers plan their levels more efficiently. A game that targets young children might not want to include realistic weapons of any kind. A level in a game that targets children 8 to 12 years old might not want to include using a severed hand on a palm scanner to open a door. **Figure 2.15** shows a gory scene where an enemy soldier gets his head cut off.

FIGURE 2.15 In this concept drawing for a scripted sequence, the player character decapitates a soldier on a hover cycle. Graphic scenes such as this one can change the rating of the game.

Ratings affect sales. Large stores that distribute video games will not carry games that are rated Adults Only. Most parents of teenagers won't buy their children a game rated Mature. Development companies might lose a lot of money if their game contains questionable content.

Localization: Making a game global

Localization simply means making a game suitable for other regions of the world. Usually this involves changing text to the appropriate language, but it can also mean changing art elements or other content in the game.

Sometimes, a level contains a display or a sign that helps the player figure out where to go or what to do, but it is not helpful in any other language than English. The level designer might need to make the level flow more smoothly without visual aids. Some of these situations evolve from the visuals rather than the gameplay. For example, settings such as hospitals, prisons, train stations, and factories require signs with text to appear more realistic. In these cases, the producer can help the level designers and artists plan for localization by creating alternate textures using appropriate languages.

In some countries, games with certain elements are banned from being sold. In Germany, any game that depicts human blood is not allowed. Games can fix most instances of blood by programmatically changing the red color of blood to another color. However, red blood will need to be modified if it exists in the environment or on textures.

Target Platform: The Game Machine

A game's platform is the system that the game is played on. Currently, games are played on the PC/Macintosh computer systems, console systems (Xbox, PlayStation 2, and Gamecube) and handheld systems (Gameboy Advance, PlayStation Portable, and Nintendo DS). While many games are developed for multiple platforms, design elements and game levels may differ depending on the platform. Some platforms can display more or less on the screen than others, which can limit the sizes and detail levels of areas. Some platforms have controllers with different buttons. Certain types of gameplay may fit better with different controllers. For example, a lot of people like to play a platformer genre game with a console controller, and those same people may prefer to play a first-person shooter with a mouse and keyboard.

Dealing with limitations

With every game platform, there are certain technical requirements the levels must pass. One requirement is the size of the level, measured in memory units (bytes). The content in levels needs to be below a certain memory size just so the level can load on each system, and these sizes vary depending on which platform it is. Even after loading a level, the game must play smoothly in every area with any possible situation.

Splitting Levels

Infinite Machine originally started developing New Legends for the PC. Most of the levels were created on a very large scale to try to simulate the epic landscape and architecture of China. About halfway through the development cycle, we changed publishers and switched to the X-Box platform, abandoning the PC version. The levels had to be split into parts so that they would load on the target platform (see **Figure 2.16**).

FIGURE 2.16 Initially, this train yard scene from New Legends was connected with the train station beside it as one large level. The two parts were eventually divided for technical reasons.

Control yourself

Certainly, how the game is controlled by the player determines the overall design of the game itself. This is called the control scheme, and it translates certain inputs from the player into actions in the game. Consoles, like the PlayStation, use a specific controller, while computer game-players can use a mouse, keyboard, game controller, or joystick. Handheld systems usually have buttons built into the device.

So, how does this impact design? For one, console controllers and handheld systems have much fewer keys or buttons than personal computers. A lot of strategy games on computer systems, such as Blizzard Entertainment's Starcraft, use "hotkeys." With hotkeys, players can customize the keys on the keyboard to do specific commands so that they can manage a lot of different tasks quickly. A player could not set up a console controller in the same way because the hotkeys would interfere with the standard game controls. A console controller, as shown in **Figure 2.17**, has a fraction of the buttons a keyboard has.

FIGURE 2.17 A generic game controller showing the number of buttons at a player's disposal. Games that require more actions might use combinations of buttons pressed at the same time.

In a lot of computer games, such as Activision's Vampire: The Masquerade – Redemption, the player uses a cursor to interact with the game. As you probably know, a cursor is a pointer on the screen, and in these games, players can click the cursor in an environment to tell their character where to go, who to attack, or what to pick up. Of course, using a cursor with a controller is much more difficult than with a mouse, and games like Vampire: The Masquerade/ Redemption would not work in the same way on a console platform.

The high concept defines the game, and contains the information you need to start isolating your level and how it fits into the overall game. But in order to design your level, you need to know what to put in it, which we discuss in the next chapter.

Assignment 1

Choosing Your Game

For this first assignment, create a "back of the box" description of the game that you want to work on throughout this book. Simply choose a genre, a theme, a target audience, and a game platform and write a brief synopsis of the game. It can contain a narrative and primary characters if that is what you want to stress.

Example

The Chaperone

Genre: Action – Shooter

Theme: Modern – Near Future

Target Audience: Teen

Platform: PC

Description: The player controls a chaperone for school field trips and facilities for children, which all coincidentally go wrong. Our hero winds up saving the kids and taking down the bad guys. The game takes place in various locations, and in the end, the player discovers that he was a target the whole time.

CHAPTER 3
Enemies and Obstacles: Choosing Your Challenges

Now that you have decided on the high concept of the game, it's time to zoom in on how the levels for the game will play. Before creating a level, both the game designers and the level designers need to work together to answer a few questions: How does the player interact with the game? What challenges the player? How does the player overcome these challenges? What changes as the player progresses through the game? The answers to these questions will determine the tools that you must use to construct your levels.

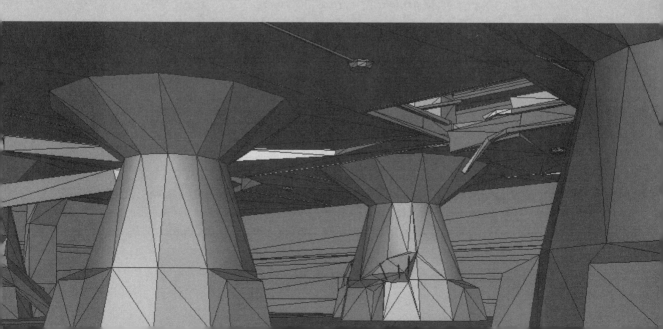

You can use two design ingredients when constructing levels: game obstacles and game skills. Game obstacles are the elements of the game that challenge the player. Obstacles force the player to react using game skills, which are the abilities players have to interact with the game. The level design team maps out in charts and graphs what obstacles will appear and what skills the player should acquire throughout the course of the game. Those charts and graphs should provide you with a clear understanding of the materials you can use in each level.

In addition to knowing all of the game obstacles and game skills, you must identify the level type before you can begin. Games have a variety of level types, including boss levels that contain special enemies and bonus levels that contain extra rewards for the player. Most of the game is made up of standard levels that set the tone for the game, but other level types break up the game into a variety of different experiences. You use the placement of your levels in the overall game to gauge what experiences you should create.

> **TIP**   Remember that the designers and level designers determine the placement of the levels during the creation of the world map or the mission flow diagram.

Your assignment, located at the end of this chapter, will be to put together what you've learned. You'll come up with a list of skills and obstacles for your game, and you'll rank them in order of difficulty. Based on your lists, you'll pick a level to design for the duration of this book. Here's where the detailed work starts, so let's get right into it, starting with game skills.

Challenging the Player

A level is really an elaborate obstacle course. Level designers take great care in constructing levels that will prolong the player's experience, packing it with fun challenges. Most players don't want to progress through an entire game in just a few minutes; that would be like paying the full price of admission at the movie theater and only seeing a 30-second short! A challenge, or obstacle, is something that causes the player to interact with the game. Barrels that block a hallway are obstacles, because the player will have to interact with the barrels in some way to get past them. In order to complete the challenge or overcome the obstacle, the player character may need to move the barrels or even blow them up.

As the level designer, your job is to keep players engaged by challenging them and by creating a sense of accomplishment. By completing a challenge and progressing to another area of a level, players feel a sense of accomplishment and they usually want to continue playing the game. You must strive to bring out this feeling as much as possible throughout your levels. You can include different kinds of obstacles to add a variety of experiences for players. Obstacles can simply block the player temporarily, like in our barrel example. Levels may also contain other obstacles, such as enemies and traps, which can cause harm to the player character. Obstacles can even be combined into a kind of puzzle that makes the player stop and think about a solution. Mix these obstacles up a bit, and you have the skeleton of a level.

Many developers create a test level with all the obstacles the game will have. This test level, which we touched on briefly in Chapter 1, is sometimes called a "sandbox level." Sandbox levels can help determine whether certain obstacles are fun and how difficult they are to defeat or get past. A sandbox level can also identify technology issues before entire levels are built.

> **TIP** ▶ Once you have built a sandbox level, you can copy sections of the sandbox level that contain a certain obstacle and paste them into an actual level. This can be used as a starting point for an obstacle in your level.

Types of obstacles

When you start designing a level, it's best to know what obstacles you have to work with. Obstacles come in many different forms depending on the game's genre and theme. Some obstacles are enemies that you need to defeat, like aliens that are invading the planet, or poisonous mushrooms that the character can't touch. Other obstacles can be physical objects that block the character's path, such as a locked door or a minefield. To create a level with a variety of experiences, you'll need to mix the types of obstacles the game provides in certain ways.

Simple roadblocks: the basic obstacles

The most basic obstacles—what I'm referring to as "simple roadblocks"—do just enough to slow down the player character without completely stopping them. An example of a simple roadblock is a fence or railing that the player character must jump over. Such obstacles mostly require just one action from the player to continue. If a player has to press a button or key to open a closed door, then the door counts as a simple roadblock. Simple roadblocks exist to add a bit of player interaction during a level.

Simple roadblocks can also make other tasks, such as combat, slightly more interesting or difficult. For example, if the player character opens a closed door, an enemy could be positioned right on the opposite side to surprise the player. The player may decide to retreat through the doorway and close the door for protection.

So, as a level designer, you can place these simple roadblocks throughout a level to intersperse player interaction and to spice up some of the experiences.

Enemies: the obstacles you shoot

Any game that involves combat will feature enemies of some kind. Enemies in games are characters, vehicles, or creatures that cause harm to the player character.

> **NOTE** ▸ Enemies are not always vulnerable to the player character. For example, in Rockstar Games' Grand Theft Auto series, when the police come, the player character can only flee to survive.

Enemies can be grouped according to a few categories: size, movement, and attack style. All of these factors contribute to how you should construct the areas in a level. In some cases, you can build areas without having specific enemies in mind, but you must then design your enemies to fit the environment.

Bosses

One special type of enemy used in video games is called a "boss." A boss is typically a unique enemy that the player has to defeat in order to proceed through the game. Each boss in a game usually only appears once in a game and it has a unique model, unique method of movement, and unique attack style. Most bosses are located in a special level type—the boss level type (more on special case levels in Chapter 5).

When building areas, you must consider the "size" of your enemies. Obviously, these characters need to physically fit in the area they inhabit. However, they also need to work well with the areas. A vast open area might suit a large monster, but players would get frustrated hunting down smaller creatures because they could be difficult to attack.

In addition to the size factor, enemies move in different ways. They can run, leap, fly, or crawl, and the environments should take their movements into account (see **Figure 3.1**). If the player character has to travel along some narrow rope bridges, enemies that walk will come from the front or behind only. Adding enemies that fly will cause the player to check all directions. Environments can also change based on the enemy's rate of speed. For example, if an enemy soldier first appears on foot but then jumps into a vehicle to attack the player, the level should accommodate for the distance the enemy can cover in the vehicle.

FIGURE 3.1 The beginning of the Altay Shan level in New Legends had a long narrow bridge that the player character needed to cross. Soldiers could run onto the bridge to attack and enemy flying vehicles could attack from the sides.

Enemies can strike in dramatically different ways. Some enemies attack the player character with melee weapons (hand to hand) and some with range weapons (projectiles). An enemy that attacks with melee weapons would be more effective in a tight hallway than on a tower in the distance. Knowing all of the enemies and their methods of attack can help designers build areas that suit them.

Once the designers have determined all of the enemies' attributes, the designers can create an enemy chart to show which enemies are more difficult to fight than others. **Figure 3.2** shows an example.

	LEVEL									
	01	02	03	04	05	06	07	08	09	10
OUTDOOR PLANT 1					X	X	X			X
OUTDOOR PLANT 2					X	X	X			X
LIGHT CREATURE 1		X	X	X	X		X	X	X	X
MEDIUM CREATURE 1		X	X	X	X		X			
MEDIUM CREATURE 2		X	X	X	X	X	X		X	X
FLYING CREATURE			X	X	X		X	X	X	X
MEDIUM CREATURE 3					X	X	X		X	X
LIGHT CREATURE 2									X	X
HEAVY CREATURE 1						X	X	X	X	X
HEAVY CREATURE 2							X		X	X

X = PRESENT IN LEVEL

FIGURE 3.2 An example of an enemy chart. The enemies are ranked according to difficulty. The level progression should show that easier-to-defeat enemies exist early in the game and more challenging enemies exist late in the game.

Of course, as you can see from Figure 3.2, some enemies may simply suit areas better than others, so they might appear to be out of order. In this case, the outdoor plants are the easiest creatures to defeat but the early levels of the game take place indoors.

Ideally, each level should present only one or two new enemies to the player. The number of enemies in a game is limited, and players like to see some variety throughout the game. If you're halfway through the levels in a game and you've already seen all of the enemy types, you don't have much to look forward to.

> **TIP** ▶ When designing a level where a new enemy is introduced, create a unique area specially designed to introduce the new enemy in a dramatic way. Players remember these kinds of moments.

Traps: the obstacles you avoid

Traps are also obstacles that cause damage to the player, but unlike enemies, they are part of the environment. A trap can be a spike that shoots out of the wall when a character stands on a certain spot or a bridge that collapses when it carries too much weight. Games, such as the Tomb Raider series from Eidos, use traps to keep the player alert.

Warning the Player – Part 1

Traps should always have some kind of warning or cue that tells the player that their character might be in danger. Players get frustrated when they can't do anything to prevent their characters from being harmed or killed. If you are designing a rope bridge that has loose boards, you could make the loose boards appear differently from the other boards and attach a cracking sound when the player character steps on them before the boards give way. You could also script an event to show the player what happens when someone steps on a loose board. An enemy could be patrolling the bridge, step on one of the loose boards, and fall.

Traps can also cause the player to progress through a level at a faster pace. Platforms that crumble require player characters to jump off them immediately. Players must rush through hallways with quickly closing walls. By accelerating the gameplay, you can control the flow of the game and sometimes the adrenaline of the player.

Puzzles: the obstacles you solve

Puzzles are just obstacles that require some brainpower to solve. Levels sometimes contain puzzles to give players the satisfaction of solving a problem with their minds and not with their reflexes. A puzzle in an action game might provide a much-needed break from the combat that fills most of the levels.

> **NOTE** Puzzles don't fit in every kind of game. Sometimes, players just want instant satisfaction, and puzzles can often slow down the pace of the game. Genres such as multiplayer shooters, racing games, and strategy games generally don't use many puzzles whereas adventure games may consist of little else.

The base of most puzzles used in level design is the lock and key. Although this puzzle type might not literally be a lock and key, the mechanics are essentially the same. For example, the player may find a rocket ship that can transport their character to a destination, but the rocket ship might need fuel. To use the rocket ship (and progress through the level) the player will need to locate fuel or figure out a way to pump the fuel into the ship. A variation of the lock-and-key puzzle type uses multiple keys instead of just one. Using the rocket ship example again, the player character may have to access three terminals that open the hoses to fuel the ship. By adding multiple "keys," the player character is forced to explore the level more thoroughly.

Puzzles, such as our rocket and fuel example, should be consistent with the style of the level. For example, in LucasArts' Dark Forces, a first-person shooter set in the Star Wars universe, a level takes place in a sewer. Player characters must open floodgates to fill an area with water so that they can swim to the exit. Although this example uses the multiple-key puzzle type (the keys are the floodgates), the elements that replace the lock and key match the style of the sewer. It wouldn't make as much sense to have the player character actually find literal locks and keys in a sewer.

Giving Players What They Need

Game levels provide challenges or obstacles that the player must navigate. But how are the challenges and obstacles overcome? The player character has a limited number of abilities, sometimes called "skills," which enable the player to progress through the game.

The player interacts with obstacles through these skills. Skills can be movement abilities, like jumping or climbing. They can also be ways of attacking. An attack skill in a first-person shooter is based on the weapon the player character has. Shooting a rocket or grenade has a different effect on enemies and the environment than shooting a bullet. The player character can defeat many more enemies with an explosion, and shooting a rocket or grenade can be considered the skill that causes the explosion.

Skills are often staggered, which means that the player character starts the game with a few and acquires more throughout the game. If all of the skills were accessible at the beginning of the game, players might be overwhelmed, and the game might be too easy to complete. A basic set of skills, sometimes called "fundamental skills," introduce the player to how the game is played and provide a foundation for other skills to be built upon. A lot of these fundamental skills exist at the very beginning of the game, and the first level of the game is sometimes a "tutorial" or training level that teaches the player how to use them.

The skills you start with

Fundamental skills are the foundation for player interaction. The player can perform these skills at the beginning of the game, and the early levels usually teach the player how to use those skills. The first level of the game contains the bulk of the instructions and is sometimes called the tutorial level.

Tutorial Levels

Tutorial levels are usually the earliest levels in the game, and their purpose is to teach the player the fundamental skills involved in the game. Tutorial levels are relatively short—typically about half the size of a normal level—and contain very simple challenges, like a pit that the character needs to jump over or a ladder the character can climb, that the player can complete quickly. If the game contains existing skills from a previous game, the tutorial level may be a bit longer. Tutorial levels are probably the most difficult levels to design because they must teach the player multiple new skills in a short amount of time. They also need to fit into the rest of the levels in the game smoothly. As a level designer, you should space out the scenarios that call for new skills so that the player isn't overwhelmed.

Players can learn skills in a variety of different ways. A voice-over audio file or a pop-up text box might tell the player how to use a skill. However, these methods may remove the player from the immersive environment. To keep the illusion intact, other characters in the game can train the player how to use a new skill. For example, in Majesco Entertainment's Psychonauts, the player controls Raz, a psychic kid who gets trained by a camp coach in the first level of the game. Raz enters the coach's mind and the coach teaches the player what skills he can use throughout the level.

The design team, including the level designers, usually collaborates when defining the fundamental skills for a game. Fundamental skills should be relatively easy to perform, which means the player should only need to press a single button or key to use them. For example, firing a gun requires the click of the mouse button in most shooters. Players would be frustrated if simple actions required key combinations. If you had a moving enemy in your sights, you might not have time for more than one action to shoot him.

It might not be obvious which skills should be fundamental and which should be more advanced. The design team may need to outline all of the skills and determine which skills should be more difficult to perform than others. This may depend on the effect of the skill. For example, let's say that your character can pilot both a jeep and a tank. The jeep "skill" might be the fundamental skill while the tank "skill" would be the more advanced simply because the tank can cause more damage to enemies and barriers than the jeep. Therefore, it might even be more difficult to control the tank than the jeep.

Certain genres contain the same set of fundamental skills. This makes it easier for players to immediately start having fun. If you know one FPS, you can probably play another without too much ramp-up time. For example, FPSs all allow the player character to sidestep or "strafe." Strafing allows the player character to dodge attacks while keeping an enemy targeted. If you removed this skill from an FPS, most players would be disappointed because they are accustomed to being able to strafe in other games.

> **NOTE** These days, many games are sequels of existing games. Many of the fundamental skills from the previous games carry over to the sequels. The designers figure out what players liked and disliked from the previous games and can decide what to keep and what to throw out. Level designers should approach every new game as if the player never learned the existing skills from the previous titles, because there will likely be players who are new to the series.

As the player masters the fundamental skills, more skills are added to the mix. Fundamental skills will be used for the entire game, but they may decrease in frequency as additional skills come into the picture.

Adding new skills

As players progress through the game, they gain additional skills. Some additional skills are as simple as obtaining a new weapon, item, or spell. Players may need to select the new weapon/item/spell from a menu, but they use the same button or key as a fundamental skill to perform the new skill. Some skills are more complex, and they may require new buttons or keys to use. For example, in Half-Life 2, soldiers join the player characters in certain areas to help them fight. The player uses a new key to direct the soldiers to a different location or command them to follow.

> **TIP** ▶ A good way to guarantee that players have a skill that they need is to block them with an obstacle that requires that skill. For example, if the player needs to find an axe that can break through wood, block off the area with a wooden obstacle such as a beam or a column. You can now hide the axe somewhere relatively close to the obstacle, forcing the player to find it before moving on. In Metal Gear Solid for the Sony Playstation, the player character needed a sniper rifle to get past a certain enemy. The rifle was hidden in a spot that was possible to miss, so the player was forced to backtrack for a while to find it. If the player had found the sniper rifle closer to the location where he needed it, the experience would have been less tedious.

Players are not necessarily granted skills when they reach certain destinations. In RPGs, such as Diablo 2, the player character gains skills by advancing in experience and "leveling up." The player can add number points to character attributes, such as "strength" and "dexterity," and choose a new skill to learn. The skills are displayed in a "skill tree" (see **Figure 3.3**) for players to make choices about which paths they want to follow. Level designers need to be aware of the character's progression as they travel through the areas to know if some skills should already be in the character's catalogue.

As a designer, you may not always have exact control over which skills are available for each area in the game. Using our example from Diablo 2, players have choices about which skills they inherit. Players can even pick different character types that have completely different skills from each other. One character can have a teleport skill that allows him into areas that other character can't enter. In these cases, you will need to plan for all skills in every area. In addition to the bugs that can crop up from these different sets of skills, the game's balance can become inaccurate and players can advance through a game too quickly or too slowly.

Design the game so that players learn additional skills gradually. If your level grants more than one skill, space out those skills so that the player has time to learn one before encountering the next. Show the player how each skill can be used to interact with different obstacles. Some levels exist purely to teach the player an additional skill and show all the ways that the skill can be used. Scenarios can be tailored for the most ideal use of the skill. For example, in a shooter a player character may find a sniper rifle in a tower with a lookout window and targets down below.

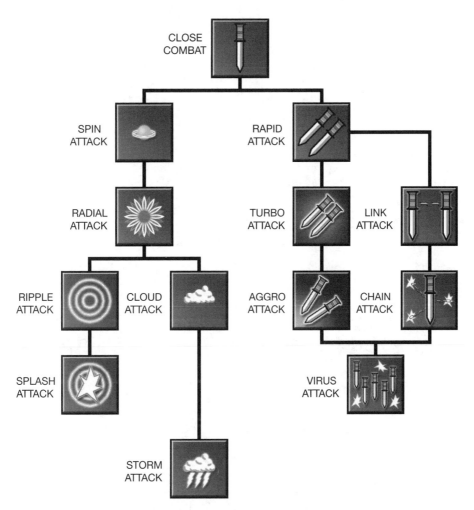

FIGURE 3.3 An example of a skill tree dialog box. Categories of skills branch out in different ways for the player to access other skills. In this example, players can choose between attacking enemies rapidly or with a greater area affected.

When I worked on Harry Potter and the Chamber of Secrets for Electronic Arts, we introduced new spells through "challenge" levels. Harry would experience many different uses of the same spell in areas designed by his professors. Spells that he had learned previously in the game would be present as well to show how combinations of spells worked. Harry could return to these challenge levels repeatedly to master a spell and to find all of the secrets.

Combining skills

Most skills in games can be combined with other skills or even by repeating the same skill. For example, if a character can cut a rope and pull a lever, a level may require that character to cut a rope to allow a lever to be pulled. Similarly, if a character can jump onto a moving platform, a level may require that character to jump onto a moving platform and jump from that platform to another moving platform. You can stack skills throughout levels to add gameplay variety and challenge your players to perform more difficult tasks. **Figure 3.4**, for example, shows the same skill repeated for various levels of difficulty.

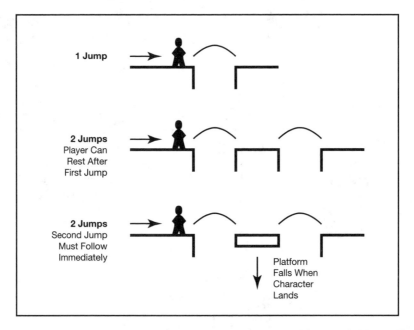

FIGURE 3.4 A diagram showing the same jump skill repeated for variations of difficulty. The player first learns a simple jump in the first sequence. The second sequence teaches that a second jump sometimes follows the first. The third jump adds a more dangerous element.

You can incorporate skill combinations in your level by placing obstacles that work together. Once you have taught the player a new skill, you can start to show them how that skill is used with other skills. Players will eventually discover solutions to problems on their own by using abilities they've already mastered. Players will find greater satisfaction combining the skills they know to overcome a series of obstacles.

TIP ▶ All of the skills used in a combination should be introduced separately before requiring players to mix them together. It's important for the players to understand what each skill does so that they can use them effectively.

Taking measurements

You must outline and detail all skills and skill combinations before creating your levels. This includes determining exact measurements for movement skills. For example, a character in a platformer game may be able to run and jump a maximum length of 128 units. Also, the same character can grab onto a ledge and climb up to extend his maximum jump length to 192 units. Armed with this information, you should not create a situation where the character needs to jump a distance greater than 192 units. **Figure 3.5** shows an example chart of the basic movement measurements for a game.

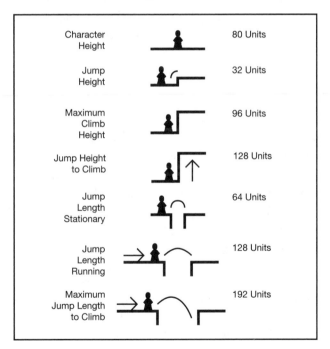

Character Height		80 Units
Jump Height		32 Units
Maximum Climb Height		96 Units
Jump Height to Climb		128 Units
Jump Length Stationary		64 Units
Jump Length Running		128 Units
Maximum Jump Length to Climb		192 Units

FIGURE 3.5 A diagram of the basic movement measurements for an adventure game. All of these sequences can be included in the sandbox level for testing and for duplication.

Warning the Player – Part 2

Once you've identified the measurements , you should start working with a background artist to establish graphical cues to show players what they can and can't do. For example, if a character can run and jump to grab onto a ledge at 192 units, and you create a gap with a longer distance to block the character, the ledge should look noticeably different. The ledge could look crumbled, or it could have a spiked fence on the edge. Graphical cues like these prevent players from trying a skill that will never work and failing over and over again.

Placing the skills and obstacles in order

Once all of the skills and obstacles have been defined and a sandbox level has been created, you must determine the degrees of difficulty. You simply rank all of the skills and the obstacles in the game from the easiest to the hardest. Then place the skills into a chart showing what skills are needed to progress through each level, as shown in **Figure 3.6**.

The level progression should show that the easier skills are present in the levels at the beginning of the game and the harder skills appear later in the game. It's not uncommon for skills to transform into new skills during a game. Players don't have to worry about an early skill if it doesn't exist anymore. For example, let's say that a game requires the player character to deliver newspapers to the neighborhood. The character might start out riding a bicycle. Later in the game, the bicycle gets upgraded to a scooter. The bicycle "skill" is no longer necessary because the scooter "skill" is much more advanced.

Some skills may not be necessary in all of the levels that follow. Players could find themselves going through one or two levels without using a specific skill, only to find that it's needed in a later level. Mixing the skills keeps the player from predicting what task will follow, and keeps the game fun

	LEVEL									
	01	**02**	**03**	**04**	**05**	**06**	**07**	**08**	**09**	**10**
PUSH TRIGGER	X	X	X	X	X			X	X	X
PUSH BLOCK	X	X	X	X	X		X			X
PUSH CREATURE		X	X	X			X	X		X
OPEN CHEST	X	X	X	X	X		X	X	X	X
OPEN LOCK				X			X			
ACTIVATE LIGHT	X	X	X	X	X					X
OBJECT DISAPPEAR	X	X	X	X	X	X	X	X	X	X
OBJECT APPEAR	X	X	X	X	X		X		X	X
RANGE ATTACK		X	X	X	X	X	X	X	X	X
CLEAR OPENING		X	X	X			X	X	X	X
CLEAR FLOOR		X	X	X			X		X	X
CLEAR WALL		X		X					X	X
CUT VINES/WEB					X	X	X	X	X	X
CUT ROPE					X	X	X		X	X
CUT CREATURE					X	X	X			X
SUPER JUMP									X	X

X = PRESENT IN LEVEL

FIGURE 3.6 An example of a skill chart. The skills are ranked according to difficulty and the player character learns the skills in this order. As the player progresses through the game, the easier skills appear less frequently.

Figuring Out Your Level Types

The obstacles and skills in the game are essentially the tools you have to create fun experiences. What more do you need to know to start designing a level? Well, you need to know what kind of level it is you're designing. Most of the levels in the game are standard, which means that they follow the high concept guidelines of the game established at the beginning of production. Standard levels support the game, but there are also a few special level types that might appear along the way. These special level types exist to connect the standard levels together, provide climaxes between levels, and add extra rewards to the game.

The base: standard levels

Standard levels are the base levels in a game. If you were asked to describe a game, you would probably describe some of the experiences contained in a standard level. These experiences are descriptive of the typical gameplay you would encounter throughout the game.

Standard levels make up the majority of the total levels in a game. Most games are about 90 percent standard levels, with the other 10 percent divided up between the rest of the level types. Since all standard levels must be played through to complete the game, a development team would probably consider them to be the highest priority. The team might also incorporate much of the game's story around the standard levels.

Even though standard levels define the gameplay for the overall game, that doesn't mean that the objectives in every standard level have to be the same. For example, in Blizzard Entertainment's RTS Warcraft III, standard levels can include taking over a map with your army, escorting a caravan from one point to another, or defending an area for a certain period of time.

The transition: hubs

Hubs are the levels that connect all the other levels together. Although you can certainly connect standard levels together one after another, hubs allow players to return at frequent intervals and provide them with a reason to return.

NOTE ▶ Not all games have hubs. Hubs are more common in RPGs, adventure games, and platformer games.

Hubs do not have the same gameplay model as the other levels. In a game involving a lot of combat you might designate a hub as a "safe" area, which means that either there are no enemies in these areas or the enemies found do not attack the player character. In RPGs like Diablo, players can trade with vendors, store equipment, and receive missions or quests in a hub called a "town."

Instead of having just one start point and one exit point, hubs usually have multiple start and exit points so that the player can access several other levels. Many of the start and exit points may be blocked until the player completes a certain task or mission. Once the game is nearly complete, hubs open up so that the player can access almost any level quickly.

By definition, hubs are complex. As a level designer, you'll need to create a hub that is functionally efficient enough to allow players to use the hubs for what they need. At the same time, you'll need to create a hub that players won't get bored with. This can be accomplished by making spatially limited hubs that are packed with the elements that players need and with bonus elements that they don't necessarily need.

You can start by determining what the most frequently used elements are. For example, how often will the player need to visit the blacksmith in the town to buy or sell weapons and armor? How often will the player need to talk with the bar patron to get extra information? If the player will visit with the blacksmith every 10 minutes and the bar patron only a couple of times during the game, you can place the blacksmith at a central point of the hub and the bar patron off in a remote corner.

The climax: boss levels

Obviously, boss levels are the levels that contain the bosses. A game can have multiple bosses and the last boss is called the "final boss." This is usually the climax of the game. Players should never feel let down at the end of the game, so the final boss level should be something quite special. Bosses are much more challenging than the other enemies, so level designers often design boss levels around how the boss attacks and how he can be defeated. See **Figure 3.7**, on the next page, for an example.

FIGURE 3.7 A concept for the final boss level in New Legends. The final boss, Xao Gon, started out a normal human size but grew to 50 feet tall. The level had to accommodate for both sizes.

Boss levels provide a break from the standard levels. They usually cover a lot less territory than other levels, and they can even have slightly different mechanics. For example, in most of the levels for Harry Potter and the Chamber of Secrets, the player could control the camera to aim in any direction. In the final boss level, the camera was locked to face only one direction. Boss levels may even contain or trap player characters so that they may not escape the area.

The gravy: bonus levels

Unlike boss levels, which are critical to the player completing the game, a bonus level usually has nothing to do with the overall story of the game, and the player does not have to complete it to proceed to the next level. Unlike boss levels, which are critical to the player completing the game, a bonus level usually has nothing to do with the overall story of the game, and the player does not have to complete it to proceed to the next level.

Bonus levels can appear throughout the game or only at a specific point. In Harry Potter and the Chamber of Secrets, Harry collected Silver Wizard Cards during the course of the game. Once he had found them all, he gained access to a Gold Wizard Card level to complete his wizard card portfolio. Harry learned about this level from a ghost in the early portion of the game; the ghost also told him how to get to the level. Knowing about this bonus level was an added incentive for players to explore all the levels in the game in an attempt to locate Silver Wizard Cards.

Designers include bonus levels to give players some kind of reward for their extra efforts. In the above example, the player gets to play a completely new level for exploring every square inch of the game. Completing a bonus level may provide the player with a special weapon that makes defeating enemies in the rest of the game easier. Bonus levels, like hub levels, provide a break from standard levels. They can be shorter and use much different gameplay. For instance, characters might have time limit to complete the level to receive the reward or they might have to complete against other characters in a race for the reward. Bonus levels should be the lowest priority on any project, and they are the first ones cut when time runs out.

> **NOTE** Developers often hide content in games called "Easter eggs." A bonus level may be an elaborate Easter egg. Easter eggs provide yet another reward for players if they play the game in an unusual way. In Requiem: Avenging Angel, one of our designers built a series of hallways that spelled out the word "FREAK" on the map. The player had to fire a grenade and jump at the same time to blast the player character into this secret area. Developers can also require certain codes or button combinations at different locations to gain access to Easter eggs.

By challenging players and giving them what they need to overcome those challenges, you have the opportunity to shape the experiences that make up the game. Levels are constructed using these elements of obstacles and skills as if they were tools or building blocks. The progression of the obstacles and skills forms an outline for the game. You can use this outline to determine what tools will be available to the player in each level of the game. Next, you'll need to brainstorm some ideas that fit into this outline so you can begin actually designing a level.

Assignment 2

Limiting What Your Players Can Do

For this second assignment, you're going to start laying the groundwork for a level that you can develop throughout the rest of the assignments contained in this book. It doesn't have to relate to the high concept you outlined in the first assignment.

Part 1—List the obstacles you want players to encounter in the level. If your game contains enemies, create a list of enemies that will appear in the level and describe the enemies in terms of size, movement, and attack style. Create an enemy chart and rank the enemies from the easiest to the hardest.

Part 2—List the game skills you want players to have when they play your level. Start by listing the fundamental skills for the game and attach the additional skills. Create a skill chart ranking according to difficulty.

Part 3—Based on your charts, choose what type of level you will be designing for this book.

CHAPTER 4
Brainstorming Your Level Ideas

Brainstorming ideas for the game happens from the very beginning of the development process, but the ideas for the level really begin to flow when the high concept and the design tools are determined. The next step is to create a level description, which you can use in several different ways. A concept artist will find it useful to have a written description of the level that you're planning to design. The level description can also be used in the level diagram, which we'll cover in Chapter 5.

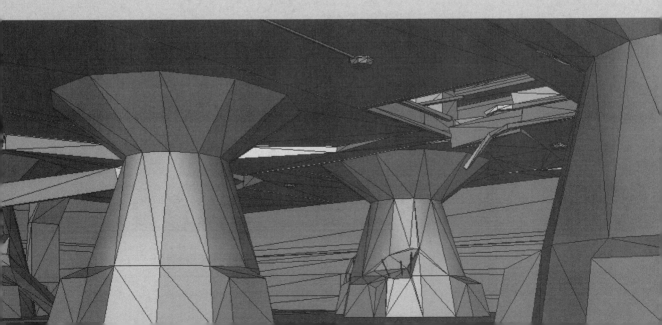

It may be unclear to you exactly how to start the level description, so let's break down some of the categories for level ideas. The first thing you as the level designer should establish is the level's location or setting. You may already know this based on the world diagram or the mission flow diagram, which we talked about in Chapter 1, but simply knowing the location by name is not always enough to give everyone a shared clear visual representation.

Level environments usually have a few general categories that need to be determined before you can begin. First of all, what is the location's functional purpose? For example, is it a mine tunnel system? Is it a military base for new recruits? Second: Does the level have interior or exterior spaces? Does it have both interior and exterior spaces that flow into each other? A third thing to consider is the level size. How big are specific areas? How much time does the player spend in the level? Fourth, what is the architecture like? Does the level have a lot of decorations, or is it much more functional? What details fill the spaces? Answering these questions can become a foundation for a level description you can work with.

Let's say you're designing a level that's been described as a camp. That's a start, but then you need to consider if it has tents or log cabins, and whether it's in a clearing or by a lake. A level description can be passed along to a concept artist who can create a concept piece for different areas in the level. This will get the team on the same page and eliminate wasted time and effort. **Figure 4.1** shows a concept sketch for a lakeside tent with cabins.

FIGURE 4.1 A concept sketch for a level in a camp. If this concept is approved by the lead artist, you have a clear understanding of the setting for the level. Concept sketches can even be replicated accurately in game form to start the ball rolling.

Once you have the setting of the level, you should develop the events that need to take place in the level based on the overall game story and the design tools defined in Chapter 3. Events can include meeting NPCs, finding items, gaining new skills, and transitioning from one area to another. The mission flow diagram should outline some of these events as well as the progression of the player character through the game.

> **NOTE** The setting, characters, and events for a level should work together. For example, if a level takes place in a red light district, the player might need to find a bartender or a dancer to get an item.

Another type of event is a scripted sequence, which is triggered based on the player character's location in a level. Some scripted sequences exist to alter the gameplay. For example, enemy soldiers can have conversations with each other that the player can overhear to gain valuable information. Other scripted sequences serve to create atmosphere. The player could witness a horrific creature feasting on corpses or a cult sacrificing an innocent. These sequences, sometimes called "scenes," are quite memorable, but they don't actually change the way the game is played. As a level designer, it will fall to you to designate where these events exist in a given level, and to define the sequences to the coders who will create them.

You will also likely need to work out the specifics of the level puzzles and how the puzzles work with the setting before integrating the obstacles and skills. Not all puzzles will fit with a location.

How do you start fitting all of these elements into your level? The level narrative may be the glue that connects everything together. The level narrative is the story within the level, as opposed to the story within the game. Level narratives can stretch across several levels, or they can only be related to one. Although they are completely optional, level narratives may make a lot of decisions easier for you later on. Personally, I find it pretty difficult to start designing a level without a level narrative. With a level narrative, you can have a few ideas and carry them all the way through to the smallest detail.

Your assignment, which comes at the end of the chapter, will ask you to create a detailed level description of the level you will be creating for this book. The level description contains the setting and the story that the setting tells as well as any scripted sequences that will make your level more memorable.

Creating a Level Narrative

The hardest part for many level designers is getting started. Even with the game skills and obstacles that we defined in Chapter 3, and your world diagram, you may feel overwhelmed by the number of options available to you. You could make just about anything at this point. One technique that I use to streamline my ideas is the level narrative. The level narrative is the story that the level tells. In a game, there's an overall story that takes the player from the beginning to the end. However, each level can also have its own story.

The level narrative isn't something that has to be based on fact. It can be something that you make up entirely. You can set up a list of rules that you, as a designer, need to follow. By sticking to these rules as best as you can, you can create a set of constraints to work within, not an open-ended blank canvas. Level narratives are not binding, which means that if something doesn't work, you can always break the rules of the narrative for the sake of the level itself.

The level narrative could come from the game's stories or central themes. On Requiem: Avenging Angel, the city levels were designed with the central game theme of good versus evil. The first level in the city made use of a nine-square grid that, if you looked at the level from the top view, resembled a yin-yang symbol. The textures throughout the levels also used this theme. We chose to represent good with water and evil with blood. Water stains seeped down from the tops of walls and bloodstains crawled up from the floors. You can see that level narratives can be incredibly subtle and might even be purely visual, but they might also be the difference that makes your level special.

The level narrative can also come from the original purpose of the areas contained in the level. So, if you're designing a level that takes place in a temple, you can fabricate a narrative about worshipers who sacrificed innocent villagers to a demon or monster. The chambers and passages should be designed with a functional purpose in mind. The level can generate from this configuration of spaces, or you can move things around to suit the level's purposes.

Narrative example: The cookie factory

To best describe how a level narrative works, let's use a level from our "Chaperone" game, which you might remember from the end of Chapter 2. In this game, the player character is a chaperone for kids' events and activities. In one of the first levels of the game, the kids go on a field trip to a cookie factory, and the chaperone is in a car following the school bus. He sees the bus enter the parking lot, but an enemy is waiting for it. Kidnappers take the children off the bus and into the factory. The chaperone must figure out a way to save them. Here's where the gameplay for the cookie factory level begins.

We can start our level narrative with the cookie-making process. To make cookies, we need the ingredients. So, we're going to make a list of areas. We'll start with the storeroom or warehouse that contains ingredients as an area in our level. The ingredients should be opened from their packaging and placed into large vats or tanks so they can be mixed together into big batches of cookie dough. We can add an area of mixers to the level and maybe some hallways with plenty of pipes and channels that the ingredients can travel through. Once the cookies are mixed, the batter needs to be separated into portions. The factory should contain an area where funnels empty the batter onto some kind of belt or track.

Then, the cookies need to be baked. Our factory will need an area where the cookies run through an oven, and where they can cool once they're baked. So, we'll add an area to the level where cookies travel and are cooled along the way.

The next step in baking cookies is, of course, to taste them. Factories can also have some kind of quality assurance area where the products are tested. Although we might not do this at home when we make cookies, our factory will need to package the cookies, so we'll need to design an area for packaging.

Our cookies aren't all just for us, so we need to have an area for getting the cookies into the hands of customers. The factory might have a section for shipping, and it might also have a storefront where customers can come in and buy them. In addition to all this, we'll need a corporate side of the operation, where the company may receive orders and process them for shipment, and a loading dock, where the raw ingredients will be brought in and the finished product will be shipped out. Now, let's list the areas in order of how they fit into the process of making cookies.

Cookie Factory Area Functions

We will now organize the level according to our level narrative brainstorming above. We'll design each area separately and then connect them all back together. We can also go back and combine some areas if the level flow works better that way. This structure gives us an idea for the scale of the level and of the building. It also provides a nice sequence of areas that players might see as they progress through the level.

1. Loading Dock

   Ingredients are brought in on one side and boxes of cookies are sent out on another. There's a parking lot area that is fenced off and leads to the street.

2. Storerooms and Warehouse

   Ingredients could be contained in smaller storerooms so that they are separated and the boxes of cookies could be kept in the larger warehouse.

3. Ingredient Tanks

   Workers open ingredient packages and pour the contents into large vats and tanks.

4. Transition Pipes

   Pipes and tubes lead from the ingredient tanks out through hallways.

5. Mixers

   The pipes carrying the ingredients dump their contents into large mixers, which might have more pipes that dump the mixes into a huge mixer.

6. Separator Funnels

   The huge mixer channels its contents through tubes that grow smaller and smaller until they reach funnels that push cookie-sized portions onto conveyor belts.

7. Ovens

   The conveyor belts carry the batter through a heating process that bakes the cookies. The cookies do not leave the conveyor belts during this stage.

8. Cooling Transition

   The conveyor belts carry the baked cookies for some distance with some separation and sliding into single-file conveyor belts.

9. Inspection Area

   The cookies, which are now cooled and on single-file belts, are randomly tested by employees for size, shape, and taste.

10. Packing

    Groups of cookies that make it past inspection are dropped into bags and sealed. The sealed bags are carried off on another conveyor belt and stuffed into boxes by more workers. The boxes are sealed and put in piles for a forklift to take to the warehouse. Some boxes are taken to the storefront.

11. Storefront

    Workers sell cookies in the store connected to the factory. The store leads out onto a different street from the loading dock.

12. Corporate Offices

    The storefront also leads to offices for business managers who process orders and have them shipped out.

We have now organized the cookie factory, and our level, into 12 unique areas. We've defined, in the form of a brief description, a functional purpose for each of these areas. The next step is to start adding details to these descriptions, including the level narrative to pull things together.

Mind those details

You can now use the rules you've set forth in your level narrative to expand the level description even further. Get as detailed as you'd like in your level narrative. This may seem extraneous and even obsessive to some degree, but it can also be something you turn to when you're stuck for ideas. Besides, it's always easier to have a lot of ideas that you can edit down than to start with that blank page.

Let's use our cookie factory as an example again. Perhaps the designers of the factory knew that they were going to hold tours in this building. They might even know the target age for their products. The best way to buy your cookies is to give them a tour of the factory and cater the experience just for kids. Maybe they painted the walls bright colors. Maybe the cookie recipe is written on signs all over the factory. Maybe they used representations of cookies and ingredients for details such as doorknobs, handles, buttons, and other devices. Maybe they modeled locking mechanisms after cooking appliances. Now, the level narrative truly connects everything the player experiences in the level and you can start to gather references for the visual qualities of the areas.

Gathering Concepts and Reference Images

Game levels start out as spaces. Visually, those spaces should resemble some kind of environment the player can understand and appreciate. While you may not actually decide on the visual style of the levels, you should design levels that work well with the established visual style as determined by the art team. In order for your art team to provide original concept art for your level, they need the detailed level description from you. You can solidify your level description even more by providing reference materials from other sources, such as photographs and even movie stills, as companion pieces. The concept art that your team creates then becomes the visual starting block for building the level.

Your reference materials, including the team's concept art, will not only make the pipeline for the levels smoother, it may also help you come up with more interesting ideas. Let's say that a level in a platformer game takes place in a circus. An artist provides a concept sketch that shows an exterior space around one of the main tents (**Figure 4.2**). Although the artist may not have intended the structures to provide the gameplay, you might look at it and come up with several ideas. You might have the player character sneak underneath the trailer, enter the trailer through the door, exit out of the top, use the sign as a tightrope bridge, and bounce across the top of the tent to the other side.

FIGURE 4.2 With this concept for a circus level, you can develop a clear understanding of the visual style. Concept art can also inspire gameplay aspects of the level.

Even though most level designers aren't skilled illustrators, they contribute a lot to the overall look and feel of the game. It is up to the level designers and game designers to determine the actual locations for the levels, and they provide artists with descriptions for these locations.

Establishing the general look and feel

As level designers, we rarely create our own concept art for levels. Usually, we provide the level description and some reference images to an artist and work together to develop a look and feel that conveys the intended mood of the game.

Not all of the spaces in a level require concept art. An entire level can just have one piece of concept art that sets the style. It may be up to us to carry that style throughout the level, using the geometry we create, and the textures we apply to those surfaces. On the other hand, a level may not have any concept art at all, but it is important to have some kind of reference materials as a base for the visual look and feel of the level. Reference materials are usually images that are taken from all kinds of media. These days, it is incredibly easy to find reference materials on the Internet. Level designers—and artists, for that matter—can search for images from photos, films, shows, comic books, illustrations, and fine art. As shown in **Figure 4.3**, on the next page, artists and designers can also use photos taken with digital cameras as reference materials.

FIGURE 4.3 A personal photo taken of cranes unloading a ship. Reference materials don't always represent spaces in the level literally. They can simply give an impression that members of the team use as a basis for other ideas. This crane could be similar to machinery in the cookie factory level.

You can take photos of everyday objects and scenes that may contain materials that you want in the level. Designers working on games that have realistic themes set in the present can directly draw from reference materials.

TIP Taking digital photos can also provide reference for the textures that are placed onto the geometry of the levels. You can gather references for both level geometry and textures at the same places.

Interior and exterior spaces

Interior spaces work very differently from exterior spaces in levels. In video games, an interior is a space that has a ceiling. An exterior space has no ceiling. The ceiling can be implied and not actually visible. The ceiling can't be the sky or anything that is immeasurable. Interiors are usually smaller and easier to control than exteriors. Exteriors typically allow the player to see more of the backgrounds (**Figure 4.4**). Therefore, the amount of detail for interiors is much greater than for exteriors. This limits some of the gameplay elements for both kinds of spaces.

FIGURE 4.4 A bird's-eye view of the refinery level in New Legends. This exterior level could not afford as much geometric detail as an interior level. Architectural pieces, such as hand railings and stairwells, had to be constructed using simple shapes.

Usually, an exterior level contains less detail, but it may display objects in the far distance. For example, for a level set in a city, you might decide to show the tops of buildings above the structures that the player moves between. The far-off buildings give the illusion that the city is much bigger than the level really is.

Terrain

We frequently use a kind of level geometry called "terrain" when creating exterior spaces. Terrain is the game representation of "organic landscape." In games, we often refer to two kinds of structures: man-made and organic. Organic landscape is landscape that appears more natural. Terrain can take the shape of rolling hills or of steep mountains and cliffs. Terrain takes up most of the real estate in many exterior levels with scattered buildings and structures as cover. Games such as Starsiege: Tribes (by Dynamix) focus on large expanses of terrain where players can battle each other over a great distance.

Spatial scale

Level descriptions can include both the scale of the entire level and the scale of specific areas. The scale of the entire level may be broad. Levels can be classified as small, medium, or large relative to the rest of the levels in the game. A medium-sized level typically takes between 20 and 30 minutes to complete. Anything shorter might be considered a small level and anything longer a large level. The scale of specific areas should be more detailed. For example, a hangar for one spaceship is very different from a hangar for many ships.

Artists frequently place a representation of the player character into a piece of concept art (**Figure 4.5**) to give a sense of scale to specific areas. Any object that you are familiar with, like a car or a piece of furniture, can work just as well.

FIGURE 4.5 A concept piece for a hangar in a science fiction game. Two human figures have been sketched in to give a sense of scale. Other objects, like stairs or railings, can also convey the scale.

Getting the scale right for a space can often be the most difficult thing for a level designer to do. It's a good idea to start with one of the simple architectural pieces and grow the space from there. So, in Figure 4.5, you could start building the stairs and then proceed to the catwalks. You can also refer to the sandbox level, which we introduced in Chapter 1. The sandbox level can contain the standard sizes for many architectural features such as doorways, crawlspaces, and windows as approved by the level designers and the artists.

Following an architectural style

Sometimes, the architectural style can dictate the design for certain areas. Columns demonstrate this point perfectly. If a large room has columns of a certain size, a player character may be able to hide behind them to avoid enemy attacks or detection. The gameplay in the area completely changes if the columns either don't exist or of a smaller size. Of course, if the room does not contain columns and you still want the player character to have cover, you can add a substitute, like debris, crates, or even heater tanks, as shown in **Figure 4.6**. It's important, of course, that these pieces make sense for the area.

FIGURE 4.6 A concept artist needs to know about gameplay elements such as columns or crates when creating concept art for a space. In this hallway, heater tanks were used for cover to fit the industrial style.

General styles can also designate the flow of a level. For example, if the architectural style is organic as opposed to man-made and orthogonal (characterized by right angles), the actual spaces of the level can have an organic structure as well. In an organic level, like a cave level, spaces might transition smoothly into each other with curves. An orthogonal level, like a hospital level, might have more predictable turns and patterns. You might choose to use less rigid angles and less repetition for smoother turns and movement through a level.

Incorporating landmarks

Every game level should contain landmarks. Therefore, your level description should include the landmarks contained in the spaces in the level. Landmarks, sometimes called "set pieces," are unique areas or features that players can use to keep from getting lost or going in circles. Landmarks can be anything in a level, as long as it's unique. Usually, landmarks are memorable either by size or by appearance. Some common landmarks in games are fountains, statues, distinct buildings, and large machines.

> **NOTE** In multiplayer games, such as Valve Software's Day of Defeat, players frequently refer to landmarks to let their teammates know where to go or what is happening. For example, a player might type "get to the bridge" or "I'll cover the church" to the other players.

Landmarks are usually the focal points of the level. They can contain a puzzle that the player needs to solve to progress, or they can simply be a special object such as a statue or a fountain. For example, the player could catch glimpses of the Buddha statue in the New Legends level shown in Figure 1.10, as the player character progressed through the level. This helped let the player know that he was on the right track.

Before designing a level, you should know or determine the landmarks for the level. Levels often contain several landmarks for the player to progress from one to another.

> **NOTE** Landmark tiles are especially helpful to players in levels with random level generation. Tiles can get repetitive quickly and players can get lost without seeing a unique piece. For example, in a dungeon level made up of random tiles, the landmark tile could be a torture chamber. Level designers can use the torture chamber as a "choke point," which is an area all players must pass through in order to progress through the game. By making your choke point a landmark tile, you ensure that all players will see your unique area. This breaks up the repetition of the level, and gives the player a sense of progression. The bridge in **Figure 4.7**, on the next page, is an example of a choke point.

FIGURE 4.7 A concept piece for the entrance to a prison. To ensure that all players will see this elaborate scene, the bridge shown should be a choke point to proceed through the level.

In our cookie factory example, we can pick out a few of the areas we have already designated and come up with some landmarks for them. The school bus in the parking lot signifies the start position for the player. The huge mixer has a lot of potential for a puzzle, so it qualifies as a landmark. The main tool for baking is the oven, so it also qualifies. The storefront façade that opens onto the street needs to draw customers in and should be different from the rest of the factory. Its unique appearance makes it a landmark area.

Writing the level description

Now we're going to take the same area list that we outlined for the cookie factory level and expand the descriptions to include the elements of the location itself. These descriptions can be given to a concept artist for possible sketches or reference materials.

1. Loading Dock

    The loading dock might have some decoration, and it could have a pedestrian entrance for tours. It is a functional area, with several doors for trucks to unload into (**Figure 4.8**). This area should be fairly large since it will contain several vehicles such as trucks, forklifts, and cars. It has both exterior and interior spaces. The doors to the loading dock are rolling doors and the facilities like pipes, vents, and tanks may be visible.

FIGURE 4.8 A concept sketch of the loading dock for the cookie factory based on its description.

2. Storerooms and Warehouse

The storerooms should only be large enough for individual ingredients. If cookies contain flour, sugar, brown sugar, butter, eggs, salt, baking soda, and vanilla extract, then there may be eight storerooms that are much smaller than the loading dock area. The storerooms are very functional and plain, with facilities visible for cooling. The warehouse section should be much larger. It is still smaller than the loading dock, but it needs to hold hundreds of boxes of cookies. Both of these areas are completely interior with little or no windows. Tons of boxes, crates, bags, and containers line shelves that go all the way up to the ceiling.

3. Ingredient Tanks

The ingredient tanks area needs to have some open spaces for workers to empty the contents of the boxes, crates, bags, and containers into the tanks. The tanks themselves are quite tall, and might have openings that are a few feet across. Workers must ascend steps and ladders for maintenance (**Figure 4.9**). At least eight tanks and labels should be visible.

FIGURE 4.9 A photo of something that could resemble an ingredient tank. This photo was taken at a junkyard in San Francisco.

4. Transition Pipes

   Pipes come from the ingredient tanks and line the hallways to the next area. This section should make the player feel claustrophobic, with pipes surrounding the occupants. There may be ladders that connect hallways vertically.

5. Mixers

   There should not be a lot of walking room in this section. The mixers should be enormous, with the one landmark mixer occupying most of the space. Ladders, stairs, and catwalks lead to areas for maintenance. The main mixing container might contain puzzle elements that the player needs to see, so it should be fairly open.

6. Separator Funnels

   The separator funnel area can be smaller, with perhaps four conveyor belts and a funnel hanging over each. The funnels should be quite tall, with ladders and catwalks for maintenance. The ceiling should be lined with pipes and ventilation.

7. Ovens

   This space, which might continue from the separator funnel area, should be approximately the same size with the same details. The oven itself is a large, flat device over and under the conveyor belts, which have changed material. **Figure 4.10** shows a photo of something that could resemble a conveyer belt.

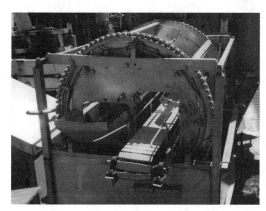

FIGURE 4.10 This piece of machinery, photographed at the same junkyard as the picture in Figure 4.9, could be used as a reference image by an artist or level designer.

8. Cooling Transition

The conveyor belts split up at this point and start to go up and down to get a lot of air around the cookies. The space can be large and open with a lot of moving conveyor belts and tracks. Windows, rather than artificial lighting, start to light the spaces.

9. Inspection Area

The inspection area needs a lot of walking space for workers. There can still be multiple sections for cookie inspection, but the area is not very large. Bins in which flawed cookies are discarded, as well as a cooler that holds milk for inspectors to drink when tasting cookies, could be included in this area.

10. Packing

The setup for this area is similar to the inspection area (lots of walking space…). However, because this area must accommodate boxes of bagged cookies and forklifts to move the boxes around, it should be quite large. If possible, the packing area should be right next to the warehouse for convenience. This could show how the cookie-making process comes full circle.

11. Storefront

The storefront is a small space about the size of a coffee shop. It features a counter with cookies lined on trays. Lining the walls are more cookies, sold by the bag. A cooler holds beverages behind the counter. There are no tables or chairs. A large window looks out onto the street.

12. Corporate Offices

The corporate office area contains just a few offices and an open space for cubicles. It might also have a small meeting room. There are a lot of windows.

When we combine these descriptions with the level narrative descriptions, we should have a clear vision of what the spaces in the level will look and feel like. Some of the areas may take on very specific forms so that the next steps in our brainstorming phase are easier.

Designing Puzzles

Puzzles are situations in levels that require the player to find a solution in order to progress. In the genres that apply to level designers, puzzles can appear in many forms, ranging from finding a key to a locked door to collecting multiple items that fit together to reveal the next area. Designing puzzles is part of designing levels. Not all levels have to contain puzzles, but there are reasons why you'd want to create puzzles.

First of all, puzzles slow the player's progression. Why is that a good thing? Well, adding puzzle elements can give players a chance to stop and enjoy the scenery as they work on the solution. Second, most players like variety. They generally want some kind of a change at least every 15 minutes or so. If the gameplay in a level is a constant line of moving and fighting, a puzzle in the middle of the level can provide that change. Puzzles can cause the player to stop and think about how the game works. Finally, solving puzzles gives the player a greater sense of accomplishment. Puzzles can integrate the gameplay with the environment in a very unique and rewarding way. Players remember levels by the puzzles contained inside and what they did to solve them.

So how do you come up with ideas for puzzles? A lot of designers work backward—from the destination to the point of entry. Most puzzles involve the player progressing in some way. You can start with where the player wants to go eventually and block the path with a barrier that makes sense for each situation. The player must be able to pass the barrier using the tools of design outlined in the previous chapter. You can imbed the tools so that the player must use multiple skills to progress. Some solutions are obvious and some are not. Use the degrees-of-difficulty charts to determine what skills and enemies are available in the level. Stack the available skills in different ways. You can repeat situations and solutions from previous levels, but add more layers of challenges on top of them or change the order around to keep the player from getting bored.

> **TIP** When you're designing a puzzle and going backward from the destination, it's a good idea to allow players to see the destination from the beginning of the puzzle. Otherwise, they might not know that it is necessary to complete the puzzle in order to move on.

During this phase of development, you should be thinking of ideas for puzzles (if your levels contain any). Going back to the level narrative is a good way to start. Pick out a section of the level that you find interesting. Maybe it has a unique feature located there. Perhaps the section just divides up the rest of your level neatly. An easy choice for our cookie factory example is the huge mixer located at the end of the mixing process. Why is it an easy choice? It's a unique feature, and it connects one large area to another. In other words, it's a choke point, at least for the cookies.

Puzzle design example: the mixer

As an example of the puzzle brainstorming process, I've provided some ideas for our puzzle in the cookie factory. Let's say that we're in the mixer area of the level, and our player wants to find a way to the other side of the room, where the exit is. We know from our level narrative and level description that this area contains machines, containers, and controls to mix the ingredients for the cookies. Following the process outlined in Chapter 2, our skill charts would show us that the player can perform certain skills. For this example, let's assume that the player character can activate controls, climb ladders, and traverse pipes. Using this knowledge, we can outline the flow of the puzzle, starting with the exit point. **Figure 4.11** shows a diagram of the following puzzle.

A. Part 1 - Controls operate the Mixer Bridge. Initially, the controls make a sound that something is wrong. A voice could say, "Ingredients not in place."

B. The player character finds a set of controls for Tank 1. When activated, the contents are emptied into the main container. A voice could say, "Tank 1contents added."

C. The player character can go back down to find the ladder for Tank 2 is destroyed.

D. Using a skill, the player character can cross on top of a pipe to get to Tank 2's controls.

E. Tank 2 controls empty its contents into the main container. A voice could say, "Tank 2 contents added."

A. Part 2 - When the player character activates the controls for the Mixer Bridge,the Mixer Bridge descends and starts to rotate slowly. The player character must jump on one end and jump off on the other side to the Exit.

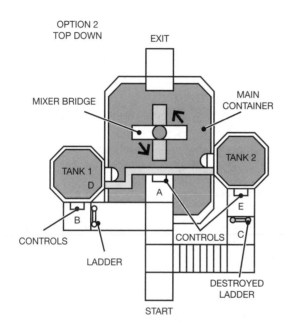

FIGURE 4.11 A basic diagram describing the mixer puzzle. A puzzle diagram can be added to a level diagram later. It helps to have a puzzle diagram first to establish the sequences of certain spaces.

Outlining the Puzzle Flow

1. Exit

The player character wants to cross over a large, open container of batter to a landing on the other side.

2. Obstacle

The batter in the container is dense, and the player character can't swim in it. The only way across it is by using parts of the mixer as a bridge. The player must figure out how to move pieces of the mixer to connect to the other side.

3. Skills

The player can activate a control overlooking the main container, but nothing seems to happen. A diagram to the side of the controls illustrates that all of the ingredients have not been added. The player character must climb a ladder to activate one set of controls, which dump ingredients from a smaller tank into the main container. The player must traverse a pipe to get to another set of controls, which dump ingredients from another small tank into the main container.

4. Result

With the main container filled with ingredients from the two smaller tanks, the player character can activate the first set of controls to move the mixer bridge down and start its rotation. The player can then jump on one end of the bridge and ride it to the other side of the container, where the exit is located.

NOTE ▶ It isn't necessary to come up with more than one option for a puzzle, but it may help later on if your first option becomes hopeless. This is rare, though, as most puzzle ideas get modified and revised over and over to eventually work even if they don't resemble the original puzzle at all.

Adding Scripted Sequences

Scripted sequences can also be referred to as "scenes." Both of these terms describe a special situation the development team has scripted for the player. Designers create some scenes to enhance the story of the game, and others to drop important clues to the player. Other scenes are meant to scare the player. Players remember special scenes in levels. Scenes make the world seem real.

Scenes can be as simple as lights turning off when the player character enters a room. For example, the introduction for one of the enemies in Epic Games' Unreal started with the player entering a hallway. The ends of the hallway were blocked off and all of the lights down the hallway turned off one by one. Each light represents a different, but simple, scripted sequence. Scenes can also be complex. In DOOM 3, a scientist turns into a zombie right in front of the player character and then starts to attack.

It's important for level designers to brainstorm ideas for scenes in their levels before the level is actually created. Scenes usually require some specific art and a lot of AI and scripting efforts. Scenes such as a conversation between two characters may require modeling, texturing, and animation for those models as well as the dialogue and voice acting. An AI programmer or a scripter may need to write a script for that specific scene, and you may need to design a specific space or geometry to contain it. It takes time to create the scenes, so you should write descriptions to help everyone understand what takes place in each scene. Submit your descriptions to the AI programmers, scripters, and animators for preparation and approval; you can also add them to the design document.

Writing scene descriptions

Let's go back to our cookie factory example, and brainstorm some scene ideas. Once again, this is a brainstorming chapter, so let your ideas flow without worrying about the implementation of all of them.

1. Loading Dock—No player control

   The bus pulls into the lot and the kids exit. Some enemies (disguised as cookie factory employees?) come out from the loading doors and lead the kids into the building. Some guards stay behind as the first enemies for the player character to fight.

2. Storerooms and Warehouse

   There might be an interior window that leads from the warehouse area to a catwalk in the packing area. The kids are shown being led on the other side of the window. One child could see the player character and give a little wave. If the player character moves past a certain point and returns, the kids are all gone.

3. Ingredient Tanks

   A pair of enemies converse up above the player character. They might reveal some clue about why the kids are being held. If they are interrupted, they can attack the player character without resuming the conversation.

4. Mixers

   Two guards are fighting and one gets pushed into the main container. He disappears into the batter. If the guard who does the pushing takes damage from the player character, the other guard still falls in the container.

5. Inspection Area

   An enemy guard is standing at an inspection post and sneaking cookies into his mouth. He keeps looking around to see if anyone has seen him. The player character can interrupt him by either passing a certain point or attacking.

6. Packing

   One child has escaped and hidden inside one of the boxes. He won't come out, though, even when he sees the player character. The player character weapon should lower when looking at the child.

7. Corporate Offices—No player control

   The kids come out of an office cheering and thanking the chaperone for saving them.

You should now have scene descriptions for your level as well as visual descriptions. With these, you have laid the groundwork to start laying out your level in a diagrammatic form, which we'll tackle in Chapter 5. This is where all of your effort so far can be shown as something that resembles a level.

Before we move on to diagramming your level, your assignment is as promised: a complete level description for your level including reference materials, landmarks, puzzle ideas, and scripted sequence ideas.

Assignment 3

Planting Your Level Ideas

Part 1—Choose a location for the level you will be designing for this book. Write a brief description of the setting including the size of the level, the kinds of spaces contained, and the architectural style you envision.

Part 2—Gather reference materials for your level. Obtain photos from the Internet or by taking your own, watching films, and looking at books that have something to do with your level's location and theme.

Part 3—Create a list of landmarks contained in your level and designate which landmarks might have scenes or puzzles associated with them.

Part 4—Select one possible area for a puzzle and write a description for what the puzzle could be about.

Part 5—Select one possible area for a scripted scene in your level and write a description of what takes place in that scene.

CHAPTER 5
Designing With a Diagram

THE DIAGRAM IS THE BLUEPRINT of the level. Like an outline for a paper or the plans for a building, the diagram gives you an opportunity to design more freely without having to build everything out in a level-editing program. Not all levels need diagrams, but a diagram can prove beneficial. As any aspiring writer will tell you, there's nothing more intimidating than a blank page. The same is often true when you're beginning to design your levels. But with a level diagram, the design factors (which we discussed in Chapter 3), and the level ideas all set up, you will have plenty to work with.

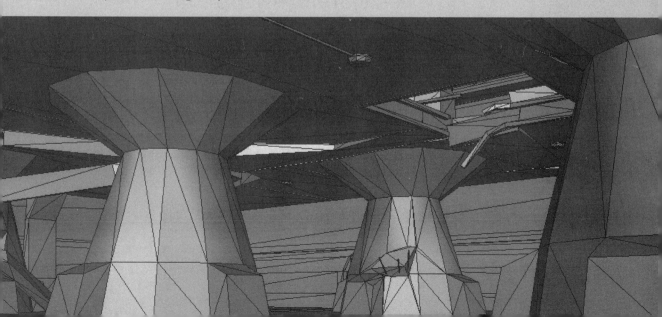

What do you need for your level diagram? The first thing to start with is the level context. In order to create your level diagram, you need to know where players are coming from, and where they are going, what skills and obstacles they faced in previous levels, and what knowledge they have acquired. The level context sets up each level with this information. Level scope, or how much of the game your level covers, is also an important part of the level context. You wouldn't want to complete your set of levels for the game only to find out from the lead designer that the game's content has been drastically reduced.

In this chapter, we'll also talk about level progression, or its sequence of experiences. For every level, there is a starting point and an ending point for the player character. Linear progressions lead the player character through a level from point to point without any real choices, while nonlinear progressions provide choices for the player to make along the way. Deciding on a progression is the first step to laying out the spaces or areas in your level diagram.

Creating your level diagram gives you a huge head start in designing your level. The order and arrangement of the spaces, the connections between those spaces, and the placement of obstacles and skills all come together in the level diagram. Once your diagram is complete, you can start creating your level with a plan. You won't have a blank page anymore. You'll also be able to clearly present your level and design ideas to higher-ups or publishers.

Your assignment, at the end of this chapter, will be a level diagram that you can present to other developers so that they can understand your ideas and design methods. You will use this diagram to construct your level in a level editor and refer back to it when you think you're getting off track. This may sound like a big task, but you can create the diagram with some small steps that we'll discuss first.

Understanding the Level Context

Game levels don't stand by themselves; most games are released with several levels, and those levels have to work together to teach players all of the skills that they will need to progress through the game and to carry the player character smoothly from one setting to another. Levels can also work together to tell the overall story of the game. A level's *context* is its relationship to the rest of the levels in the game. To understand a level's context, it's best to start with the world diagram, which we covered in Chapter 1. The world diagram should show the total number of levels in the game, which in turn indicates the scope of each level; the order of the levels in the game; and the indications for special-case levels.

The *scope* of the level refers both to the amount of gameplay in a level and the percentage of the game contained in each level. There's a big difference between a level that covers 10 percent of the game versus one that covers 5 percent of the game. Knowing this number will help you plan the length of certain segments.

As we discussed in Chapter 3, the level order determines the skills and obstacles that you'll place in the game. Not only will knowing the order of the levels give you a breakdown of the skills you'll need for your specific levels, but it will also show you the skills and obstacles you should introduce in subsequent levels.

Special-case levels exist to break the rules. Breaking the rules is a great way to keep the player's interest. For example, in New Legends, we added a level where the player character had to run and slide down a mountain to escape an avalanche. Up to this point, the player character had to battle many enemies using a variety of weapons and a small team of other characters. The avalanche provided a short recess from the core gameplay defined by the earlier levels in the game. Designers will use these types of levels to add variety to a game, so if you're working on one, you'll need to figure out the unique gameplay involved in the level before starting your diagram. These special-case levels can be outlined during the creation of the world diagram by the level designers and the lead designer.

Determining level scope

Before you start to design your level through a diagram, you should know the scope of the level, or how much of the game the level covers. This isn't necessarily the physical size of a level. Small levels can contain complex gameplay that keep players occupied for a long time, while large levels can contain simple gameplay that players can run through quickly. The scope has more to do with gameplay time. If the team decides that the level that you're designing should take between 15 and 20 minutes to complete, as outlined in the design document and the world diagram, the scope of the level becomes much more clearly defined than knowing the physical proportions.

The level scope is determined by several factors: the total playing time for the entire game, the number of levels in the game, and whether the level is played just once or can be revisited. The total playing time for the game is a value that you probably won't have any control over. Project leads and executives may discuss this value and come up with something that sounds like it's long enough for the player to feel satisfied but short enough for the team to finish on time. The number of levels and the rules for revisiting can be determined by the project leads and the level design team.

> **NOTE** Of course, the time it takes to play through a level is greatly dependent on the experience of the player. A player who is familiar with a certain genre might complete a level in half the time it takes for a beginner. This is one reason why play-test sessions are so important. It may take several play-test sessions with players of varying degrees of experience to find the right amount of gameplay for a level.

Since most players like to experience some kind of change in the game every 15 minutes or so, level designers usually strive to limit the level gameplay to 30 minutes or less. The change can be a simple one, such as a different enemy to fight or a new weapon to use. Or it could be more dramatic; let's say, for example, that the player character has been traveling through a cave on foot for a while. You could decide to flood one section of the cave with water, so that the player needs to wade or swim to get across. Both of these changes would require a different look to the level.

Some games contain levels that can be revisited during the game for various reasons. For example, if item collection is a major part of the game, a hub used for trading or finding secrets might involve a lot of content. These levels may not have a time stamp on them, but they may have other methods for measuring size. For example, in Harry Potter and the Chamber of Secrets, Harry can encounter story elements, trade with other students, collect items, and find secrets in three hubs: the entrance hall, the grand staircase, and the grounds. He also needs to revisit these areas to find connections to other levels. These hubs aren't measured in size or time but in the frequency the player character interacts with their functions.

Level scope determines both the amount of gameplay in the level as well as the amount of time you should spend creating the level. Many game-development projects have rigid schedules, and if you know that you need to complete a certain number of levels before a deadline, you'll have to manage your time accordingly. In other words, it's not wise to spend too much time on one level that covers only 5 percent of the game when you still have five other levels to design that collectively make up 50 percent of the game!

Knowing the level order

The sequence of the levels outlines which skills and obstacles are available to the player in each level of the game. Before you create your level diagram, you'll need to know the sequence of the levels to associate each of those skills and obstacles with a specific space in your level. The level order can even determine what the purpose of the level is. Some levels, like the "challenge level" shown in **Figures 5.1a** and **5.1b**, on the next page, have the sole purpose of introducing a new skill that the player character can use. Each space in the level becomes an example of how the new skill overcomes a different obstacle.

Levels, and the challenges contained in those levels, tend to grow as players progress through a game. A level that appears later in the game could be substantially bigger than a level that appears at the beginning because the player character has a wider range of skills to use and a wider range of obstacles to face. You can gauge level size by using your skills and obstacles chart (Chapter 3). Using your chart, you can see just what the player character can do and exactly what obstacles the character will face in a particular level.

> **NOTE** As levels grow larger, they also become increasingly challenging to complete. The order of the level sets up a foundation for the initial difficulty of the entire game. The first level should be the easiest to complete, and the last level should be the most difficult. The level diagram can start to convey some of the difficulty through the density of the obstacles and the skills used to overcome them.

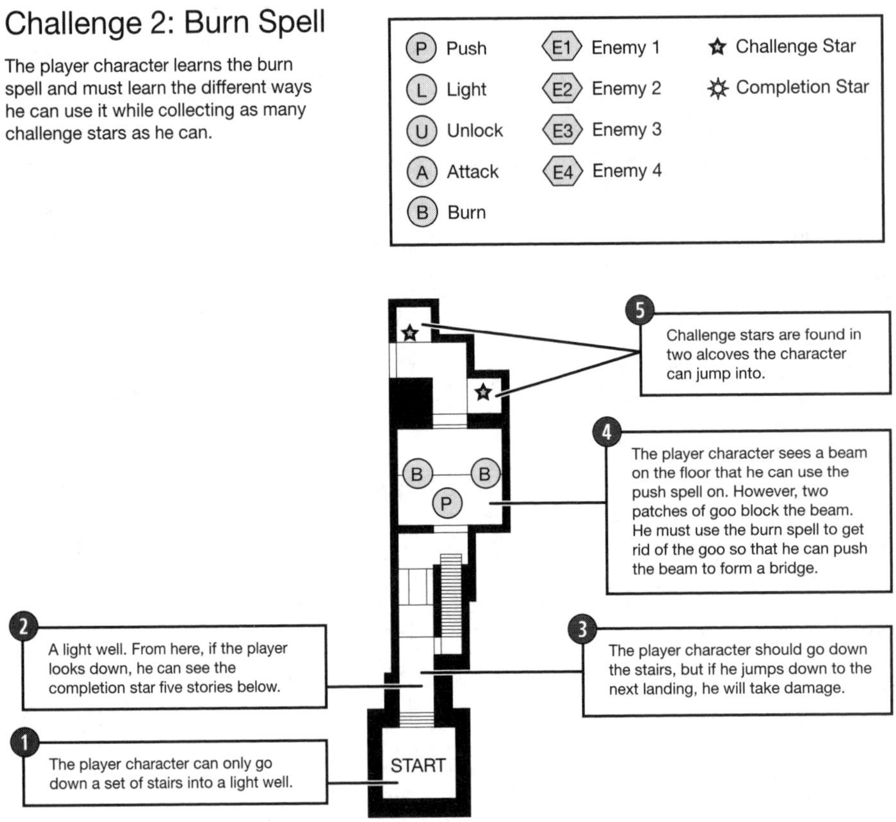

Challenge 2: Burn Spell

The player character learns the burn spell and must learn the different ways he can use it while collecting as many challenge stars as he can.

Legend:

- (P) Push
- (L) Light
- (U) Unlock
- (A) Attack
- (B) Burn
- ⟨E1⟩ Enemy 1
- ⟨E2⟩ Enemy 2
- ⟨E3⟩ Enemy 3
- ⟨E4⟩ Enemy 4
- ☆ Challenge Star
- ☼ Completion Star

5 Challenge stars are found in two alcoves the character can jump into.

4 The player character sees a beam on the floor that he can use the push spell on. However, two patches of goo block the beam. He must use the burn spell to get rid of the goo so that he can push the beam to form a bridge.

2 A light well. From here, if the player looks down, he can see the completion star five stories below.

3 The player character should go down the stairs, but if he jumps down to the next landing, he will take damage.

1 The player character can only go down a set of stairs into a light well.

START

FIGURE 5.1A The level diagram for a challenge level to introduce a new skill (or, in this case, spell).

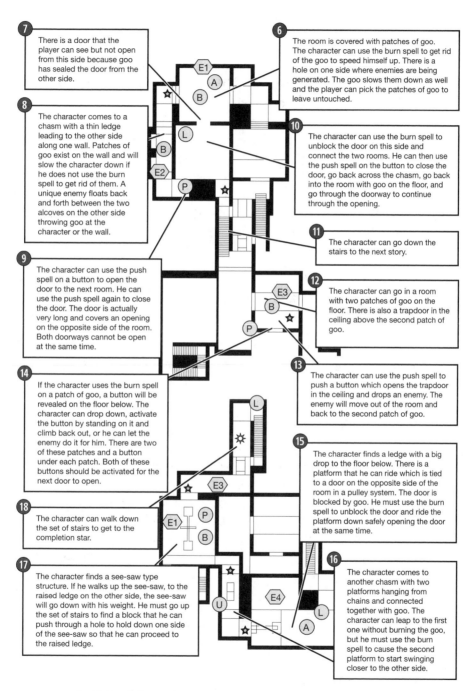

7 There is a door that the player can see but not open from this side because goo has sealed the door from the other side.

8 The character comes to a chasm with a thin ledge leading to the other side along one wall. Patches of goo exist on the wall and will slow the character down if he does not use the burn spell to get rid of them. A unique enemy floats back and forth between the two alcoves on the other side throwing goo at the character or the wall.

9 The character can use the push spell on a button to open the door to the next room. He can use the push spell again to close the door. The door is actually very long and covers an opening on the opposite side of the room. Both doorways cannot be open at the same time.

14 If the character uses the burn spell on a patch of goo, a button will be revealed on the floor below. The character can drop down, activate the button by standing on it and climb back out, or he can let the enemy do it for him. There are two of these patches and a button under each patch. Both of these buttons should be activated for the next door to open.

18 The character can walk down the set of stairs to get to the completion star.

17 The character finds a see-saw type structure. If he walks up the see-saw, to the raised ledge on the other side, the see-saw will go down with his weight. He must go up the set of stairs to find a block that he can push through a hole to hold down one side of the see-saw so that he can proceed to the raised ledge.

6 The room is covered with patches of goo. The character can use the burn spell to get rid of the goo to speed himself up. There is a hole on one side where enemies are being generated. The goo slows them down as well and the player can pick the patches of goo to leave untouched.

10 The character can use the burn spell to unblock the door on this side and connect the two rooms. He can then use the push spell on the button to close the door, go back across the chasm, go back into the room with goo on the floor, and go through the doorway to continue through the opening.

11 The character can go down the stairs to the next story.

12 The character can go in a room with two patches of goo on the floor. There is also a trapdoor in the ceiling above the second patch of goo.

13 The character can use the push spell to push a button which opens the trapdoor in the ceiling and drops an enemy. The enemy will move out of the room and back to the second patch of goo.

15 The character finds a ledge with a big drop to the floor below. There is a platform that he can ride which is tied to a door on the opposite side of the room in a pulley system. The door is blocked by goo. He must use the burn spell to unblock the door and ride the platform down safely opening the door at the same time.

16 The character comes to another chasm with two platforms hanging from chains and connected together with goo. The character can leap to the first one without burning the goo, but he must use the burn spell to cause the second platform to start swinging closer to the other side.

FIGURE 5.1B In this level, the player character learns the "burn spell," which burns away a gooey substance. The level shows several examples of how to use the spell as well as combining obstacles that have been seen before in slightly different ways.

Using special-case levels

Some levels in games contain quite unique elements of gameplay. For example, player characters that usually travel by foot might pilot a vehicle, or perhaps enter an environment, like an anti-gravity chamber, that changes their movement altogether. These levels, called *special-case levels*, might simply provide more variety to the overall game, or they may be an inherent quality of the game itself. Many levels in the platformer Psychonauts take place inside the minds of different characters, and each one offers a different experience to the player. **Figure 5.2** shows two screenshots from the Waterloo World level in Psychonauts. In this level, the player character, Raz, can switch back and forth between three different sizes. The figure shows Raz standing on the game board at medium and small sizes (Scales B and C, respectively).

At the beginning of the diagram stage for a level, you should know if the level is a special-case level and what features make the level special. This should all be determined by the design team and outlined in the world diagram to fit into the overall context of the game.

Special-case levels don't follow all of the same rules as the rest of the levels in the game. You can establish a new set of rules that the player must learn and adapt to quickly. The Waterloo World level, for instance, is the only level in Psychonauts where Raz can change his size. It adds a great deal of variety to the gameplay at a late stage in the game.

The special features in these levels don't have to be as extreme as changing the scale of the player character. Sometimes, a change of camera angle is enough to vary the gameplay. For example, in the original Crash Bandicoot, developed by Naughty Dog and Sony Computer Entertainment, the camera usually follows the player character, Crash, from behind. In special-case levels, the camera shows the front of Crash and a huge boulder chasing him. The player must direct Crash through an obstacle course of pits and barricades while preventing him from being crushed by the boulder.

SCALE B

SCALE C

FIGURE 5.2 Screenshots of the Waterloo World level in Psychonauts. This level takes place inside the mind of a character named Fred. The level is set up like a board game where the player's character, Raz, can change between three different sizes.

Progressing Through a Level

The level context deals with how the player progresses through the entire game. The level progression involves how the player character moves through one individual level. Even if you have a good idea of the specific areas in your level, you'll need to start placing those locations in some kind of order and give them an organizational structure. This structure is the first step in creating a level diagram.

By using the game's story, the level narrative, and the level's context, you should know where the character needs to go to complete the level. The player may start the level where the last level left off and may end the level where the next level begins. The single objective or multiple objectives for the level may require a task to take place in a specific area. It might not be obvious at this point, though, and you will have to decide on these locations independently.

Linear levels: The levels that guide

In video games, the term linear refers to players having no choice in how to play the game. In game levels, linear refers to players having no choice in the locations to move to or the sequences of the tasks. Linear levels typically flow in a straight line from the start to the exit. In other words, the player is guided along a path from beginning to end (**Figure 5.3**). They may contain open areas that the player character can move around in freely, but in the end, there really isn't a choice about what to do next.

These days, linear levels have a negative connotation because every player has a similar experience playing through the level, but they are often necessary to propel the game and the game story forward. They can also be the most fun to design and play. From a design perspective, linear progressions allow you to control what the player experiences every step of the way, and the level can benefit a great deal from this advantage. For example, in Chapter 4, we brainstormed ideas for scripted sequences that the player can encounter while playing a level.

OIL REFINERY
LINEAR

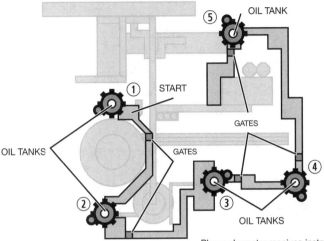

Player character receives instructions
to plant explosives at each oil tank.

A locked gate at each oil tank forces the
player to perform the tasks sequentially.
Each of the gates open when the explosives
are planted for its oil tank.

Once all the explosives are planted, a
cinematic plays of the player character
escaping and the refinery blowing up.

FIGURE 5.3 A diagram showing a linear level progression that forces the player to perform tasks in a specific order. As this diagram illustrates, a linear level progression doesn't always have to be a straight line.

In a linear level, you know which scripted sequences play before others. So, if you ultimately want the player to witness a sacrifice of an innocent villager to a demon, you can script sequences to allow the player to watch the whole sequence of events. In a nonlinear level, these sequences might be experienced in a different order; sometimes the player won't see them at all.

TIP ▶ It is often a good decision to make early levels in a game linear. Players sometimes need to be shown where they are supposed to go, especially early on. At the beginning of the game, linear levels can drive players deep into the gameplay experience quickly.

Nonlinear levels: The levels that split

Nonlinear levels give the player choices. Some of these levels simply have branches or forks at certain locations. The branches could go in different directions, or they could meet up later on. Some nonlinear levels have objectives that require the player character to travel to multiple destinations and perform a task. The tasks can be performed in any order and this sequence of the tasks becomes the choice (**Figure 5.4**).

Nonlinear levels are much more difficult to design because it's not possible for you as the level designer to completely control the player's experience. Since players are given real choices about where they want to go next, you'll need to design certain events, like scripted sequences, so that they work in any order. For our sacrifice example from earlier, you might need to plan for several villagers to be captured in different parts of the level and force the player to see at least one of them. The villagers can be taken to different preparation stations and pushed into the sacrificial pit one at a time.

There are also difficulty issues that go along with player choice. For example, let's say a level allows the player character to go down one of three paths to get to a destination. A character can get to the destination and then head back down one of the other paths back to the start position. The character may have acquired a new skill along the way so that the journey back is now too easy. Of course, you can't alter the path that the character takes back to the start because that might be the path that they choose in the beginning. In addition, if the players backtrack, they could acquire double the amount of items, such as health and ammunition, which makes subsequent levels easier.

OIL REFINERY
NONLINEAR

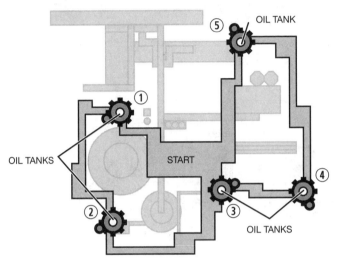

Player character receives instructions to plant explosives at each Oil Tank.

The player can choose to plant the explosives in any order.

Once all the explosives are planted, a cinematic plays of the player character escaping and the Refinery blowing up.

FIGURE 5.4 A diagram showing a nonlinear level progression that allows the player to perform tasks in any order.

Some nonlinear levels offer many ways to get to the same destination, and not all of the paths are necessary to complete the level. If players choose one way over another, they may miss some content. The content and assets created for that area may only be experienced a percentage of the time. For example, in **Figure 5.5**, the player has a choice about which path to go and either path will take the player character to the level exit. There are five landmarks created for the level, and the player will only see three of those five landmarks.

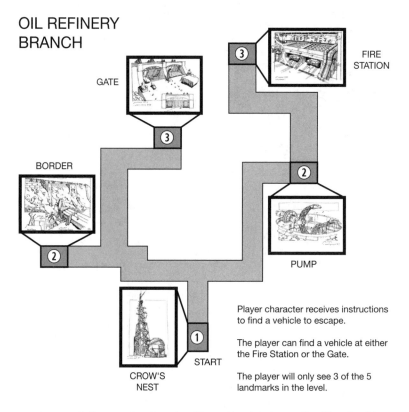

OIL REFINERY
BRANCH

GATE

FIRE STATION

BORDER

PUMP

Player character receives instructions to find a vehicle to escape.

The player can find a vehicle at either the Fire Station or the Gate.

The player will only see 3 of the 5 landmarks in the level.

CROW'S NEST

START

FIGURE 5.5 A diagram showing a level branching into two paths. Thumbnail images of the landmarks in concept form show the intricacy of the art. The player will travel from one landmark to another, and the landmarks help to outline the entire level

RPGs often encourage the player character to return to areas multiple times to gain more experience or find new items or more challenging enemies. Players may see all of the content created for a level if they play through an area in a different way than before. In other genres, however, it probably isn't worth spending a lot of time to create content that might be missed.

Creating a Diagram

You're now ready to create a diagram for your level. The diagram allows you to document your level ideas and get the rest of the development team on the same page concerning the level size, the level progression, and the amount of content that the level contains.

What should your diagram look like?

There is no standard for creating diagrams. Diagrams can be quick pencil drawings or they can be elaborate presentations done in computer programs such as Adobe Illustrator, Adobe Photoshop, or Microsoft Visio. Some designers like to model simple geometric representations of the spaces for their level in a 3D modeling program like Maya or 3D Studio Max. This way, they can take screen captures that best show where the scenes take place.

Everyone has his or her own methods of planning and documenting levels. Pick up any strategy guide at the bookstore and you're likely to see images that look like treasure maps, architectural plans, or even artist sketches. It's not important for all of the level designers on a team to adopt the same methods—unless the team has to present the diagrams to a publisher for approval. It's more important to get your ideas in place before the building phase begins.

Most level designers like to design in a top-down or "plan" view. To get a sense of what this would look like, imagine cutting a building horizontally and looking down into it. Sometimes, this view doesn't work well with the kind of level you're creating. You may need to switch to a side or "section" view, which is like cutting a building vertically and drawing what you would see looking into it from the side. **Figure 5.6** shows a sectional or side view of a level from Lucasarts' Indiana Jones and the Infernal Machine. A level diagram for this level might be drawn from the side to explain the verticality of the spaces. You may even need to go to a three-dimensional view to get your ideas across.

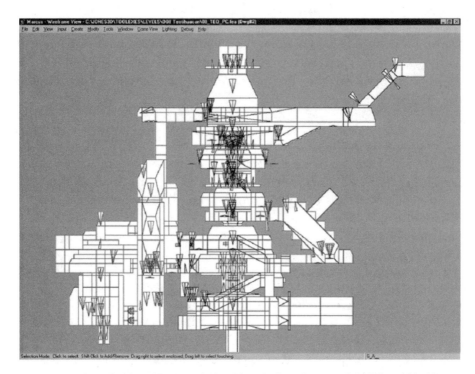

FIGURE 5.6 A sectional or side view of a level from Indiana Jones and the Infernal Machine displayed in "Marcus," the level editor Lucasarts used to create their levels. A top-down diagram for this level would not convey the level progression as well as a sectional diagram. Level image © 2003 LucasArts and LucasFilm Ltd.

To start creating your diagram, you'll first list the areas you outlined in Chapter 4 and lay them out in a sequence or arrangement appropriate to your level progression. Try not to worry about getting this basic layout right the first time. Almost all level designers constantly rearrange spaces as they go. Next, you'll connect all of the areas together, placing the areas you've reserved for skills, obstacles, and scripted sequences. Then, you'll evaluate your diagram for basic problems or issues and revise accordingly. Finally, you'll clean up your diagram and add concept art or other materials to help everyone on the team visualize the final level.

Although this may sound overwhelming, remember that you're not starting with a blank page anymore. You should now have all of your areas loosely defined and all of the design factors you'll need to contain in your level. It might be best to pick up a pen and a sheet of paper and start laying out your level.

Laying out the areas

If you have created a level narrative for your level and broken down the level according to the functions of each area, as we did in Chapter 4, you're already close to laying out your level. Using a pen and a sheet of paper, create basic geometric shapes, such as rectangles and circles, for all of the major areas and label them. It might help to base the shape sizes on the relative size of the area in the level, although you can always modify the shape sizes as you start to develop the level further.

> **TIP** This first step in creating your diagram doesn't deal with the gameplay in the level yet. It's just meant to get the ball rolling and the creative ideas flowing.

Figure 5.7, on the next page, shows all of the areas for the cookie factory level in an organization based on the level narrative. You can see how the diagram takes the list of areas from our descriptions in Chapter 4 and simply presents them in a sequential order.

Let's go through the sequence of the areas as I've diagrammed them. For the cookie factory level, the parking lot was an easy choice for the start of the level. The level narrative starts with the loading dock, but the parking lot provides the opportunity to be in an outdoor space and transition to an interior. This can also give the player an understanding of the level as a building. If, after reviewing the diagram or the template the team decides the level is too big, I can combine the parking lot and the loading dock areas.

From the parking lot, the player character will move to the loading dock. I assumed that employees of the factory will also park in the parking lot and enter the building from the back as opposed to the storefront. So, I placed the entrance to the corporate area adjacent to the loading dock. However, the corporate area is also supposed to be the last area in the level narrative, which means that the player character should not be able to access that area yet. So, perhaps I'll design the gameplay to include a key of some sort for the player to find in order to access the corporate area. Because a regular door might be too typical, I'll use an elevator to get to the corporate offices above, and that elevator will need an access code to move up. From the loading dock, the player character can see the elevator but can only travel through the warehouse and the storerooms to the ingredient tanks and then to the mixing area. This follows our level narrative closely.

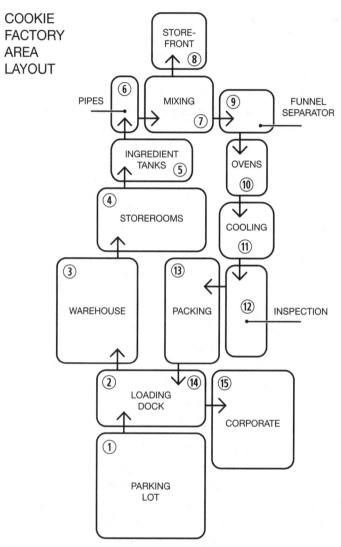

FIGURE 5.7 Here's a first stab at a diagram that lays out the areas for the cookie factory level. The shapes are simple blocks that represent the sizes of the areas.

Many stores and restaurants allow customers to see how they create their products. So, let's design the storefront in the cookie factory level to show the mixing process and its complex machinery. The mixing area can have a connection to the storefront and also to the funnels.

Continuing with the level narrative, the player character travels through the ovens and the cooling section to the inspection and packing areas. We should design the level so that the access code for the elevator is located in either the inspection or packing area. The packing area opens into the warehouse again, but it's a one-way entrance so the player character could not have gone from the warehouse to the packing area. Once in possession of the access code, the player character can move back to the elevator and into the corporate offices, where the character now faces a boss enemy and tries to free the hostages.

> **NOTE** It's perfectly fine if you haven't nailed down all of the decisions for the layout at this early stage. There may be a lot of possibilities without any definitive answers. If you have the time, you could even create multiple layouts based on your choices.

Gluing it all together

Once you've laid out your level areas, you can begin to connect them. The actual connections depend largely on the kind of game and level you are creating. Some connections might be additional spaces, such as interior hallways or outdoor passageways, while others might be ladders, elevators, tunnels, or bridges. You might decide to give the player a break from the gameplay with a cinematic or cut-scene. **Figure 5.8**, on the next page, shows the connections I've added to the cookie factory level.

Keep in mind that you might decide to change the connection types later, when you add obstacles. For example, you might decide to collapse a bridge over a waterway, and give your player a boat to cross to the other side.

> **TIP** Once again, variety is very important. When adding your connections, try to mix up the way that the player character gets from one space to another.

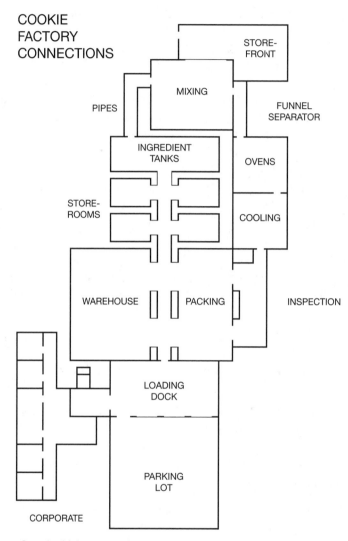

FIGURE 5.8 Once I add the connections to the area layout, the cookie factory starts to look like an actual level.

Placing the Gameplay Elements

Now that the level is starting to take shape, it's time to place the skills, obstacles, and scripted sequences you've outlined from Chapters 3 and 4 into the level diagram. The skills and obstacles in particular can serve as anchors for you to start.

I usually begin by establishing symbols for the skills that the player character will use, for each of the obstacles, and for items the player needs. Symbols should be grouped according to their category: skill or obstacle. All of the skills should have a similar look, as should all of the obstacles. Although symbols are grouped in this way, they should still appear distinct from each other. **Figure 5.9** shows some examples of skill symbols.

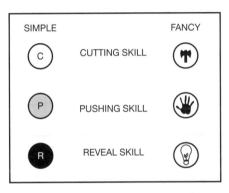

FIGURE 5.9 Here are examples of skill symbols for a diagram. Most of the time, you'll use simple symbols, but you might create more elaborate symbols for a presentation.

I'll label each of the symbols in a legend, and then place the symbols into their respective areas in the level diagram. Sometimes, it helps to imagine the individual areas in the diagram containing the architecture or physical features that they would have. You can then form obstacles from those features. For example, in the cookie factory level, if we zoom in on the loading dock area, we might imagine that the platforms where the cargo is taken off the trucks are higher than the player character can jump up to. In order to jump to the platform, the player character might need a skill to move another object to use as a step.

> **NOTE** At this stage, you should try to imagine "playing" through the level as you go through the diagram. This can be a difficult task, especially if the game engine has not been developed or if no concept art exists. It might help to model some areas with simple geometry in a 3D modeling tool and take screenshots to envision some scenes.

After establishing the symbols and placing them within the diagram, you must figure out how the skills can be used or stacked in each location of the level. If you plan to introduce a new skill during the level, be sure to exploit that skill in an appropriate location. You wouldn't want to give the player characters a skill that they can't try out right away.

Next, focus on placing the enemies within the different areas of the level. To place enemies, consider how they attack and how they move. You might not want to place a symbol for every actual enemy or item found in an area. Not only does this make your diagram look cluttered and difficult to read, it may also hinder your progress if you worry about the difficulty issues this early in the process. Place one symbol that represents the idea that the enemy or item exists in that location.

TIP If your diagram starts to get too cluttered, insert sequential numbers into the locations and write descriptions separately.

Figure 5.10 shows the final working level diagram for the cookie factory. In order for the level diagram to make sense to the team, it's a good idea to review it with the level description that follows. The level description is optional, but it describes each of the areas, as well as the player's intended progression through these areas, in greater depth.

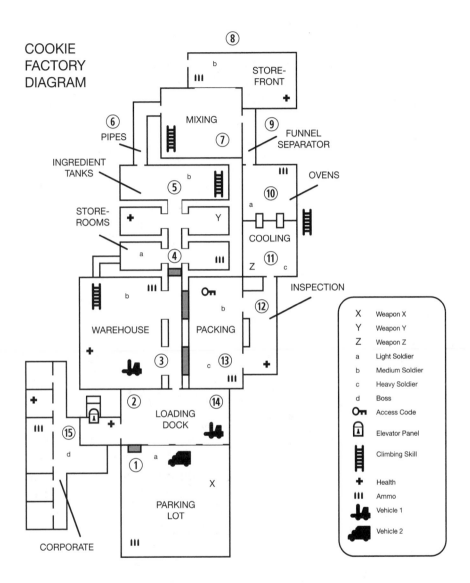

FIGURE 5.10 The final working level diagram for the cookie factory. To elaborate on each area in depth, this level diagram is combined with a level description. The numbers contained in the diagram correspond to the numbered points in the level description.

Cookie factory level description

You can include a supplemental level description document with your diagram to explain what happens in your level—provided that all of this information doesn't render your diagram unreadable. Insert numbered points into the diagram that correspond with the numbers in your level description. If you can fit the level descriptions into your level diagram without it becoming too cluttered, then do so.

1. A cut-scene plays off the chaperone arriving at the parking lot and seeing the kids taken off the bus into the building. Light soldiers, the easiest enemies to fight, see the chaperone and run behind a truck. There are three loading bays and the truck is parked at the second bay. The chaperone takes a handgun out of his glove compartment and gets out of the car. The cut-scene ends at this point, and the chaperone becomes the player character. The player must defeat the light soldiers behind the truck. If the chaperone checks the pedestrian entrance to the factory, he'll find it locked. The loading door at the third bay has been left open.

2. The chaperone can jump up into the loading dock through the open loading door, but he'll find himself enclosed by walls in front and to the right, and by crates and boxes on the left. There's a button on the wall that can be activated. Light soldiers come out of the door from the warehouse and shoot down at the chaperone. If he activates the button on the wall, the loading door on the opposite side of the crates opens. Once the door opens all the way, it starts to close. The chaperone must activate the button, run out of the loading door he came through, run around the truck, and jump into the first bay before the door closes. He can see an elevator in the hallway to the left, but he needs to enter an access code into a panel beside it to operate it. He can only proceed up a set of stairs to a hallway between the warehouse and the packing area.

3. The service doors on the left are closed; they lead to the packing area. Crates and boxes block the hallway in front of the chaperone. The doors on the left are open, and they lead to the warehouse. The warehouse has two stories, and the second story is a series of catwalks with medium soldiers (more difficult enemies) shooting down at the chaperone. There are light soldiers on the ground floor, too. Using a ladder, the chaperone can climb to the second story and find a ventilation shaft to crawl inside to the storerooms.

4. Dropping down into a storeroom, the chaperone surprises a couple of light soldiers expecting him to come from the doorway. After shooting them, he can explore three more storerooms for a shotgun, health, and ammunition. After obtaining these items, the chaperone proceeds down a hallway to the ingredient tanks.

5. Medium soldiers are protecting the ingredient tank room, and they start to attack the chaperone as he enters the room. Some medium soldiers are perched on higher levels, where the ingredient tanks are loaded, and some are on the ground floor. The chaperone uses the hallway for cover to take out the closer soldiers and moves behind a tank structure to take out the rest. He then proceeds to the pipes hallway.

6. Upon entering the pipes hallway, several light soldiers run down toward the chaperone. The chaperone uses the shotgun to clear the way and enter the mixing area.

7. The mixing area contains a large vat for mixing the ingredients together. There are tanks on the right and left sides of the vat. From the entrance, the chaperone can see the exit door on the opposite side of the vat, as well as a mixing device hanging from above. It's too far for the chaperone to jump to the mixing device, but the mixing device is shaped like a bridge. The chaperone sees controls straight ahead for the mixing device but they won't activate. He climbs a ladder to the left of the controls to get to another panel, which dumps contents from the tank on the left into the vat. There's a pipe traveling from that tank to the tank on the right. The chaperone uses the pipe to cross over and dump the contents from the right tank into the vat. Now that the ingredients are combined in the vat, the chaperone can activate the controls for the mixing device, which causes it to rotate slowly. He jumps onto an end as it comes close and sees a window on the left side that opens up into the store. The chaperone can shoot out the glass and jump through into the store.

8. In the store area, the chaperone finds health and ammunition. Medium soldiers guarding the front of the store come over to attack him when he jumps through. He can defeat these enemies before collecting the items. He goes back through the window onto the end of the mixing bridge and jumps off on the side of the exit to the funnel separator. The store area can be skipped entirely if the chaperone remains on the mixing bridge past the window.

9. The funnel separator area is split into two parts. The first part consists of a hallway for visitors to view the cookies being created in dough form on a conveyor belt. They can see this process through a large window. The second part is the start of the conveyor belt that the chaperone can get to if he decides to break the windows. The chaperone can go down the hallway to the ovens or cross over a short barrier and ride a conveyor belt to the ovens.

10. The oven area has several light soldiers waiting for the chaperone to enter from the hallway. This would be the more difficult route. However, the chaperone can enter the room without being seen by the soldiers if he rides the conveyer belt into the area. He can leave the conveyor belt and come around the other side to avoid combat completely or come at the soldiers from behind. The conveyor belt continues into the ovens, which are too small for the chaperone to crawl through. A ladder takes the chaperone up to a catwalk and through to the cooling area.

11. In the cooling area, the chaperone finds a rifle near the catwalks. Heavy soldiers (the most difficult enemies) occupy the ground level and the chaperone can pick them off from above. The heavy soldiers appear to have an opening in the head portion of their armor, so it's ideal for the chaperone to shoot from above. He may learn this from the animations of the soldiers or how they react when shot anywhere but the head. Once he's shot all of the heavy soldiers, the chaperone drops down to the ground level and moves on to the inspection area.

12. In the inspection area, the chaperone finds a light soldier sneaking bites of cookies. He needs to take out this soldier to move on to the packing area.

13. Medium and heavy soldiers are holding factory employees hostage in the packing area. The chaperone shoots all the soldiers and talks to the workers. One worker gives him the access code for the elevator. A button on the wall opens the service doors to the hallway back to the loading dock.

14. Back in the loading dock, the enemy has brought in reinforcements by vehicle into the parking lot. The chaperone watches as a van pulls up, and out of it come soldiers, who attack him. He disposes of them and enters the access code to the elevator to bring him to the corporate offices.

15. The boss soldier is waiting for the chaperone when he arrives. The kids are contained in the conference room. The soldier has some heavy artillery and the chaperone will have to use the offices for cover and also to find extra health and ammunition. Once the chaperone has defeated the boss, a cut-scene plays where the kids come out and thank the chaperone.

Evaluating the diagram

Once you have created your diagram and level description, the development team will evaluate the level. This is one of the main purposes of creating a diagram in the first place. The team will discuss several issues at this stage, including the level size, the feasibility of the gameplay, and the overall level flow.

Of course, these are all of the same issues you considered as you created your level diagram. At this point, the team will serve as a second (and third, and fourth) set of eyes on your level, helping you answer the following questions: Is the level too small or too big? Are there enough areas that will contain unique elements of gameplay? Are there too many areas that require unique elements of gameplay? Does the level introduce new features? If so, what are they? Does the level offer variations in gameplay or is it the same thing over and over? Are the skills and obstacles appropriate for the level? Answering these questions at this stage can save a lot of time and assets later on. The team may even decide to cut an entire level from the game.

How do you evaluate a level by its diagram? It definitely takes a bit of imagination. Members of the team will likely have enough imagination to be able to visualize playing the level by scrutinizing the diagram.

Judging the size and scope

Based on the goals of the level—which are defined in the design document and the world diagram—the team can determine whether the level is too big or too small. Some games have fewer levels than others, but those levels are generally quite large to encompass more playing time. If one piece is too big, players might get bored or they might feel as if they're not progressing fast enough. If a level is too small, players might feel that they are never fully immersed in the environment.

Levels are a way of breaking a game up into different pieces. If the team determines that a level is too big, you might need to start cutting areas out or combining areas together. If the level appears too small, you might need to add more areas before getting final approval and presenting the diagrams to the publisher.

To determine whether the level size is appropriate, the team looks at the skill and obstacle chart to see if all of the intended elements made it into the level. This investigation may show that the level designer introduced new skills or obstacles too closely to each other. To fix that, you would create additional areas or longer connections. On the flip side, the level may contain too many areas that use the same skills or obstacles. The team will likely recommend that some areas be removed.

Of course, the time budget also directly impacts the level size. If a certain amount of time is budgeted for the level and it's too big for the schedule, then the level designer must condense it accordingly.

Will this work?

At this stage, the team leads will have established the technical limitations, and the programmers will raise a red flag if a level exceeds those limits. For example, the programmers may not be able to implement a feature the way the designers intended, or they can't implement a feature at all. Maybe some AI doesn't behave the way that the level requires. Maybe the designers are asking for too many new features, and some cuts need to be made if the game is to ship on time. If features are compromised, you might be able to substitute other gameplay components. Sometimes, you might be required to completely replace certain areas.

> **TIP** With any luck, you won't have to replace areas because of technical limitations or feature interpretations. To prevent this, level designers should always let the lead programmer know what they are thinking and how they intend for a feature to be used. Designers and programmers should be in constant communication during the diagram phase to avoid issues down the line. Of course, one purpose of the level diagram is to give programmers an idea of what the level will contain. It's better to catch problems at this stage than later on in the development cycle.

Gauging the level progression

As the development team scrutinizes your level for size and scope, they will also be checking the level progression. The level progression is probably the easiest element to judge in a level diagram. You can look at a diagram and follow the progression along and see potential problems with the level. One issue is lack of variety within the level. In Chapter 3, we talked about players requiring some amount of variety throughout a game; this also holds true for the levels within the game.

For instance, if you've created a large group of connecting spaces that are approximately the same size or shape, you might need to change or rearrange them so that the player encounters some variety. Certain shapes stand out once a level has a diagram. In an interior level, for example, long hallways usually mean that the player doesn't have a lot of choice in where to go. If the hallway leads to a dead end or requires them to backtrack through it (**Figure 5.11**), the players won't see anything new for a long time. Of course, they might lose interest during sections of a level that are repeated.

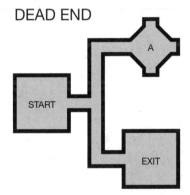

FIGURE 5.11 A basic diagram for a level that requires the player to perform a task at A to proceed to the exit. The player needs to go down a long hallway and then come back. The level designer might decide to have enemies come out of the exit and try to trap the player character once the task at A is complete. This can solve the boredom issue.

Let's say that you've created a big loop in your level. This was appealing because you could reuse art assets and give the player a sneak peek at what was coming or what the player needed to accomplish. However, if players need to repeat any large areas again, as in **Figure 5.12**, they may get frustrated.

LOOP 1

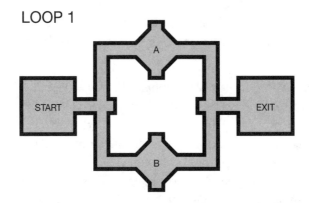

FIGURE 5.12 In this level diagram, the player needs to perform tasks at A and B to proceed to the exit. This requires the player to repeat some areas of the level. If the level is large, this can take a long time. A solution for this layout might be to only require either task A or B to proceed to the exit.

Just as it's easier to flag potential problems when the level is in diagram form, it's also easy for the team to explore solutions for these problems. Solutions for problems at this stage can take a mere afternoon to solve, whereas if the level were permitted to progress further, the problems could take days to iron out. Each team member can add input concerning their areas of expertise and they can see problems with solutions that won't work sooner. **Figure 5.13** shows a different solution to the problem identified in Figure 5.12 that minimizes back-tracking while still giving the player a choice of which task to perform first. By adding a middle path, players can perform tasks A and B and not end up at the start position with no new paths to choose. They can take all three routes, which grows the level in size and eliminates forced repetition.

LOOP 2

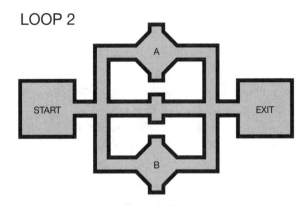

FIGURE 5.13 With this configuration, the player can perform tasks at both A and B and proceed down the middle route to the exit. This minimizes backtracking.

In **Figure 5.14**, the player can perform the tasks at A and B without having to travel a great distance to find the exit.

LOOP 3

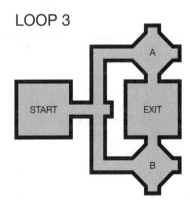

FIGURE 5.14 This layout explores a different solution where the player is not required to backtrack a long distance.

Once the issues with level size and scope, technical limitations, and progression have been addressed to the team's satisfaction, you can start cleaning up your level diagram and putting it into a presentable form.

Presenting your work

By creating a diagram, you can plan out a majority of the level before you actually build it. A lot of design takes place during the building phase, but the diagram gives you a great start. Diagrams also convey your ideas to the rest of the development team. The members of the team who have decision-making responsibilities can approve levels at the diagram stage and allow level designers to focus on actual production. Even more important, the rest of the development team can get excited about the levels and about the game before they begin production.

The Design Test

A lot of companies that are looking for level designers (or game designers, for that matter) ask that you complete a design test for potential consideration. Design tests are sometimes written questionnaires that ask for your opinions about specific games or levels and your approach to design. They might also require you to design a level in diagram form. A solid visual presentation can greatly increase your chances of getting hired.

To prepare a presentation, assemble your resource charts, level diagram, level description, and reference materials in a way that is simple and clear. You may need to break up your level diagram into pieces or show one diagram of the whole level and other diagrams of areas that are expanded. Levels that are already divided by floors or stories may be presented in the same fashion.

Example Presentation: Waterloo World Level

The following presentation contains development documents for the Waterloo World level in the game Psychonauts. Because the level is so complex, the Double Fine development team needed to create several documents to explain the full design.

The level did not ship in exactly this form. Several elements changed during production. The designers added some new elements and removed other existing elements as the level went through play-testing and revisions. A few of the elements, such as the confusion puzzle, were not yet nailed down even upon completion of the diagram.

Psychonauts is a game that blends the adventure genre with the platformer genre. The player controls Raz (short for Rasputin), a psychic kid who can jump into other characters' minds. Raz progresses through the game by conversing with other characters and finding items, which is characteristic of an adventure game, and by a combination of physical and psychic maneuvers that emulate a lot of platformers. It is a fairly complicated game, and its eccentric design was groundbreaking in many respects. Although a lot of the game mechanics stayed consistent from level to level, many levels added new twists to keep the experiences fresh and unique. For instance, in one level, called "Black Velvetopia," the visuals of the game changed to appear as if Raz was inside a black velvet painting.

Figure 5.15, on the next page, is the level progression chart for the entire game. It shows the order of the levels, the areas or "sublevels" in each level, and the level type. In Psychonauts, Raz can travel through the physical world and the mental world. For example, the psychic camp areas, represented by [CA] for "camp," are in the physical world, whereas the Waterloo World level, represented near the end of the chart as [WW], is a mental level.

The level progression chart helps to explain the position of the Waterloo World level within the game world. You can create a chart like Figure 5.15 after creating your world diagram. Level progression charts are used frequently in games with many levels, or games that have a complex story, like Psychonauts.

LEVEL	SUBLEVEL	LEVEL TYPE
Camp [CA]		Physical
	Kids' Cabins	
	Main Area	
	Reception	
	GPC & Wilderness	
	Boat House	
	Sasha's Lair	
	Janitor's Lab	
Basic Braining [BB]		Mental
	Area 1	
	Area 2	
	Log Tunnel	
[NI]		Mental
	Main Path	
	Brain Tank Arena	
Sasha's Shooting Gallery [SA]		Mental
Milla's Dance Party [MI]		Mental
	First Lounge	
	The Race	
	Last Lounge	
Lungfish Lair [LL]		Physical
Lungfishopolis [LO]		Mental
	Main	
	Coach Battle	
Camp Night [CA Night]		Physical
Asylum [AS]		Physical
	Grounds	
	Courtyard	
	Upstairs	
	Lab	
Milkman Conspiracy [MM]		Mental
Gloria's Theater [TH]		Mental
	Main Stage	
	Catwalks	
	Phantom Boss	
Waterloo World [WW]		Mental
Black Velvetopia [BV]		Mental
	Edgar's Sanctuary	
	Running Against The Bulls	
	Wrestler Arenas	
	Matador Arena	
Meat Circus [MC]		Mental
	Meat City	
	Butcher Boss Battle	

The psychic camp level — Camp [CA]

The Waterloo World level — Waterloo World [WW]

FIGURE 5.15 The level progression chart for the game Psychonauts. The Waterloo World level appears toward the end of the game.

To explain how each level connected to the rest of the game, the designers at Double Fine created a goal outline. The goal outline determines the goals for the player throughout the game. **Figure 5.16** shows a portion of the goal outline. Each level is represented by a two-letter abbreviation in brackets, which was first introduced in the level progression chart shown in Figure 5.15.

PSYCHONAUTS - GOAL OUTLINE - PART I

IV. Rescue Lili: Rescue Lili

    A. [LL] Defeat Lungfish: Pursue and defeat Lungfish

    B. [LO] Free Lungfish: Free Lungfish from influence of Kochamara

        1. Destroy Tower: Get to Kochamara Tower and destroy it

            a. Learn Psi-Shield: Smash jail and free dissidents

            b. Giant Cannon: Rendezvous with dissidents at dam

            c. Blimp Pilot: Free blimp pilot from his prison

                i. Tunnel: Find way to get through laser-shield tunnel to prison

                ii. Smash Prison: Destroy the prison to free pilot

            d. Dam: Use blimp to get over dam

            e. Skyscraper Island: Reach Skyscraper Island

            f. Destroy Planes: Destroy all planes so freighters can dock

            g. Tower Island: Proceed to Tower Island to destroy radio tower

                i. Defeat Kochamara: Battle Kochamara

                ii. Climb Tower: Climb tower and destroy antenna

    C. Asylum Gates: Get through Asylum Gates

        1. [MM] Boyd's Mind: Find Milkman

            a. Clairvoyance: Find Clairvoyance Badge in Boyd's house

            b. Try Clairvoyance: Practice Clairvoyance on living subject

            c. Find Graveyard: Go to graveyard and search Milkman's grave

                i. Road Crew: Get past road crew

             d. Disguise: Find disguise for graveyard

            e. Graveyard: Use flowers to infiltrate graveyard

            f. Sewers: Take sewers to book depository

                i. Plunger: Find disguise to pass as sewer worker

            g. Assassin: Get inside book depository

            h. Spy Copter: Get better view of entire neighborhood

            i. Hideout: Get inside Milkman's hideout

            j. Den Mother: Fight Den Mother

FIGURE 5.16 A portion of the goal outline for Psychonauts. By listing all of the player's goals in the game, the objectives for each level match the outline of the overall game story.

The main objective for Raz in this portion of the goal outline is to rescue a girl named Lily from the summer camp area of the game. To get to her, Raz battles, and ultimately enlists the help of, a giant lungfish to transport him to the island where Lily has been taken captive. Once on the island, Raz faces more challenges: he must enter the asylum gates, behind which Lily is being held prisoner.

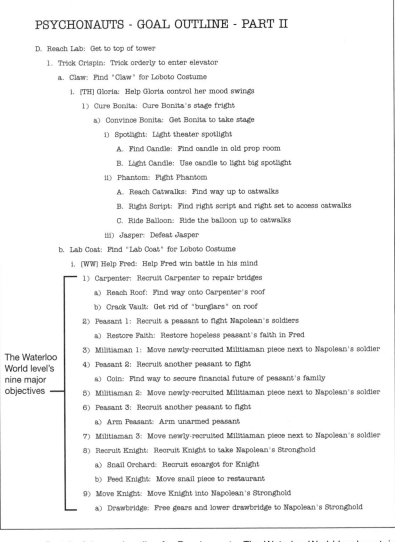

FIGURE 5.17 Part 2 of the goal outline for Psychonauts. The Waterloo World level contains nine major objectives.

Figure 5.17 takes over where Figure 5.16 leaves off. Once through the gates, Raz sees that Lily has been taken to the lab of an evil doctor. He discovers that he needs to find some objects around the island to fool the person who guards the entrance to the lab. One of the items he needs is a lab coat, and one of the asylum residents, named Fred, is wearing a straightjacket that might just do the trick.

At this point, Raz enters Fred's mind and goes into a den. In the den, he sees Fred playing some kind of board game against his ancestor, Napoleon. Because the gameplay gets a little complicated at this point, the designers at Double Fine created two diagrams to help explain the gameplay in the den (**Figure 5.18**), and on the game board (**Figure 5.19**). To further complicate things, Raz can be three different sizes in the Waterloo World: in the den, which you'll see in Figure 5.18, Raz is sized at "Scale A," which is about the same size as Fred and Napoleon. This is the largest size he can be in this level. Raz can speak with Fred in this area of the level and interact with different items in the room. If Raz interacts with the ladder on the side of the game board, he changes scale and becomes part of the board game.

Most of the gameplay for the Waterloo World takes place inside the game board (Figure 5.19). Here, Raz shrinks down to Scale B, or the medium size, which is about the size as tree or building on the game board. He can shrink down even further to Scale C, which allows him to enter buildings and interact with smaller pieces on the board. Throughout the level, Raz switches back and forth between the different scale sizes as he accomplishes his objectives. Use the numbered event progression (on next page) to follow along with Raz's objectives (Figures 5.18 and 5.19, shown on pages 154 and 155).

1. Talk to Fred and get the plot intro.

2. Shrink to Scale B, do TK/orders tutorial, and get tactical briefing (overview of each location, description of the bind Fred's in, description of victory terms).

3. In Scale C, go to the Carpenter's Workshop. The Carpenter won't emerge to do his job because there's a thief on the roof who won't leave. Get up to the roof to find a vault running in circles. Take out the vault, get a slideshow, and return to the Carpenter. He'll thank Raz and turn into a game piece.

4. Move the Carpenter over to the broken bridge, and tell him to fix it. He'll do so. However, on the other side of the bridge is a soldier. If the Carpenter crosses the bridge, he'll get killed. So you'll need someone who's able to engage the soldier in combat.

5. Go to Peasant House 1. The inhabitant will say he's not coming out until he gets answers from his ruler (Fred).

6. In Scale A, talk to Fred. Tell him what Peasant 1 said. Fred will give you an honest, earnest answer in which he assumes responsibility for everything he's put the citizens through.

7. In Scale C, tell Peasant 1 what Fred said. The Peasant admires his honesty and agrees to take up arms against Napoleon's forces. Militiaman 1 appears in the space adjacent to Peasant House 1.

8. Move Militiaman 1 onto the newly repaired bridge. Once in that space, you'll see a dialog box with the militiaman asking if you want to attack the soldier. The answer is yes! The militiaman and soldier pieces are both removed from the board and the way is cleared.

9. In Scale B, TK the wine glass off the playfield.

10. Bring the Carpenter piece back and get him to repair the second broken bridge.

11. In Scale C, go talk to Peasant 2. He wants something, a yet-undefined object. This object can be found in the den in Scale A. It should be something subtle enough that the player wouldn't have picked it up just for the heck of it, but overt enough that you won't miss it if you're looking for it.

12. Give the item to Peasant 2. The Militiaman piece will appear next to Peasant House 2.

13. Move Militiaman 2 over to Soldier 2 and do battle.

14. Talk to Peasant 3. In order to be promoted to a game piece, he needs <TBA mission on Scale C>.

15. Complete <TBA mission on Scale C>. Return to Peasant 3. Militiaman 3 is spawned.

16. Direct Militiaman 3 to battle Soldier 3. Both pieces are removed.

17. As the player's already been told, only the Hearty Knight piece can actually take Napoleon's Stronghold. The Hearty Knight is at the Hotel location tile, pining away for some quality cuisine.

18. Go to the Abandoned Orchard in Scale C and chase down all of the snails infesting the orchard. Once all are collected, the Bucket of Snails piece spawns in the next hex over.

19. In Scale B, move the Bucket of Snails down to the Hotel and order it to become dinner. This will spawn the Hearty Knight piece, as he's finally gotten a quality meal.

20. Maneuver the Hearty Knight piece up to the retracted Drawbridge tile protecting Napoleon's stronghold.

21. In Scale C, use TK to pull the Drawbridge Lever that's behind the big gates. The Drawbridge will lower.

22. Move the Hearty Knight piece onto the now-lowered Drawbridge tile and order him to take Napoleon's stronghold.

23. You win! Go high-five Fred.

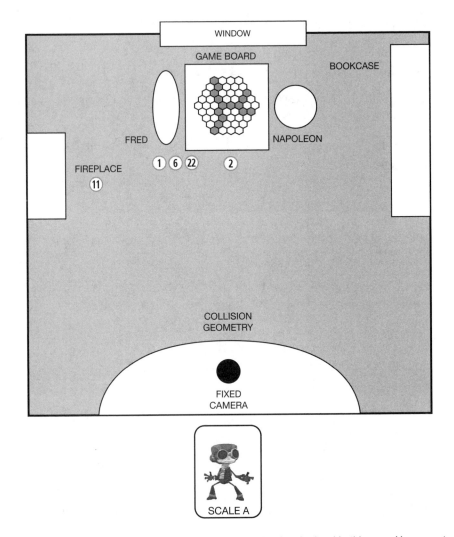

FIGURE 5.18 A diagram of the Den (Scale A). Raz begins the level in this area. He can enter the game board with a ladder on the side.

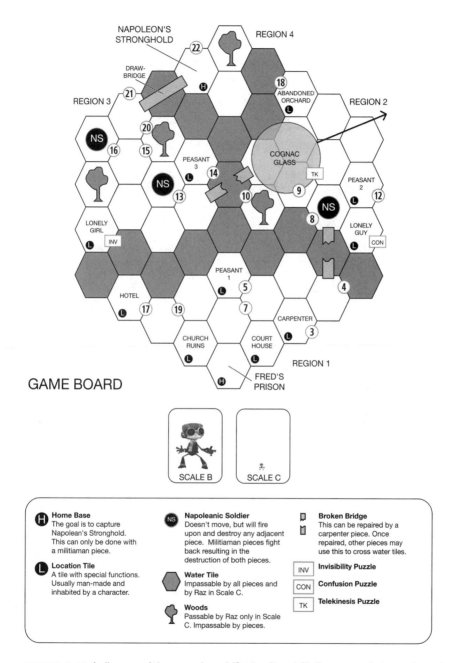

GAME BOARD

FIGURE 5.19 A diagram of the game board (Scales B and C). Raz moves between these two scale sizes by interacting with citizens. Raz can exit the back to the den by climbing a ladder on the inside of the game board.

This presentation is just an example of the kinds of documents that game developers use to get from the preproduction phase to the production phase. The production phase, which we are about to begin, will use all of the design work you have completed so far to provide you with a concrete plan. Once you have a plan that has been critiqued and approved by the members of your team, you can proceed to the actual creation of the level in the level editor.

Assignment 4

Laying Out Your Level

Part 1—Create a list of areas for your level and arrange them in order of progression. Decide if your level is going to have a linear or nonlinear progression.

Part 2—Create an area layout diagram arranging the areas of the level.

Part 3—Add connections to the area layout diagram.

Part 4—Add symbols to the diagram representing skills, obstacles, items, and a label point for descriptions.

Part 5—Describe each area of the level sequentially according to its label point.

Part 6—Assemble the resource charts, final diagram, descriptions, and reference materials for a presentation of your level.

CHAPTER 6
The Template

THE TEMPLATE IS THE ROUGH draft of the level. For level designers, creating a template is the beginning of production for a level. Up to this point, the preproduction process was more or less conceptual, meaning that you didn't have a concrete medium to actually play your level. During production, your level will take shape, and that shape starts with translating your diagram into a three-dimensional form.

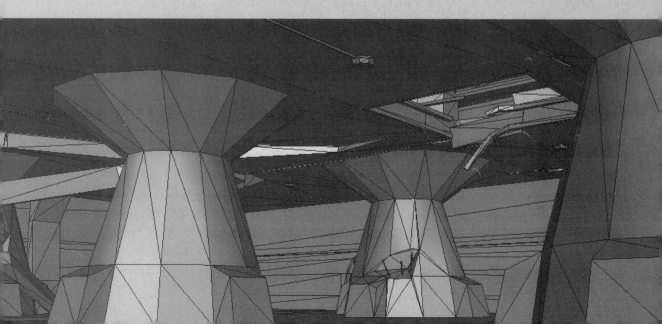

You may have to take some liberties with some of the scaling and the alignment of spaces, but basically, it should stay very similar to the level diagram. Your level will begin to take on a more interesting configuration as the vertical elements of the level take shape. Adding stairs, ramps, bridges, and walkways can help you understand the spaces that may have been difficult to imagine with the diagram. **Figure 6.1** shows the level template of the cookie factory created in UnrealEd. You can start to see how the spaces relate vertically as well as horizontally.

FIGURE 6.1 The template for the cookie factory level created in UnrealEd. During construction of the template, each area begins to feel like a 3D space or volume.

Level designers create templates quickly using simple geometry. They sometimes use previously created pieces that are copied and pasted from other levels, including pieces straight from the sandbox level. Templates should encompass the entire level so that all of the areas are properly tested and the overall scale of the level is revealed. Some areas of the level may be more thoroughly constructed than others. Having well-defined areas in the template phase, however, will make things much easier later in the production pipeline.

The level, in its template form, will probably not look like a game level yet. It will use placeholder textures and will not have any extra details. Template levels don't even have to have lighting. The development team can play through levels in special modes where the entire level has the same level of brightness. Most of the time, you won't have all of the obstacles the level needs until later in the development process. Maybe the art team has only created a few enemies and those enemies might not have all of their animations. Some of the experiences will require some imagination to fill in what is missing or incomplete.

In this chapter, you'll create a template for your level using a level editor. You might already be familiar and even comfortable with a level editor. If not, the CD accompanying this book includes tutorials on how to use UnrealEd to get you started. However, you are free to choose another level editor if you are more comfortable with it.

> **NOTE** The version of Unreal, both the editor and game, contained on the CD is a demo. Therefore, several features have been removed from the retail versions. Most notably, the "game engine," where you will be playing and testing your level, does not feature any skills other than running, jumping, and activating triggers. Your character will not be able to attack, pick up items, or even encounter enemies. I highly recommend purchasing a retail version of a game that contains a level editor for full editing and gameplay features. Full retail versions often come with models and textures that shipped with the game that you can use in your level. I would also recommend using an editor that is best suited to the kind of game level you're creating. For example, Valve Software's Hammer is the level editor for Half-Life 2, which contains gameplay elements that might be more suitable for single-player levels than the editor for Unreal Tournament 2004, which would be more suitable for a deathmatch level.

Once your template is complete, your level will be playable. This sounds like a big leap from being a drawing on a piece of paper, but once you learn just a few operations in the level editor, you'll have your level up and running in no time. You'll also see that the prep work you've done up to this point—the level narrative, the descriptions, the puzzle designs, and the level diagram—will allow you to build more quickly.

Translating the Diagram

The level diagram is the plan for the level. The template is the foundation for the level. When buildings are constructed, the architects, engineers, and contractors need to follow the plans to pour the foundations precisely. Although changes can be made with smaller details and slight adjustments, the foundation itself is not very flexible. With game levels, however, designers can move spaces and elements around with the click of a button. So, as you're building your template, keep in mind that you can easily rearrange and modify the level as you see fit. Of course, you might not be able to rearrange and modify the level after a certain point, such as the beta stage, but you aren't entirely committed to the layout of the level for a while. It can be difficult to just jump right into a level editor or 3D modeling program and start building, but it's a relief to know that you don't have to get it perfect the first time around.

Creating a template should start with a straightforward construction of the level based directly on the diagram you created in the previous chapter. You'll use simple geometry shapes, such as boxes, cylinders, and wedges. These shapes will be of various sizes and can be combined to make all of the areas in your level. While you're constructing the level geometry, you'll apply some placeholder textures to the geometry so that you can distinguish the different sides of the spaces you're building. These textures will likely be swapped out later by a background artist, but as I'll discuss shortly, it's important to have something in place for the template phase.

In order to translate your level diagram into a template, you'll need to become familiar with a level editor. As I mentioned in the introduction, we'll be using UnrealEd, Epic Games' level editor for the Unreal game series, and the runtime demo is included on the CD that accompanies this book. To get you up and running, I've written several tutorials for you. These tutorials are divided into three major sections: basic operations, additional geometry tools, and gameplay elements. In the basic operations section, you'll install the demo, get a feel for the interface, and use some of the functions that will help you start creating some simple rooms. The tutorial on additional geometry tools will show you how to make slightly more complex geometry that might be necessary in your template. After you've constructed the template's geometry, you'll need to add the gameplay elements so that people can actually play through your level.

If the idea of using a level editor sounds difficult, don't worry—we're going to start with some simple operations to help you get started.

Using simple geometry: boxes, cylinders, and wedges

Level designers use simple geometry to create level templates. For example, rooms are represented by boxes, cylinders, or wedges, and combinations of simple shapes can result in areas that follow the diagram more closely. If you combine a box shape and a wedge shape, you can create room corners with angles other than 90 degrees. In **Figure 6.2**, three simple box shapes make up three separate rooms. When we combine some wedge shapes (triangles) to the middle room, the shape starts to change into something more complex, as shown in **Figure 6.3**.

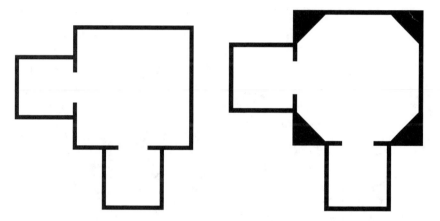

FIGURE 6.2 The shapes of rooms can be constructed by combining simple shapes together. Here, three rooms are made up of three block shapes.

FIGURE 6.3 The middle room from Figure 6.2 has been made more complex by combining wedge shapes in each corner.

To make the construction of the template even simpler, you can create primitives, or reusable pieces that you can copy and paste throughout the level. These primitives should use the measurements and scale that relates to the skills and obstacles we discussed in Chapter 3. So, if the player character can jump up a maximum of 64 units, you can create a block that is 64 units high, and you can reuse that block as an obstacle wherever the maximum jump height is used. If the lead level designer puts together a sandbox level, you can import those primitives into your template level.

You may need to develop some decorative elements during the template phase if it is essential to the design. For example, large columns or supports in the middle of a room can affect the gameplay in that area. These elements can exist in the template, but they should still be fairly simple. Instead of creating a round column with a capital and a base (the pieces at the top and bottom of columns), you can create a cylinder instead. You can even use simple geometry as a placeholder for much more complex elements such as statues and vehicles. For example, in **Figure 6.4**, the player character needs to sneak around this train yard to find the entrance. In the template, the level can contain simple blocks to represent train cars for the player character to hide behind. In **Figure 6.5**, the simple blocks can later be replaced with actual train cars.

FIGURE 6.4 Plain, rectangular blocks are placeholder pieces for train cars in this template version of a train yard level.

FIGURE 6.5 The blocks in Figure 6.4 have been replaced with actual train cars.

Using placeholder textures

Level designers don't need many textures to create a level template. A handful of textures that differentiate between walls, floors, and details should be enough. You may be wondering why the template should have textures at all if they are going to be replaced by background artists during the art passes. Well, having the same default texture all over a level can be confusing and distracting. Since the level may not contain lighting information, it would be impossible to navigate the level if it consisted of just one texture.

In addition, a lot of pieces in levels are repeated over and over for consistency purposes and because realistically, a structure such as a building or a space station probably doesn't need every hallway to be unique. So if you don't use placeholder textures to line up how the texture will be placed in the final level, then instead of simply replacing the placeholder texture with the final texture, you might have to line up the final texture on every piece of geometry even if that piece has been repeated. For example, let's say that a level has a lot of walls that are 256 units high. When you're creating your template, it's much more efficient to create one wall that has a texture lined up correctly, with the bottom of the texture at the bottom of the wall and the top of the texture at the top of the wall. Once that's in place, you can duplicate that wall all over your level. If you didn't use a placeholder texture that represented the wall, you might not know whether the wall texture lines up with the form of the wall at all. When you go back to replace the texture, you would have to line up every wall that you constructed. Some companies, such as Valve, have a set of developer textures that show how other textures can align to level geometry without giving the player an artistic impression of the level. You can see a hallway using the wall and floor development textures in **Figure 6.6.**

FIGURE 6.6 A hallway constructed in Valve Software's Hammer, the level editor for the games Half-Life 2, Counterstrike: Source, and Day of Defeat: Source. Using placeholder textures with guidelines, you can make sure textures line up without giving the impression that the textures are final.

Placeholder textures can also be final textures that were originally created for other areas of the game. For example, let's say that a background artist has already created some final textures for one level in the game. This level contains a brick texture that was specifically made for another level. You may choose to use this brick texture to represent a brick wall in your level. This may give the false impression that the level is closer to completion than it actually is, but you can give the background artist assigned to the level a clearer direction of the textures the level will eventually contain.

Using simple geometry and placeholder textures, you'll be able to construct a playable framework of your level. The tool you'll use to construct that framework is the level editor.

UnrealEd tutorial: basic operations

UnrealEd is a very popular level editor. Several books and Internet resources are available that can take you through the program step by step. The demo contained on the CD also contains a link to the Unreal Developer Network, which provides a lot of information that you might find useful. This tutorial is meant to give you the basics for creating a template for your level.

You'll start by installing the UnrealEd Demo from the CD included with this book. You'll be prompted to agree to Epic's UnrealEngine2 Runtime End-User License Agreement. Once all the directories are set up on your hard drive, you can copy some of the files from the CD in appropriate folders to save you from tracking down individual files.

1. From the Unreal\Textures directory on the CD, copy the file Tutorial.utx into your Unreal\Textures directory.

2. From the Unreal\Maps directory on the CD, copy the file Tutorial01.urt into your Unreal\Maps directory. If at any point during this tutorial you're unclear about what's being described, just open up the Tutorial01.urt level for an example.

User interface

Several versions of UnrealEd are available, and they are all based on similar functions and interface. Now let's launch UnrealEd and take a look at the interface shown in **Figure 6.7**, on the next page.

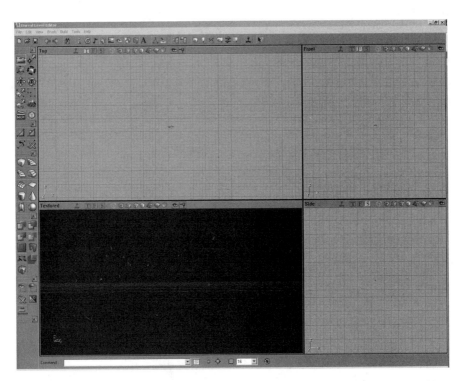

FIGURE 6.7 UnrealEd, like many 3D modeling programs, allows you to look at your level in four different views. This is the default configuration, but you can customize your views. The top-left window is the "Top" view; the top-right window is the "Front" view; the bottom-left window is the "3D" view; the bottom-right window is the "Side" view.

TIP ▶ Hover your mouse over any of the icons in the menu bar (shown in **Figure 6.8**) for a tool tip label.

FIGURE 6.8 The menu bar at the top of the screen provides icons that let you perform basic file-management tasks such as New Map, Open Map, and Save Map, and access dialog boxes for browsers, certain tools, and options.

By default, UnrealEd opens to Camera Movement mode, which allows you to navigate around the views.

To pan in the Top, Front, and Side views, hold down the left or right mouse and drag. To zoom in and out in the same views, hold down both the left and right mouse buttons and drag. In the 3D view, the navigation is a bit different:

Holding down the left mouse button and dragging moves the camera around horizontally along the XY plane. To rotate the camera in any direction, hold down the right mouse button and drag. Both buttons held down and dragged simultaneously move the camera up and down along the z-axis.

Using the toolbar that is shown in **Figure 6.9,** you can switch to other modes when you want to edit geometry, position textures, and position actors, which are nongeometry elements of the level.

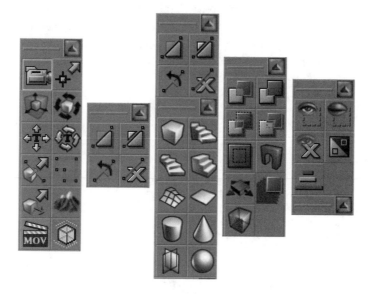

FIGURE 6.9 Buttons on the toolbar let you switch between editing modes and perform certain operations. Hover your mouse over any of the icons to view a tool tip that identifies it.

Many modeling programs and level editors start with an empty space and require the user to add solid pieces in that space. Rooms are built by creating floors, walls, and ceilings. Unreal operates in the exact opposite way. In Unreal, you create spaces by choosing variously shaped "brushes" from the toolbar and subtracting those shapes from a solid block using the active brush (**Figure 6.10**), which you can manipulate into various shapes and dimensions (**Figure 6.11**). Rooms are simply boxes of negative space. Once the spaces are subtracted, you use brushes to then add shapes back into them. The geometry is then built or processed by the editor for the game to use. Building the level cuts up all the geometry into convex polygons and tells the game engine how to draw the level. This data structure is called Binary Space Partition (BSP).

FIGURE 6.10 When you open the editor, the active brush appears as a red square in your views. To choose a different active brush, such as a cylinder or a set of stairs, you just select its icon from the toolbar.

CubeBuilder		
Properties		Build
Height	256.000000	Close
Width	256.000000	
Breadth	256.000000	
WallThickness	16.000000	
GroupName	Cube	
Hollow	False	
Tessellated	False	

FIGURE 6.11 Right-clicking on a tool in the toolbar lets you can change its parameters, including dimensions. This image is of the CubeBuilder dialog box.

NOTE Convex polygons are simpler than concave polygons. If you draw a line using any two points along the outline of a convex polygon, you won't exit the shape. So, squares, rectangles, and triangles are convex. With concave polygons, you will exit the shape if you draw a line using any two points along the outline. For example, the shape of the letter "c" is concave because a line drawn between its ends exits the shape of the letter. Concave polygons need to be cut into convex polygons during the BSP process.

UnrealEd also has a menu bar at the top of the screen that contains buttons for several management operations, including saving and loading levels, the undo and redo commands, and opening dialog boxes. You can also open the browser window, which is shown in **Figure 6.12**, from the menu bar.

FIGURE 6.12 The tabs in the browser window let you view elements such as textures, actors such as lights and game items, static meshes that can decorate your level, and even sounds before you place them into your level.

Creating a simple room

The easiest thing to create first is a simple room. For now, the room is just going to be a box that is subtracted from the world. You'll also need to place a couple of elements into the room to play it in the game: a "PlayerStart," which is where the player will start in the room, and a light so you'll be able to see inside the room.

1. Right-click the Cube icon on the toolbar to open the CubeBuilder dialog box. Type a Height value of 512, a Width value of 1024, and a Breadth value of 1024, and click the Build button (**Figure 6.13**). Your active brush should change size accordingly in your views. Close the CubeBuilder dialog box.

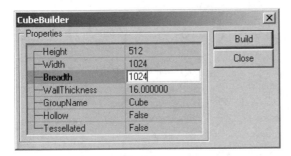

FIGURE 6.13 Click the Build button in the CubeBuilder dialog box to create an active brush with the specified dimensions.

2. Click the Subtract icon on the toolbar or press Ctrl+S to subtract a cube with the designated dimensions. You can see that a subtracted brush is displayed with a brown color in the 2D views and the Wireframe mode of the 3D view.

3. In the 3D view, hold down the right mouse button and drag the mouse to point the camera at the subtracted space and hold down the left mouse button and drag to move the camera to the middle of the room. Hold down the right mouse and drag again to rotate it down to point at the floor. Left-click on the surface of the floor to select it. You should see the surface change color slightly to show that it's selected.

4. Right-click on the middle of the surface and select Add Player Start Here from the contextual menu that appears (**Figure 6.14**). You have now determined where the player character will start when the level loads.

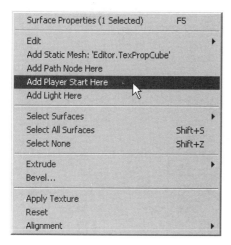

FIGURE 6.14 Right-clicking on a surface will bring up a contextual menu for you to select from.

5. Hold down the right mouse button and drag to rotate the camera so you're looking up at the ceiling, and with the left mouse button, select the ceiling surface.

6. Right-click on the middle of the surface and select Add Light Here (**Figure 6.15**). You have now added a light to the room.

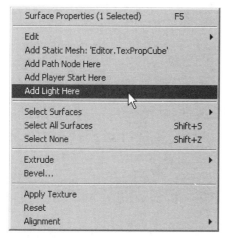

FIGURE 6.15 The contextual menu that appears when you right-click on a surface makes several common operations simple, such as adding a light.

7. From the menu bar, click the Build Options icon (**Figure 6.16**) or press the F8 key to bring up the Build Options dialog box, which is shown in **Figure 6.17**. For now, leave the options at their default settings and click the Build button in the dialog box. Your level will now "build," which means that the editor will get it ready for the game engine to use.

FIGURE 6.16 You can open the Build Options dialog box with the Build Options icon found on the menu bar.

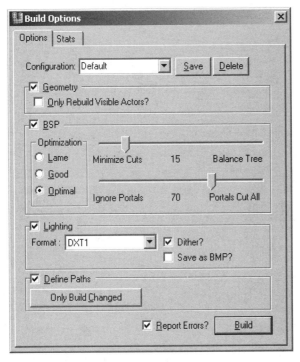

FIGURE 6.17 The Build Options dialog box. You can build geometry, BSP, lighting, and paths all at the same time or in any combination.

NOTE When you build your level without applying textures, you'll see an error message that says that your brush "has NULL material reference(s)." Ignore this warning for now and click the Close button.

With your level built, you can view how the room will look, including how it is lit, by clicking the Dynamic Light icon on the 3D view menu (**Figure 6.18**).

FIGURE 6.18 The 3D view has several modes in the 3D view menu. You can use the Dynamic Light icon to switch to the Dynamic Light mode, which enables you to see your level with lighting.

To save the level, click the Save icon on the menu bar or press Ctrl+L. Check out the level in the engine by clicking the Play Map! icon on the menu bar or by pressing Ctrl+P. The level will appear inside the game engine, and you will be able to walk around the room. Press the Esc key and select Exit Runtime to go back to the editor.

Texturing a simple room

The room you have just created probably doesn't look like any of the spaces you've imagined in your level. Without spending too much time, you can expand on the room to make it more complete.

1. Open the Texture Browser window by clicking the Texture Browser icon on the menu bar (**Figure 6.19**). Textures are organized into packages and then into groups within those packages.

FIGURE 6.19 To open the Texture Browser, click the Texture Browser icon on the menu bar.

2. In the browser window, select Open from the File category. Select the Tutorial.utx package and click the Open button. You should see several textures appear in the browser window. You can change the texture group in the Texture Group menu (**Figure 6.20**). Select the Floors texture group. Select Texture Floor01 in the browser window to make it the current texture.

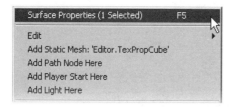

FIGURE 6.20 Textures in texture packages are often divided into groups, such as "walls," "floors," and "details." Switch between texture groups with the Texture Group menu.

3. In the 3D view, right-click on the floor surface of your room and select Apply Texture. Your floor should now have the floor texture applied to it.

4. To change some of the properties of your surface, you can select the surface and right-click. Select Surface Properties (**Figure 6.21**) to open the Surface Properties dialog box (**Figure 6.22**). In the Pan/Rotate/Scale tab, you can change the position, rotation, and scale of the texture.

Surface Properties (1 Selected)	F5
Edit	▶
Add Static Mesh: 'Editor.TexPropCube'	
Add Path Node Here	
Add Player Start Here	
Add Light Here	

FIGURE 6.21 The Surface Properties dialog box can be opened by right-clicking on any surface and choosing Surface Properties from the contextual menu.

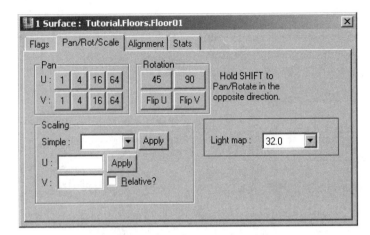

FIGURE 6.22 The Surface Properties dialog box allows you to change the properties of a surface, including fitting textures in the Pan/Rotate/Scale tab.

5. Back in the Texture Browser window, select the Walls texture group and then select Texture Wall01.

6. Select all of the walls of your room in the 3D view by pressing and holding down the Ctrl key while left-clicking on the surfaces. Holding Ctrl down while selecting allows you to select multiple surfaces.

7. Press and hold down the Shift key and left-click in the 3D view to automatically assign the current texture to the selected surfaces. Your walls should now be textured appropriately. Perform the same operations on the ceiling of your room to give it the texture of your choice. Your room should now look more like a real room.

Adding to a simple room

Although your room is now textured to look more like a real room, it is still simple and a bit stale. To give your room more detail, you can add geometry back into the space, and change the way the room works in the game. For example, you can add columns or supports back into a room to provide cover for the player character to hide behind.

1. Open the CubeBuilder dialog box again to create an active brush for a simple column. Change the Width and Breadth values to 64 but leave the Height value at 512. Click the Build button in the CubeBuilder dialog box and close the dialog box.

2. In the Top view, press and hold down the Ctrl key, then hold down the left mouse button and drag the active brush to a corner of the room so that two of its edges touch the inside of the subtracted brush that represents your room (**Figure 6.23**).

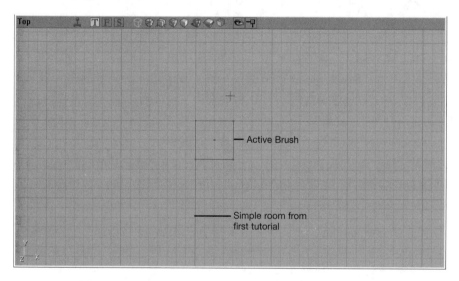

FIGURE 6.23 To add a column into a corner of the room, move the active brush that will represent the column so that it is flush with two sides of the room.

3. Click the Add icon on the toolbar or press Ctrl+A. A column to support one corner of the room appears. You can see that an added brush appears blue in the 2D views and in the Wireframe mode of the 3D view.

4. Move the active brush to another corner and click the Add icon on the toolbar to create a second column.

5. Now, move the active brush out of the way so that you can select the column you just added by left-clicking it in the Top view.

6. Press and hold down the Ctrl key and left-click on the first column to select both columns.

7. Right-click on either of your selections and choose Duplicate from the contextual menu (**Figure 6.24**). You can also duplicate any object in the editor by pressing Shift+D. Your column brushes will appear to duplicate in the 2D views and the Wireframe mode of the 3D view.

FIGURE 6.24 Right-clicking a brush will bring up another contextual menu where you can find the Duplicate command.

NOTE Some modes of the 3D view will not update geometry with certain functions, like Duplicate, for example, until the level has been built.

8. Move the duplicated column brushes into the remaining two corners of the room. Build the level to see the changes.

You can also add brushes to break up flat surfaces. For example, let's add a brush that shares the same plane as the brushes we just created to add a different texture to the surface of the floor.

1. Open the CubeBuilder dialog box and enter a Height value of 32, and Width and Breadth values of 256. Click the Build button and close the dialog box.

2. Move the active brush to the middle of the room and lower it so that the top of the active brush lines up with the bottom of the subtracted brush of the room.

3. In the Texture Browser window, select Texture Floor04 from the Floors texture group.

4. Click the Add icon in the toolbar. You should see a special piece on the floor of your room. Build the level and click the Play Map! button on the menu bar to see the result in the game.

Because you can add and subtract brushes that share the same planes, the order that you create brushes is very important. To change the order of brushes after they've been created, select a brush and right-click on it to bring up its menu (**Figure 6.25**). Select Order and you can move the order of that brush: To First makes it the first brush you created in the level; To Last makes it the last brush you created in the level; or Swap Order swaps the order of two brushes you have selected.

FIGURE 6.25 The Order list consists of three options to change the order of a selected brush in a level.

Select the special floor piece in the Top view and right-click to bring up its menu. Select To First from the Order list to change its order. Rebuild the level and the special floor will not appear in the game. The subtracted brush you first used to create the room now comes after the special floor piece and the subtracted brush texture is used over the entire floor. You can still see the special floor brush in the 2D views and the Wireframe mode of the 3D view so that you can choose To Last to change the order again. Rebuild the level to bring the special floor piece back into the room.

You can also rotate brushes, which you'll use when you want to create geometry with different angles. Let's use rotation to change the angle of our column.

1. To rotate a brush, hold down the Ctrl key while right-mouse-dragging.

2. Duplicate one of the room's columns and move it into the room away from a wall.

3. Keep the column selected and in the Top view, rotate it 45 degrees so that it appears as a diamond. Build the level to see the result.

Brushes are rotated according to their pivot point. Select the rotated column and a bright red crosshair should appear in the center of it. This is the pivot point for that brush. You might want to move the pivot point to rotate a brush relative to another point in the world. For example, if you want to rotate two columns around the center of the room, you would need to select the brushes that represent the columns and drag the active pivot point to the center of the room. Now, when you rotate the columns, they rotate around the center of the room, not the center of one column.

1. To move the pivot point to a different location, press and hold down the Alt key while holding down the left mouse button and dragging.

2. Duplicate the rotated column and move it directly on top of the original rotated column.

3. Keep the column selected and in the Top view, move its pivot point to the very center of the room.

4. Rotate the column 180 degrees so that it is on the opposite side of the room from the original rotated column. The results should appear similar to **Figure 6.26**, on the next page. To reset the pivot point, right-click on the brush to bring up its menu. Select Reset, which will expand into more options, and then select Rotation.

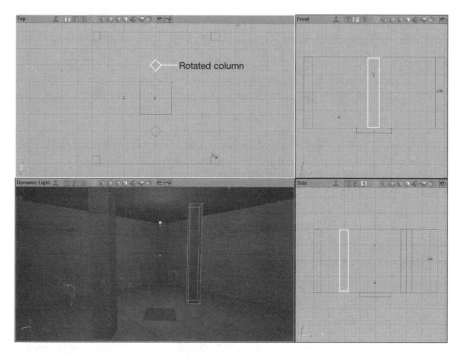

FIGURE 6.26 Use brush pivots to place columns in a symmetrical form.

Try some of the other brush tools in the toolbar, such as the Linear Staircase and the Cylinder. They work in the same way the Cube tool works. You will see your active brush change shape (to a set of steps or a cylinder), and you can change its settings in the builder dialog boxes just like you've already done using the CubeBuilder dialog box.

Placing an actor

In your first room, you already placed two actors into your level: the Player Start and a light. Some actors that are frequently placed in levels are contained in the surface drop-down menu, which you may recall can be accessed by right-clicking on a surface in the 3D view. To place other actors into a level, you will need to select one from the Actor Class Browser window to make it your current actor. You can then place it from the surface drop-down menu.

1. Click the Actor Class Browser icon on the menu bar to open the Actor Classes browser window.

NOTE The Actor Classes browser contains several tabs, including Textures, Actor Classes, Static Meshes, and Sounds. If your browser is already open, you can simply click the tab of the corresponding browser that you wish to select from.

2. Expand the Actor list by clicking the plus sign next to Actor. Expand the *Light list and select *Spotlight (**Figure 6.27**).

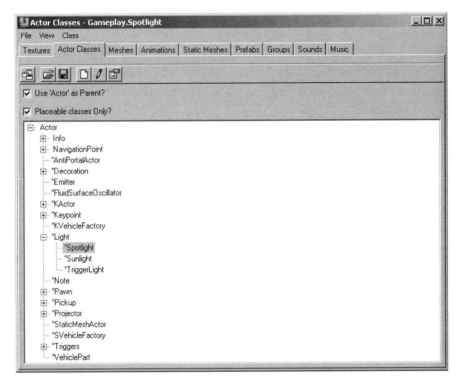

FIGURE 6.27 You can select a variety of different actors, such as a spotlight, in the Actor Classes browser.

3. In the 3D view, right-click on the ceiling of the room and select Add Spotlight Here from the contextual menu. You have just placed an actor from the Actor Classes Browser list.

You can select, move, and rotate actors with the same controls as selecting, moving, and rotating brushes. The only difference is that actors don't have pivot points that you can edit.

4. Select your spotlight and you should see a red arrow coming out of it. This is the direction that the spotlight is facing. In the Front view, rotate this arrow so that it is pointing straight down to the floor. Rebuild the level to see the results.

Lighting a simple room

Lighting can make all the difference in a level. In the template phase, you can light areas in a general way to get feedback during the initial testing phase. If lighting is essential to the gameplay to help hide the player's character or enemies, the template phase of lighting might be more crucial.

Although the actual light source models, such as light fixtures, torches, and lamps, are very important to add detail and realism to a level, the template might not contain them. It will be easier to move lights around to get the right scheme without having to move around the light source models.

1. Select the first light you created for the room and move it down about 64 units. If a light is too close to a surface, it won't light the whole surface and it might wash out the area closest to the light.

   NOTE You can get a sense for distance in the editor by changing the Drag Grid Size setting, which is found under the 3D view. To move an object down 64 units, for example, change the setting to 64 and move the object down one grid square.

2. Move the light into one quadrant of the room in the Top view.

3. Duplicate the light and move it to another quadrant of the room.

4. Duplicate both lights and move the new lights so that each light is in its own quadrant.

5. Click the Build Lighting icon in the menu bar to create the results of the lights. Click the Dynamic Light icon in the 3D view menu to see the room with your new lights.

6. Select all of the lights except the spotlight and right-click to bring up their menu. Select Light Properties to open the Light Properties dialog box. Click the plus sign next to Light Color to expand the Light Color list.

Here, you can change the LightBrightness, LightHue, and LightSaturation settings (**Figure 6.28**). All settings range from 0 to 255. LightBrightness affects the light's intensity, LightHue changes its color, and LightSaturation specifies how much of the surface is affected by the light's color. LightBrightness is straightforward: the higher the value, the brighter the light. To reflect more color, you should decrease the LightSaturation value: the higher the value, the less color is reflected from the surface. LightHue follows an RGB color chart that is explained in **Figure 6.29**.

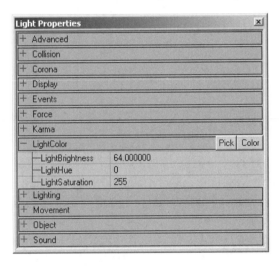

FIGURE 6.28 The Light Properties dialog box contains settings for LightBrightness, LightHue, and LightSaturation.

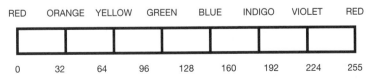

FIGURE 6.29 A chart showing how the LightHue value works.

7. Change the LightBrightness value to 80, the LightHue value to 32, and the LightSaturation value to 64.

8. To expand the Lighting list, click the plus sign next to the Lighting option. The most frequently used parameter under Lighting is LightRadius. By changing this value, you can adjust the light's fall-off, or the distance at which the light loses its effect.

9. Change the LightRadius value to 48. Rebuild the lighting to see the results.

   With these settings, you can start to establish a mood or atmosphere for the room. Now, try changing the LightHue value to 128 for a cooler blue tone. Try changing all of the settings to experiment with the lighting parameters. Rebuild lighting to see the results.

Adding a Skybox

Many game levels contain portions of outdoor areas. Sometimes, a window or skylight allows the player to see outside a room to the exterior. Other times, the space itself is outdoors. Because most games can't technically afford to create a huge open sky above every level, they need to portray the sky in a different way. Unreal uses a Skybox to create a realistic sky. A Skybox is essentially a small, subtracted brush that has a sky texture applied to it. A special actor called a SkyZoneInfo is placed inside it to take on the role of a camera. Surfaces in the level are marked with the Fake Backdrop flag. When the game's camera looks at a surface marked with this flag, the Skybox is seen.

1. Open the CubeBuilder dialog box and type a Height value of 64, and Width and Breadth values of 256.

2. Click the Build button and move the active brush to the middle of the room.

3. Move the active brush up so that the bottom plane lines up with the ceiling of the room.

4. Click the Subtract icon on the toolbar to create a skylight in the room.

5. Assign a wall texture to the skylight brush.

6. Select the top surface and right-click to bring up its menu. Select Surface Properties to open the Surface Properties dialog box.

7. Under the Flags tab, select the Fake Backdrop check box (**Figure 6.30**).

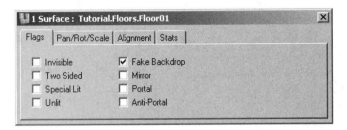

FIGURE 6.30 The Surface Properties dialog box has four tabs. In the first tab, Flags, you can set a surface to have special properties, such as Fake Backdrop.

8. Open the CubeBuilder dialog box again and enter a Height value of 256, and Width and Length values of 512.

9. Click the Build button, and move the active brush so that the bottom edge is more than 128 units above the top of the skylight brush.

10. Click the Subtract icon in the toolbar to create the Skybox brush.

11. In the Texture browser, select the sky texture group and select Texture SkyTop. Assign this texture to the top surface of the Skybox. Now, assign Texture SkyBack, Texture SkyFront, Texture SkyLeft, and Texture SkyRight so that the textures all line up. The bottom surface of the Skybox can have any texture on it because it will not be seen.

12. Select all of the Skybox surfaces except the bottom and right-click to open their menu. Select Surface Properties to open the Surface Properties dialog box.

13. Under the Flags tab, check the Unlit box. This will cause the sky textures to appear fully lit.

14. In the browser window, select the Actor Classes tab and click the plus sign next to Actor to expand its list. Click the plus sign next to Info to expand the Info items, and click the plus sign next to ZoneInfo to expand its list. Select SkyZoneInfo from the list (**Figure 6.31**).

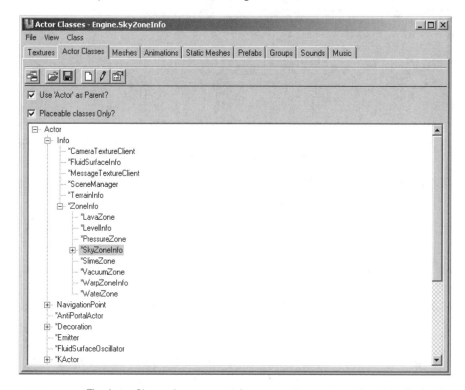

FIGURE 6.31 The Actor Classes browser contains more actors you can place into the level, such as the SkyZoneInfo actor.

15. In the 3D view, right-click on the bottom surface of the Skybox and select Add SkyZoneInfo Here.

16. In the Top view, move the SkyZoneInfo to the middle of the Skybox brush. Build the level and play the map to see the Skybox through the skylight in the ceiling.

UnrealEd tutorial: additional geometry tools

Most levels aren't constructed entirely of simple geometric shapes like cubes. UnrealEd has some additional geometry tools that will help you create different kinds of shapes. The Intersect and Deintersect tools can take groups of brushes and combine them or fill gaps made by them forming an active brush that you can use as a primitive. The Vertex Editing tool can change the shapes of existing brushes as well as the active brush. You can select a vertex, or endpoint, of a brush and move it around. The 2D Shape Editor tool can help initially create different kinds of shapes for the active brush. Basically, you can draw a shape in two dimensions and manipulate that 2D shape into a 3D brush. The Terrain Editing tool can create a new kind of geometry that simulates landscape, such as rolling hills or rocky cliffs. You may need to use some or all of these tools to create the template for your level.

From the Unreal\Maps directory on the CD, copy over the file Tutorial02a.urt into your Unreal\Maps directory. If you're ever unclear about what is being described, open the Tutorial02a.urt level for an example.

Intersect and Deintersect

Level designers sometimes need to group or combine brushes to accomplish the desired effect. UnrealEd uses Intersect and Deintersect for grouping and combining brushes. With the Intersect tool, you can surround a group of brushes and "capture" their faces and textures into the active brush. Then, you can add or subtract the active brush for the group of brushes to function as a single brush.

1. Start UnrealEd and open the room you created in the first tutorial. You can also open Tutorial01.urt if you'd prefer.

2. Open the CubeBuilder dialog box and enter Height, Width, and Breadth values of 1024. Click the Build button to change your active brush.

3. In the Top view, move the active brush so that it lines up with your original room. In the Front view, move the active brush down so that its top is 256 units below the floor of the original room.

4. Select a texture from the Texture browser and subtract the brush. Let's call this separated subtracted brush the "construction area."

TIP Level designers typically create side rooms, which we're calling our "construction area," where they can construct geometry. Think of the construction area as a scratch pad. Players will not be able to access this area during the game.

5. Open the CubeBuilder dialog box and enter a Height value of 32 and Width and Breadth values of 64. Click the Build button to change your active brush. In the Front view, move the active brush down so that the bottom is 256 units above the floor of the construction area brush.

6. Add the brush.

7. Move the active brush up so that the top of the active brush is 256 units below the ceiling of the construction area brush and add another brush.

8. Open the Cylinder Builder dialog box by right-clicking the Cylinder icon on the toolbar. Enter a Height value of 448 and an OuterRadius value of 24. Click the Build button to change your active brush.

9. In the Top view, move the active brush so that it's in the middle of the two added brushes. In the Front view, move the active brush so that its top is lined up with the bottom of the upper added brush and its bottom is lined up with the top of the lower added brush (**Figure 6.32**).

10. Add this new cylinder brush. All three of these latest brushes together form a column. You can texture this column however you like.

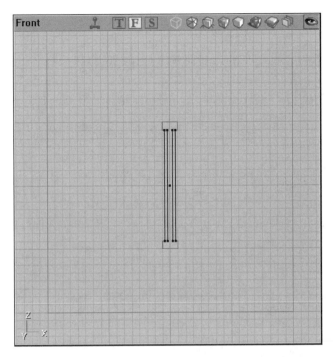

FIGURE 6.32 Line up the active brush to form a column with a base and a capital.

11. Now, open the CubeBuilder dialog box and enter a Height value of 528 and Width and Breadth values of 80. Click the Build button to create an active brush just slightly larger than the column. Make sure the active brush completely surrounds the column but does not make contact with any other brushes. Intersect the column brushes by clicking the Intersect icon on the toolbar (**Figure 6.33**).

— Intersection icon

FIGURE 6.33 Use the Intersect icon on the toolbar to "capture" the faces of everything inside the active brush.

You'll see a new active brush that has captured all the faces of the column. Move this new active brush into your room so that its top lines up with the ceiling of the room and its bottom lines up with the floor of the room. You can replace the columns you had in the corners by deleting them and adding this new column in all four corners. Rebuild the level, save it, and play the map to see the results.

Next, we'll use the Intersect tool to capture a group of brushes that form a broken column.

1. Create a Cube active brush with Height, Width, and Breadth values of 80.

2. Move the active brush back into the construction area and in the middle of the column brushes.

3. Subtract the brush so that it looks like the column has a top half and a bottom half.

4. In the Side view, rotate the active brush 45 degrees in either direction.

5. Subtract the brush so that both halves of the column look like they have a piece missing.

6. In the Top and Front views, rotate the active brush slightly in either direction. Subtract the brush so that the column now looks like it is broken.

7. Create a Cube active brush with a Height value of 256 and Width and Breadth values of 80.

8. Reset the active brushes rotation by right-clicking on it and selecting Rotation from the Reset list (**Figure 6.34**).

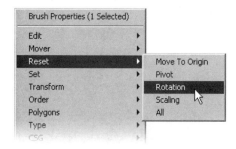

FIGURE 6.34 It's a good habit to reset the rotation of the active brush after every rotation procedure. It may keep a rotation for when you try to change its dimensions in the CubeBuilder dialog box.

9. Position the active brush so that it completely surrounds the bottom half of the broken column but does not make contact with the top half.

10. Intersect the broken column by clicking the Intersect icon on the toolbar.

11. Move the new active brush into your room so that its bottom is lined up with the floor of the room. Add the brush to the room and rebuild the level. Save and play the map to see a broken column in the room.

The Deintersect tool does the opposite of what the Intersect tool does. Instead of surrounding a group of brushes and capturing what is already there, the Deintersect tool can capture the inverse geometry. You'll now use the Deintersect tool to create a missing piece from the broken column above.

1. In the construction area, right-click on the cylinder brush you added to create the shaft of the column (from Figure 6.32) and select To Brush from the Polygons list. This forms an active brush in the shape of the column shaft.

2. Click the Deintersect icon on the toolbar (**Figure 6.35**). The active brush now fills the space where the column has been disconnected.

Deintersect icon

FIGURE 6.35 Use the Deintersect icon on the toolbar to capture a space in between geometry.

3. Move the active brush 128 units to the side and add the brush. You should see your broken column and off to the side, the piece that is missing from the broken column.

4. Move the active brush up into your room and rotate it 90 degrees in the Front or Side view so that it looks like the piece is lying on the floor.

5. Add the brush. Rebuild, save, and play the map to see the results in the game.

Vertex editing

Brushes are made up of faces. Faces are the planes that connect endpoints known as vertices (the plural form of "vertex"). You can move an individual vertex or a group of vertices with the Vertex Editing tool. This operation can change basic shapes like cubes into more irregular shapes. These irregular shapes can change a basic level progression into a more interesting one.

1. Near the bottom of the construction area in our current level, create an added brush with a Height value of 128, a Width value of 32, and a Breadth value of 64.

2. Move the active brush out of the way.

3. Click the Vertex Editing icon on the toolbar to access the Vertex Editing tool (**Figure 6.36**).

Vertex
Editing icon

FIGURE 6.36 Click the Vertex Editing icon on the toolbar to switch to vertex editing mode.

4. Select the newly added brush by left-clicking on it.

5. In the Side view, select the bottom-right vertices by pressing and holding down both the Ctrl and Alt keys and dragging a box around the bottom right corner of the brush with the left mouse button.

6. Press and hold down only the Ctrl key this time, then left-click and drag to move the vertices to the right 32 units. The brush should now angle out to the right as it gets to the bottom.

7. Duplicate the brush and move it up into the room so that the bottom of the brush lines up with the floor of the room.

8. In the Top view, position the duplicated brush so that the straight side lines up with a wall and the angle slopes down toward the middle of the room.

9. Duplicate this brush again to add more wall supports around the room. Rebuild, save, and play the map to see the results.

> **NOTE** ▶ Vertex editing is another operation that will require you to rebuild the level to see the results in the 3D view.

You can use the Vertex Editing tool on all kinds of brushes, including the active brush, to change their shapes. I use the Vertex Editing tool all the time to make slight adjustments to existing brushes. For example, let's say you want to make a room slightly taller. In either the Front or Side view, simply select the top vertices of the room brush and move them up. This can save you from going back to the CubeBuilder dialog box and creating a completely new brush to add on the top.

The 2D Shape Editor

The 2D Shape Editor allows you to customize the shape of the active brush based on a 2D shape of your creation. You can then perform operations such as Extrude to project the shape a specified distance and form a brush with the space inside. This allows you to start with a brush that has more or fewer vertices than the standard number of four for a cube. You can create a wedge brush starting with a triangle, for example.

1. Open the 2D Shape Editor by clicking the 2D Shape Editor icon on the menu bar (**Figure 6.37**). The 2D Shape Editor window will appear. The default 2D shape is a square, and you can use this to start with (**Figure 6.38**, on the next page).

FIGURE 6.37 You can open the 2D Shape Editor window with the 2D Shape Editor icon on the menu bar.

2. Select the top-left corner of the square by left-clicking on it. The top-left vertex should turn red.

3. Move the vertex down to two grid squares above the bottom-left vertex by left-clicking and dragging the vertex down.

4. Now, select the top-right vertex of the square and click the Split Segment icon on the menu bar to add a new vertex below it.

5. Drag the top-right vertex so that it is one grid square to the right of the top-left vertex.

6. Drag the middle right vertex (the newest one created) so that it is one grid square below the top-right vertex.

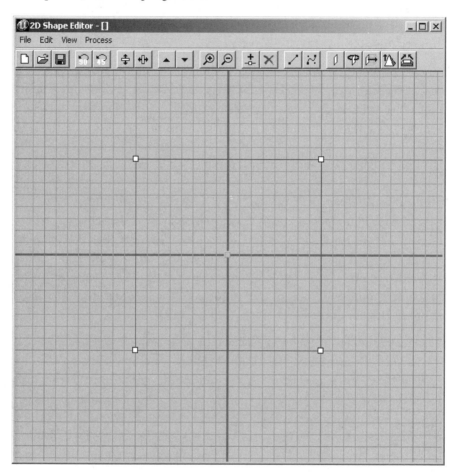

FIGURE 6.38 The 2D Shape Editor window with its default shape.

7. To complete the shape, drag the bottom-right vertex to the left so that it is two grid squares to the right of the bottom-left vertex. Your result should look similar to **Figure 6.39**.

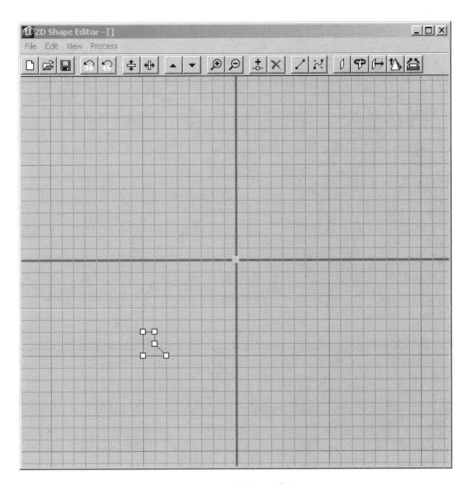

FIGURE 6.39 The new shape created in the 2D Shape Editor.

8. Now, click the Extruded Shape icon (**Figure 6.40**) on the menu bar to open the Extruded Shape dialog box. Enter a Depth value of 640 and click the OK button to change the active brush to an extruded 2D shape.

FIGURE 6.40 The Extruded Shape icon will open the Extruded Shape dialog box.

9. In the Top view, move the active brush so that it lines up with the left wall of the room. In the Front view, move the active brush so that the bottom of the active brush lines up with the floor of the room.

10. Add the brush to the level. You have now created a bottom trim to the room. You can move the wall supports you created in the Vertex Editing exercise to border the trim.

11. Duplicate the trim and wall supports and position them on the other three walls in the room. Rebuild, save, and play the map to see the results.

> **TIP** You can change the grid size in the 2D Shape Editor by opening the Grid list from the Edit drop-down menu.

Terrain

If any part of your level is outdoors, there's a good chance you'll need to add terrain. (Of course, you could always make an outdoor level in a man-made setting, such as a city square, that won't need terrain.) The Terrain Editing tool in UnrealEd allows you to sculpt a ground plane to simulate natural terrain. This terrain geometry is completely different from the brush-based, BSP geometry the Unreal engine uses for its indoor levels.

From the Unreal\Maps directory on the CD, copy the file Tutorial02b.urt into your Unreal\Maps directory. If you're ever unclear about what is being described, open the Tutorial02b.urt level for an example.

1. Start a new Unreal level and create a large subtracted brush with a Height value of 2560, and Width and Breadth values of 5120. This will actually be much smaller than a typical level with terrain, but it will be easier to manage for a first level.

2. Select all of the faces of the brush and open the Surface Properties dialog box.

> **TIP** To easily select all the faces of a brush, select one of the faces in the 3D view and press Shift+B.

3. In the Flags tab, select the Fake Backdrop check box.

4. In the Pan/Rot/Scale tab, select a Simple Scaling value of 16. This makes the brush a little less distracting.

5. Create a Skybox underneath the large subtracted brush.

6. Open the Actor Classes browser and expand the Actor list. Expand the Info list and select *ZoneInfo (**Figure 6.41**).

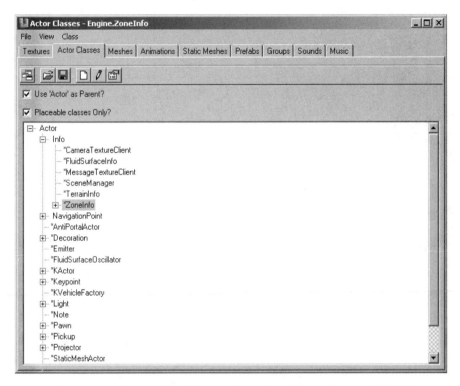

FIGURE 6.41 You can find the ZoneInfo actor in the Actor Classes browser. A kind of ZoneInfo actor was used to create the Skybox in Tutorial01.

7. In the Top view, place the ZoneInfo in the middle of the brush.

8. Open the ZoneInfo Properties window by double-clicking on the ZoneInfo actor you've just placed. Expand the ZoneInfo list in the ZoneInfo Properties window and change the bTerrainZone value to True. This will allow terrain to be created in this zone.

9. While still in the ZoneInfo Properties window, expand the ZoneLight list and enter an AmbientBrightness value of 64. You'll be able to see the terrain better with this value raised. Close the ZoneInfo Properties window.

10. Click the Terrain Editing icon on the toolbar to open the Terrain Editor
(**Figure 6.42**). The Terrain Editing window (shown in **Figure 6.43**) should
appear.

FIGURE 6.42 Clicking the Terrain Editing icon opens the Terrain Editing window.

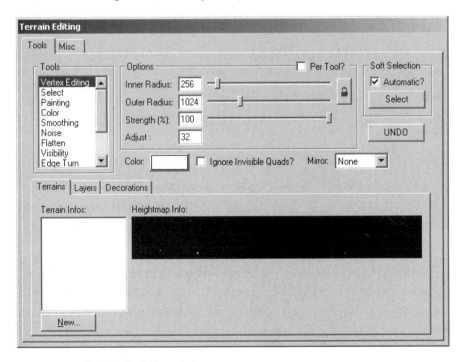

FIGURE 6.43 The Terrain Editing window.

11. Click the New button to create a new terrain. A dialog box will appear asking for several parameters for the new terrain (**Figure 6.44**). For now, just type a unique name in the Name field and click OK. This creates a TerrainInfo actor you can place in your level.

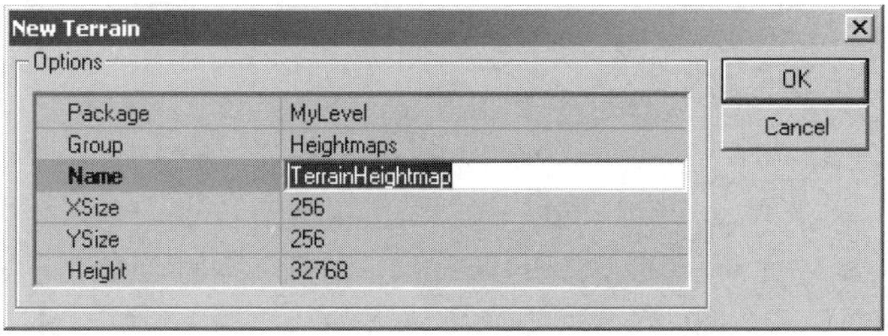

FIGURE 6.44 The New Terrain dialog box with its default settings.

The TerrainInfo is essentially the center point for your terrain, and its properties control the properties of the terrain itself. You have also just created a new height map that your terrain will use to figure out the height of each vertex. This height map is located in a texture package called myLevel, which will be associated with your level. You should now associate the appropriate textures for each layer of the terrain. There is a base layer that needs a base texture, and you can add more layers to make paths and patches of different textures.

1. Switch to the Layers tab in the Terrain Editing window. Highlight the top Undefined field in the Layers tab by left-clicking on it (**Figure 6.45**, on the next page).

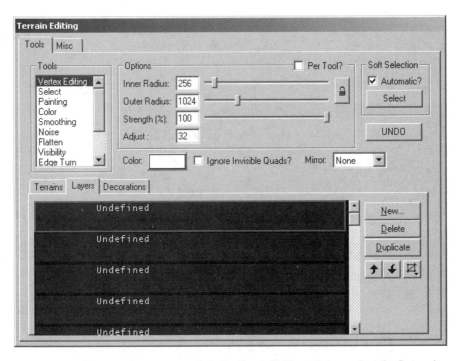

FIGURE 6.45 After creating a new terrain in the Terrain Editing window, select the first undefined layer to make it active.

2. Open the Texture Browser and open the Tutorial.utx texture package. Select the Terrain texture group and select Texture Ground01* from the group of textures.

3. Go back to the Terrain Editing window and click the New button. This will make the current selected texture the base texture for the terrain. The New Terrain dialog box will appear. Highlight the second Undefined field in the Layers tab and select Texture Rock01* from the Texture Browser. Click the New button in the Terrain Editing window to create a layer on top of the base terrain texture.

   Repeat this procedure one more time using Texture Path01* as the last layer. Build the level and you will see the terrain appear in the 3D view. Terrain does not draw from the bottom side, so if you don't see it in the view, move the camera up. You may also need switch to the Textured mode in the 3D view so that the terrain is fully lit. You will need to add some lighting to the terrain. Since most terrain is outdoors, let's add a Sunlight actor to the level.

4. In the Actor Classes browser, expand the *Light list and select *Sunlight.

5. Place the Sunlight actor anywhere in your large subtraction brush.6. In the Top view, select the Sunlight actor and rotate the direction 45 degrees in either direction. In the Front view, rotate the Sunlight direction 45 degrees down toward the ground.

6. Close the Terrain Editing window by clicking the Camera Movement icon on the toolbar.

7. Open the TerrainInfo Properties window by double-clicking on the TerrainInfo actor. Expand the TerrainInfo list and the Layers list below that. Expand the [0] list and enter UScale and VScale values of 8 (**Figure 6.46**).

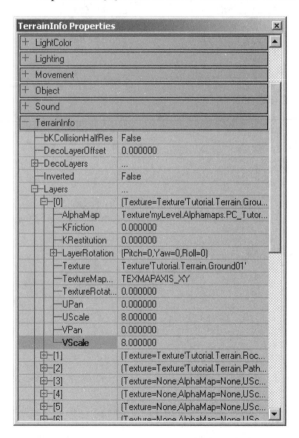

FIGURE 6.46 You can change the scaling of the textures, or how often it repeats, using the UScale and VScale values in the TerrainInfo Properties window.

This is the base texture for the terrain, and by changing the UScale and VScale, you can change how often the texture repeats.

8. Expand the [1] list and enter the same value of 8 for its UScale and VScale. This is our rock texture layer.

9. Expand the [2] list and enter a value of 4 for its UScale and VScale. This is our path texture layer.

10. Expand the TerrainScale list and enter X, Y, and Z values of 24 (**Figure 6.47**). Your terrain should now better fit the subtraction brush. Close the TerrainInfo Properties window.

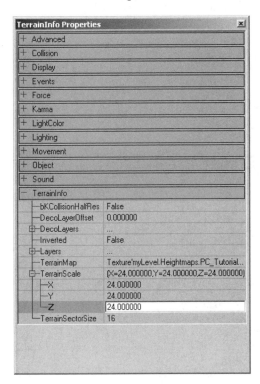

FIGURE 6.47 You can change the scaling of the terrain easily using the X, Y, and Z values under the TerrainScale list in the TerrainInfo Properties window.

11. Open the Terrain Editing window again and switch to the Terrains tab if it isn't already selected. Double-click on the height map to make sure it is selected. Now, select the Painting option from the Tools menu.

12. In the 3D view, while holding down the Ctrl key, right-click in the middle of the terrain to start pushing the terrain down. The longer you hold down the Ctrl key, the further the terrain will be pushed down. Continue this process to push the terrain down the middle of the level and keep the borders relatively intact.

> **TIP** ▶ If you push down too much, you can Ctrl+left-click to pull the terrain back up.

13. Form an enormous pit that will be the walkable area of the level. Once you have a rough area formed, pull up the edges in a random way so that it resembles a crater.

14. Switch to the Smoothing tool and Ctrl+left-click to smooth out some of the height differences that are too abrupt. Experiment with the sliders under the Options menu for Inner Radius, Outer Radius, Strength (%), and Adjust. Inner Radius is where the paintbrush starts, and Outer Radius is where it ends.

15. Use the Strength option to alter how much the smoothing affects the terrain, and use Adjust to change how many differences of heights will occur.

    When you're happy with your terrain's shape, rebuild the level. The Sunlight actor should now affect the terrain and make the heights a little clearer. Place a PlayerStart and move it just above your terrain. Save and play the map to test the area.

Keep in mind that the terrain you have just created still has only one base texture on it. Sometimes, other textures layered on top of the base texture can make it less repetitive and more realistic. You can also create a path for players to follow. The following exercise will show you how to do both.

1. Open the Terrain Editing window and switch to the Layers tab. Click in the second field, which should be the rock texture layer.

2. Select the Painting tool, and in the 3D view, Ctrl+left-click to paint on the rock texture and Ctrl+right-click to erase the rock texture. Paint the rock texture on anything too steep to walk on and randomly paint a few patches all over to break up the ground texture.

3. Select the Noise tool and Ctrl+left-click to splatter some small patches of the rock texture and break up the repetition of the base texture.

4. Click in the third field, which should be the path texture layer. Use the Painting and Noise tools with the path too, but only on the flatter areas where the player can walk. Rebuild, save, and play the map to test the results. Your level in the editor should look similar to **Figure 6.48**.

FIGURE 6.48 The tutorial terrain level in the 3D view.

Assignment 5

Creating a Template for Your Level: Level Geometry
Using your level diagram as a blueprint, create the basic geometry for your level. Use simple shapes and add some placeholder textures and lighting.

UnrealEd tutorial: gameplay elements

Creating the spaces for a level is just one part of the building process. You'll also need to add several gameplay elements for the level to function in a game. Some of these elements can be placed through the Actor Browser window in UnrealEd. For example, you can add items like weapons and ammo for player characters to pick up, or objects like crates and barrels that player characters can break or open. Other elements require a bit more mechanics. You can create geometry that moves and can "collide" or block and even transport a player character in UnrealEd. Pieces of moving geometry are called *movers* in Unreal. Movers can be simple doors or platforms that move when a character collides with them. They can also be activated to move when a *trigger* sends a message to do so. For example, you can set up a button in an elevator that the player character must bump up against to cause the elevator to move.

From the Unreal\StaticMeshes directory on the CD, copy the file PC-StaticMeshes.usx into your Unreal\StaticMeshes directory. From the Unreal\Maps directory on the CD, copy the file Tutorial03.urt into your Unreal\Maps directory. If you're ever unclear about what is being described, open the Tutorial03.urt level for an example.

Static meshes

The Unreal engine uses a few different types of geometry. The brush-based, BSP geometry from the first tutorial is one type, and the terrain-based geometry from the second tutorial is another. The final type is called *static meshes*. Static meshes are models that are brought into levels for various purposes. Static meshes can be highly detailed decorative pieces, such as machinery, statues, and furniture. They can also be features essential to the gameplay, such as trees in a forest or pipes to walk along. Static meshes can be converted into movable geometry.

Static meshes are usually created in external 3D modeling programs such as 3D Studio Max or Maya. They are imported into UnrealEd and can be organized into packages and groups similar to textures. Let's add a static mesh to the room for some decoration.

1. Open the Static Mesh browser by clicking the Static Mesh Browser icon on the menu bar.

2. In the browser window, select Open from the File category. Select the PC-StaticMeshes.usx package and click the Open button. You should see a list of static meshes on the left frame of the browser. You can select any of these static meshes and view them in the main frame of the browser.

   The main frame is a view similar to the 3D view: You can navigate around the view in the same way to see the selected static mesh, and you can change the static mesh group in the Static Mesh Group menu.

3. Select the Basic static mesh group. Select PipeMesh01 in the left frame to make it the current static mesh. You will see an object in the main frame that looks like a pipe (**Figure 6.49**).

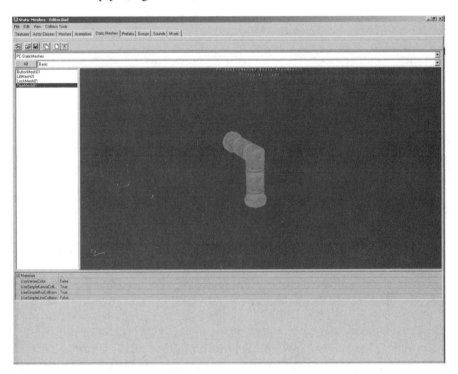

FIGURE 6.49 A pipe static mesh in the Static Mesh browser.

4. In the 3D view, right-click in a corner of the floor in your room and select Add Static Mesh: 'Editor.PipeMesh01' from the contextual menu. The pipe will appear in the room. It will be green in color because it is currently selected.

5. Move the pipe up so that the bottom intersects the floor slightly. Move and rotate the pipe so that its other end intersects a wall slightly.

You can edit some properties of static meshes:

1. Right-click on the static mesh pipe and select StaticMeshActor Properties from the contextual menu. Expand the Display list and type a DrawScale value of 0.5; then press the Enter key (**Figure 6.50**). The static mesh pipe will appear 50 percent of the size it was when it was placed.

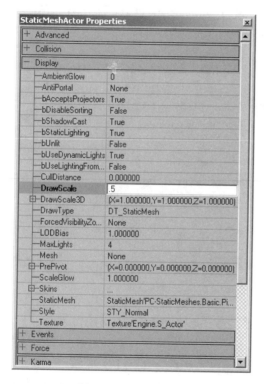

FIGURE 6.50 You can change the DrawScale value of a static mesh to make it bigger or smaller.

2. Change the DrawScale value back to 1 and press the Enter key to revert the pipe to its original size. Expand the DrawScale3D list and enter a Z value of 0.5; then press the Enter key. DrawScale3D allows you to change the scale of a static mesh along any axis. Change the pipe back to its original scaling.

Rebuild the level to see the static mesh properly lit. Save and play the map to test the room with the pipe in it.

Although static meshes should be imported from external 3D modeling programs, it is possible to create them using UnrealEd. If you are not familiar with or don't have access to a 3D modeling package, you can build simple static meshes in UnrealEd:

1. Create a piece of geometry and use the Intersect tool to capture the faces of the geometry together (this was covered in the Intersect and Deintersect section earlier).

2. Add the captured brush in another location.

3. Right-click on the brush and select To Static Mesh from the Convert list (**Figure 6.51**). Enter names for the Package, Group, and Name fields and click the OK button. Save the new static mesh package.

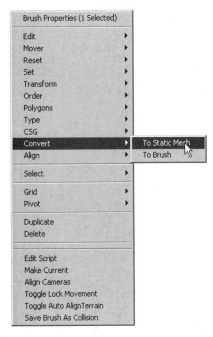

FIGURE 6.51 Right-click on a brush to bring up a contextual menu that will allow you to convert a brush to a static mesh.

NOTE You'll need to choose unique names for the static mesh package, group, and name. The Unreal engine can become confused if more than one file shares the same name, and you may not see your static mesh in the game.

Movers

A *mover* is a type of static mesh, and movers can only be created from static meshes. Level designers create gameplay elements such as doors, lifts, and platforms by using movers. In the exercise that follows, I'll show you how to add an elevator to the middle of your room.

1. Open the CubeBuilder dialog box and type a Height value of 32, and Width and Breadth values of 256. Click the Build button in the dialog box to change your active brush to these settings.

2. Move your active brush to the middle of your floor and down so that the top of the active brush lines up with the top of the floor.

3. Click the Subtract icon on the toolbar to subtract the brush.

4. Keep the active brush in the same position as it was when you subtracted the pit in your floor.

5. If it isn't already open, use the Static Mesh browser to open the PC-StaticMeshes.usx static mesh package. Select the Basic static mesh group and then select LiftMesh01.

6. Click the Add Mover Brush icon on the toolbar (**Figure 6.52**). This will create a mover in the form of the static mesh cube with its center point where the active brush is.

FIGURE 6.52 Use the Add Mover Brush icon to create a mover from the static mesh you have selected in the Static Mesh browser.

7. Open the Mover Properties dialog box by either right-clicking on the mover and selecting Mover Properties from its contextual menu or by double-clicking on the mover. Expand the Display list and enter a DrawScale value of 0.75; then press the Enter key. The mover should now fit into the shallow pit you created in the middle of the floor.

Movers can travel from point to point and back again. UnrealEd uses a series of key frames that you can set for the mover to go between.

1. Close the Mover Properties dialog box and right-click on the mover to bring up its contextual menu. This time, highlight the Mover selection and you will see the Key Frame list appear to the side (**Figure 6.53**). Currently, the mover is in Key 0. Select Key 1 to set the next frame.

FIGURE 6.53 To animate a mover, you can select different key frames for that mover and translate the mover however you like.

2. Position the mover up to the middle of the room.

3. Right-click on the mover and go to the Mover Key 0 again. The mover will pop back to its original position.

4. Build the level and play the map to test it. Walk to the mover and stand on it. It should raise your character up to the middle of the room. You have now created a lift or a platform. Other kinds of movers, such as doors and buttons, are created in the same way.

In addition, movers can have more than two points to travel between. You might use a mover like this when you have a train that travels along a curved path or even to animate a mover getting blown up and flying through the air.

1. Select the mover again and right-click to select Mover Key 2.

2. Position the mover in the middle of the room again, as you did in Step 2 from the previous tutorial. This time, in the Top view, rotate the mover 90 degrees clockwise.

3. Right-click on the mover and select Mover Key 3.

4. In the Top view, rotate the mover 90 degrees clockwise but keep its height position the same. Save and play the map. Stand on the lift. It should lift your character up, then rotate 90 degrees and come back down.

You can add sounds to movers quite easily. Each mover contains information in its properties that attaches sounds to different actions it performs. For example, you can select a sound for the mover to play when it opens and when it closes.

1. Open the Sounds browser by clicking the Sound Browser icon on the menu bar.

2. Select SoundEffectsTest from the list and click the Play button in the browser to hear what the sound is (**Figure 6.54**, on the next page).

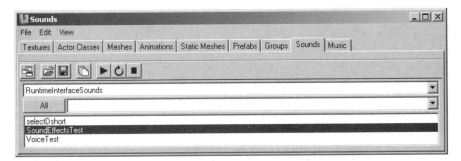

FIGURE 6.54 You can preview sounds in the Sounds browser. This is quite useful so you don't have to play the whole level to find out if you got the right sound.

3. Open the Mover Properties dialog box and expand the MoverSounds list. Click on the text ClosedSound and three more buttons should appear to the right of the value box (**Figure 6.55**).

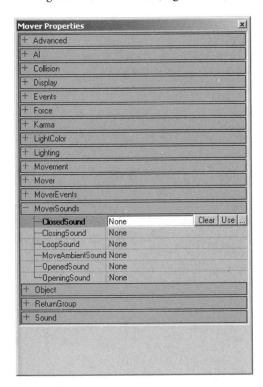

FIGURE 6.55 UnrealEd helps you by providing commands to easily clear the field box or to use the currently selected sound in the Sounds browser.

4. Click the Use button to assign the current sound. Perform the same operation for OpenedSound. Save and play the map. Ride the lift to hear the results.

Triggers

A *trigger* is the mechanism used to activate certain events in Unreal. Triggers send messages to activate movers, effects, enemies, sounds, and music. In the following exercise, we'll set up a trigger in your room to activate the lift remotely. Currently, the mover in the room is activated by the player character colliding with it.

1. If you open the Mover Properties dialog box and expand the Object list, you'll see that its InitialState option is set to BumpOpenTimed. This means that the mover is waiting until a player character bumps into it to activate. You can change the InitialState setting by clicking on the text InitialState and then clicking the down arrow that appears next to BumpOpenTimed. When the drop-down menu appears, select TriggerOpenTimed (**Figure 6.56**).

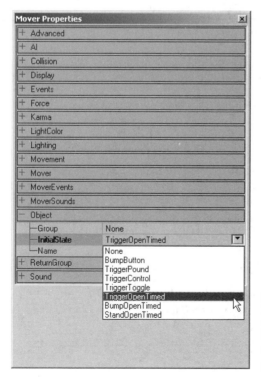

FIGURE 6.56 By changing the InitialState to TriggerOpenTimed, you're telling the mover to wait until it receives a message from a trigger to move instead of a bump from a player character.

2. Open the Actor Classes browser and expand the Actor list. Expand the Trigger list and select the *Trigger item.

3. In the 3D view, place the trigger in a corner of your room near the floor.

4. Open the Mover Properties dialog box of the lift by double-clicking on the lift. Expand the Events list and check the Tag value (**Figure 6.57**).

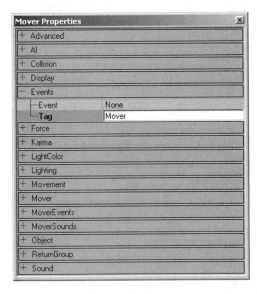

FIGURE 6.57 The tag value is the name you give to the mover.

5. Open the Trigger Properties dialog box by double-clicking on the trigger. Expand the Events list and for the Event value, type whatever the Tag value was for the lift (it should be Mover if you have not changed it).

6. Save and play the map. Go to the corner where you placed the trigger. Look to the middle of the room and you should see the lift rise, rotate, and go back down.

Let's add a button on the wall that triggers the lift:

1. Open the CubeBuilder dialog box and enter 64 for the Height, Width, and Breadth values. Click the Build button in the dialog box to set your active brush to this size.

2. In the Top view, position the active brush in the middle of the right wall in your room. The left side of the active brush should line up with the right wall. In the Side view, move the active brush so that the center of the brush is 192 units above the floor.

3. Subtract the brush to form a square hole in the wall that is eye-level to the player character.

4. In the Static Mesh browser, open the PC-StaticMeshes.usx static mesh package if it isn't already open. Select the Basic static mesh group and select ButtonMesh01.

5. Keep the active brush in the same position as it was in Step 10. Create a ButtonMesh01 mover by clicking the Add Mover icon on the toolbar.

6. Double-click on the new mover to open its Mover Properties dialog box. Expand the Display list and enter a DrawScale value of 0.32. Press the Enter key to change the new mover's DrawScale. It should fit perfectly into the subtracted brush.

7. Rotate the mover by holding down the Ctrl key and right-clicking and dragging so that the hand symbol points out into the room. In the Top view, move the new mover 32 units to the left so that it is sticking halfway out of the wall.

8. Right-click on the new mover and select Mover Key 1. Drag the mover until the face with the hand symbol is flush with the surface of the wall.

9. Right-click on the new mover and select Mover Key 0 again.

10. Open the new mover's Properties window and expand the Events list. Change the Tag value from Mover to Mover1 so that the lift is the only mover with the Tag value of Mover.

11. Select the trigger that was in the corner of the room and place it in the hole in the wall just to the right of Mover1 in the Top view.

12. Open the trigger's Properties window and expand the Trigger list. Change the TriggerType value to TT_AnyProximity (**Figure 6.58**).

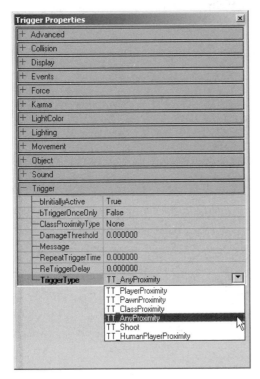

By changing the TriggerType value to TT_AnyProximity, you're telling the trigger to send its message when any object collides with it—in this case, the button.

13. Expand the Collision list and change the CollisionHeight and CollisionRadius values to 2. Save and build the level.

14. Play the map and run to Mover1, which should look like a button. Collide with the button by moving your character into it and turn around. The button should collide with the trigger, which activates the lift.

Movers and triggers are the basic components of the gameplay elements in a level. Of course, there are many others that are more specific to the skills and obstacles that you create for your individual game, but knowing how to use movers and triggers should allow you to build a valid template.

Creating a Template for Your Level: Gameplay Elements
Part 1—Add all of the mover gameplay features to your level such as doors, lifts, and platforms.

Part 2—Place the triggers to make the level function as you have planned with your diagram.

Creating a level template is the first step of the production process for level designers. You actually get to see your level take a 3D form and, when it's complete, you can play through the level to see if it lives up to the ideals that you originally set out to accomplish. Other people can also play the level and give you feedback. With that feedback, you can find solutions to problems and revise your level to improve it. This next stage, the play-test and revision stage, is probably the most important part of the level design process.

CHAPTER 7
Improving Your Level

THE PRIMARY REASON TO CONSTRUCT a template for your
level is for you to analyze the level before it's actually done. In Chapter
5, we talked about how the level could be judged by the team in diagram
form. Since judging the diagram takes some imagination and the template
phase still contains some design work, the template should give the
team a better means to evaluate the level. The template may also reveal
problems or issues in the level that were not apparent in the diagram.

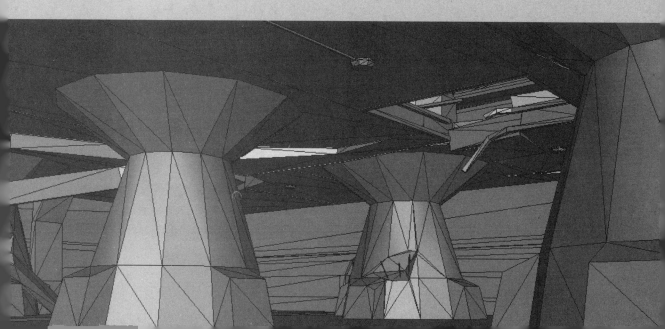

The process of playing and evaluating is called *play-testing*. Play-testing a level can happen at any time once the template is complete. The team should play-test levels continuously for the remainder of the development cycle or until it becomes impossible to make any changes. Play-testing can be done by members of the team (including the level designer who creates the level), members of the company who aren't part of the development team, or even the general public. Most companies hold play-test sessions with an exterior collection of individuals called a *focus group* to gather information and feedback about the game and specific levels. Typically, a member of the team watches a focus group tester play through a few levels and takes notes about the experience. The tester can also fill out a questionnaire for additional comments.

Multiplayer Levels

A lot of games have both single-player levels and multiplayer levels. Of course, it's impossible for you to play-test a multiplayer level alone. For some games, like Unreal Tournament, players can compete in multiplayer levels against AI characters called *bots*, but even bots don't play exactly the way that other human players do. Human players have ways of exploiting unfair advantages in levels that bots could never understand.

For a multiplayer level, companies should be sure to play-test with varying numbers of players. For example, let's say that the minimum number of players for your level is two, and the maximum is 32. Play-testing for this level should involve sessions with the minimum number of required players, the maximum number of players, and everything in between. And ideally, the level should work well in all scenarios.

For a level designer, observing a play-test session can often be a horrific event. Someone could struggle to complete a puzzle in your level for several minutes while you had estimated that the puzzle would be quite simple. At the same time, play-testing can be incredibly educational and rewarding. Just a few minutes of observing your testers can tell you more about your level than your own testing could reveal in hours. It's the hardest thing in the world to play through your own level as if you hadn't designed it yourself—you're just too close to your level to analyze it properly. Play-testers should be within the target audience of the game, but it might also be helpful to add a wider variety of testers to cover all of the bases.

Play-test sessions provide level designers with the information they need to improve their levels. In its template form, a level can reveal many flaws that don't appear during the diagram stage. Some common problems in levels exist and can be avoided if you are aware of them. Even when these common problems come up, there are almost always methods to solve them.

Although play-testing continues for the rest of the project, you can't stand around for weeks and weeks waiting to receive all of the feedback based on the first template. You need to keep updating and improving your level to get feedback on possible solutions or to turn attention toward other issues that the level may contain.

> **NOTE** Many play-testers tend to focus on the few major issues that they really want changed in a level while ignoring other portions that they deem less important. Play-testers even focus on the same issues that others have already addressed. To make a level the best it can be from beginning to end, you should update your levels frequently so that other areas get more attention from future play-test sessions.

A revision for a level can sometimes take longer than the initial design—in fact, the revision may even seem more intense. You can get caught up on a solution for one issue and stare at your screen for hours at a time without actually creating anything. These are important decisions that need time and thought, but taking the time and effort will be worth it in the end. It might be humbling and depressing to watch someone play through your template, but it could be incredibly rewarding and uplifting to watch someone play through your revision.

Setting Up a Play-Test Session

The simplest play-test session happens when someone new to the level plays through it while the level designer watches. More complex play-test sessions occur when the game is in its beta stage and members of the general public sign up to be beta testers. These kinds of play-tests are usually games that require many people to play the game at the same time, such as a Massively Multiplayer Online Role Playing Game (MMORPG). Most commonly, play-test sessions occur at regular intervals that coincide with a weekly build or a monthly milestone. Members of the team usually can start play-testing the game in its template form, but outside individuals may be invited as well.

Pretty much anyone can be a play-tester. In fact, you will always be a play-tester as you tweak the level and make sure it is playable. Obviously, a member of the target audience would be the ideal play-tester, but a slightly different audience is also fair game. In most cases, a company will initially expose the level in its template form to team members. Later on, when the level starts to both look and feel like a shippable product, external players can be brought in.

Who should play-test?

Once the template is completed, team members are usually the first play-testers. The template is not going to resemble the final level in an artistic sense, and it may be difficult for players outside of development not to focus on the visuals.

It's best to find a play-tester who has not only never played the level before, but who also has never seen the level diagram. Although this perfect play-tester might be easy to find at first, more and more of your team members will start to play the level and you might have to resort to someone who's already familiar with it. Right after you've completed the level template, you can approach any team member to play-test, even though some of them may have been involved with the level diagram. In fact, you might want to start with the other level designers on the team. It's a good idea to start with one play-tester at a time so that you have more "fresh" play-testers as you revise and edit the level.

The Ideal Play-Tester

During production, a company may hire new team members or move existing employees to other projects. These are the best candidates to play-test levels. They usually have little or no information about the levels since they were not around during preproduction. Be sure to get these new team members to play-test before they get "tainted" by team conversations, meetings, and email.

Members of the team who have not been exposed to the game levels also make great play-testers. For example, at Blizzard we created a group of team members known as the "level design strike team." This group consisted of programmers, artists, and designers who had no knowledge of the levels we were going to critique yet. They did, however, have a lot of experience playing the game. Once I designed the level in template form, we would all play the level and meet back in the conference room to discuss problems or issues.

NOTE It's okay for team members who have played the level before and who have seen the level diagram to play-test a level with new revisions and additions. Their feedback can be limited to the new or changed areas.

Creating a test plan

Play-testers are sometimes given a document called a *test plan* to give feedback to the developers. Test plans can be simple questionnaires for play-testers to answer once they have completed the level, or they can be a list of specific areas that the team requested feedback on. Test plans work well when the level designer or another team member cannot be present to observe the play-test session. But even if a team member is there taking notes, it's still a good idea to have a test plan for the player to fill out. You can watch someone play through a level, but you still might not know what they were thinking when they performed a specific task. The test plan can allow the developers to get inside a player's head.

To create a test plan, start with general questions about the level size, the difficulty, and the progression. You can ask more detailed questions about specific sections of the level as well. For example, you might ask if players saw the solution to a puzzle right away or it took some time and experimentation to find out what they needed to do.

> **TIP** ▶ Try to use terms that all players can understand. Most players won't understand a question that refers to areas of the level that only you have labeled and that don't have final art associated with them. For example, you won't be able to refer to a part of your level as "the maintenance room" before a texture of the maintenance room sign has been created and placed.

Sample General Test Plan Questions:

1. Is the level too difficult or too easy to complete? Do you remember any specific situation that is too difficult or easy?

2. Does the level feel too long or too short? Are there parts of the level that seem unnecessary? Is there a part that could be expanded?

3. What are your favorite parts of the level? What are your least favorite parts?

Sample Specific Test Plan Questions:

1. Did your character have any trouble getting into the air vent?

2. Do you think your character should be able to climb over the fence at the final platform?

3. Is the last piece of the relic too difficult to find?

Test plans are meant to supplement the play-test session. A member of the development team should observe play-testers as they play through a level. If the company holds a focus group session, one development team member should be assigned to each play-test station.

The role of the observer

Any member of the development team can observe players during play-test sessions—it doesn't necessarily need to be the level designer who created the level.

However, it's very important for these team members to know their roles while participating. Too much observer involvement can taint the experience for a play-tester. Each observer should follow certain rules to avoid contamination.

First, the observer should not speak or give clues in any way during the play-test session. This is probably the most difficult rule to follow. Players can get stuck in an area and retrace their steps to the beginning of the level while the solution seems so obvious to you as the level designer. You may need to give a brief description of the game's story, or teach a skill that's necessary for the player to know before playing through the level. But once the player starts the level, it's best to watch in silence. If play-testers ask specifically about an area that's giving them trouble, you may want to ask what they are trying to do in that area before answering their question.

The observer should also keep track of the time it takes for the players to complete sections of the level and the entire level. Measuring a level in terms of time is probably more revealing than measuring it in terms of square footage.

Time Limits

The development team may set a ballpark time limit for each area of a level to ensure that the entire level is analyzed. Certain areas or puzzles may have major issues that need to be solved before another play-test session can start. So if a play-tester is struggling in an area or with a puzzle for a very long time, the observer can intervene and skip the player to the next area.

After the first few play-test sessions, the development team can refine this time limit for the level areas. The observer may choose to extend or shorten that time limit depending on the situation. For instance, if a player seems close to solving a puzzle, the observer can give the player just a little more time.

The observer should take notes on the player's experience. It is important to document any unexpected actions players make in the level, or any comments they make while playing. As I mentioned earlier, as the level designer you may not always serve as the observer for these play-test sessions, and you'll rely on these notes to get the feedback you need to make changes to your level. Of course, it's also difficult to remember every problem with every area of the game, and you can refer to these notes later during the revision phase.

Notes can vary from bugs that you need to fix for the next play-test session to comments that a play-tester makes while playing the level. Here is an actual list of notes taken while I observed someone playing the cookie factory level:

- Jumped on top of vehicle to jump inside loading dock. Move vehicle closer for easier jump.

- Did not find shotgun in crates. Picked up shotgun from dead soldier.

- Add item crates in the storage rooms.

- The button for the mixer room puzzle "looks like a tripwire."

- Died at the second jump in the mixer room puzzle.

- Soldiers can shoot through catwalk.

- Add railing around cooling pit.

- Double-jumped over the generator. Add player clip brush.

Once the player has completed the level, the observer is free to ask questions about the experience. This can sometimes take the place of a test plan. You can ask play-testers why they performed a certain action or if they expected something more in a specific section of the level. They may mention something that you didn't notice during the play-test. For example, here are comments made by a play-tester after playing the cookie factory level:

- Some of the doorways in the beginning felt too tall.

- After coming out of the air vent, the two enemy soldiers are directly lined up so that one is hidden from view. You're expecting to only fight one, but another pops out behind him.

▶ A few areas seemed empty. There should be more stuff, like crates, boxes, and barrels.

▶ There should be another enemy type thrown in that's different.

The observer should gather up all of the notes taken from the play-test session and create a task list. All task list items should be treated equally at this point.

Learning from a Play-Test Session

Your next step is to take the feedback from a play-test session and decide how to improve your level. This may sound easier than it really is. Sometimes, play-testers can contradict what other play-testers have said, or they may even contradict themselves. Hopefully, though, some issues or problems will stand out more than others, and you will most likely be able to determine which ones demand immediate attention.

Levels tend to have several common problems. Play-testing sessions during the template phase can expose some of these problems and can lead to solutions that improve the level a great deal. Some of the common problems involve the progression of the level. Play-testers may have complained about a lack of direction, repetitiveness within the level, or impassable obstacles that were frustrating to them. You should expect to spend a reasonable amount of time and effort fixing these problems and improving the level.

You can also use the feedback from play-testers to help make the level "feel right." Players experience the game through the levels, and certain factors in levels can contribute to the player's feeling of progression through the game. You should evaluate the level for both its size and its difficulty.

It's a good sign if a play-tester doesn't want to stop playing the game or if they want to play another level after their session is over. In most cases, it shows that the player is having fun and that other players will want to play the game in a similar way. You can learn a lot about the level simply by watching the reactions players have as they experience it.

> **NOTE** Play-testers can't always reveal their true reactions for a level while being observed—especially if the observer is the level designer. It might be difficult to get an accurate reading from play-testers from the things that they say. As an observer, though, you can deduce a lot from their actions and even their facial expressions as they play through the level.

Receiving feedback

Whose feedback should you address? What actions should you take to address the feedback you receive? Receiving feedback from play-test sessions can be more difficult than you'd expect. You might agree with an issue but not with the suggested solution.

> **NOTE** Depending on your team structure and company organization, you might be required to change your level if just one individual makes a comment about it. A team lead, the company president, or even someone in marketing might insist on a change that you'll need to implement—even if you don't concur entirely.

The level design team can meet with the lead designer to discuss what issues need solutions immediately and which ones can wait until further testing begins. The lead designer works with the producer and project lead to develop a task list for the level designer to complete before another play-test session.

Tracking Feedback with the Bug Database

In Chapter 1, I mentioned that a D-bug is a comment or suggestion made by a tester. All documented bugs, including D-bugs, are contained in the bug database. The producer usually works with the lead tester to set up the bug database with capabilities to input feedback. It's a good idea to start the bug database at the beginning of the production process to track feedback for all aspects of the game. The leads can meet with the producer and go over each of the comments or suggestions in list form and assign a priority to each. As the level designer, you can access the same database and see the list of tasks you should address in a specific order. This gives you clear direction as to what you should do next to improve the level.

Solving common problems in levels

Each game genre has its own set of problems that are specific to it, but some common problems span many genres. And most of these problems are usually uncovered during the template phase. For example, many levels in all sorts of different game types have issues with "impassable" obstacles, or obstacles that the player can't overcome. Impassable obstacles might be essential to a level, but there are dangers that should be avoided when placing them.

Another common problem in levels is too much repetition. When level designers place obstacles that use the same skills in the same ways, players can lose interest. The spaces contained in the level itself should also vary. Going through spaces that are the same size and shape can get confusing and the gameplay associated with those spaces becomes repetitious.

There will be times when you want the player to stop and think for a minute. At the same time, you also want to provide the player with enough direction to be able to complete the challenges of the level. This brings us to our next common problem: lack of direction. Level designers can provide direction within levels in very simple ways, but sometimes, the level might require an entirely different arrangement of its spaces to help the player along.

These kinds of problems can be fixed relatively quickly while the level is still in its template phase. Spaces can be rearranged, expanded, or compacted to break up repetition, add variety, or add direction for the player. Even impassable obstacles, if they cause problems in the play-test phase, can be changed or moved to serve a better purpose for the game.

The use of impassable obstacles

Levels sometimes contain obstacles that the player character is not supposed to pass. Some of these impassable obstacles are meant to push or steer the player in another direction. For example, a level designer might place a thorn bush obstacle in their level. Because it might cause damage to the character if they make contact with it, the obstacle eventually teaches the player to avoid going near it.

TIP ▶ The player character should never have to get hurt or die to find out that an obstacle is dangerous. Obstacles can be designed with visual clues that it can cause harm. For example, the first thorn bush the player character encounters could have long, obvious thorns with blood dripping from them. Another method to convey danger is with AI-controlled characters. The player might witness an enemy come into contact with a thorn bush and scream in pain.

Other impassable obstacles help to set up a special scene that the developers want players to experience. A see-through fence may allow a view of an objective, such as the level exit or a necessary item that the player needs to find later. Or, the developers may decide to place a scripted sequence behind the fence that the player can't interfere with. For example, the player character could observe an execution scene between an enemy soldier and a civilian from the other side of the fence. And while the player could not prevent the execution, the scripted sequence—and the impassable obstacle—serve the purpose of conveying the atmosphere of the game world.

Impassable obstacles are sometimes necessary to the level and the game, but they should also be used carefully to avoid frustrating players. Players might not recognize that an obstacle is impassable. In the first level of New Legends, the player character comes to a dead end and fights a number of enemy soldiers. Once a certain number of soldiers are killed, an enemy tank appears and blasts a hole in the wall that the player character can escape through. The enemy tank, the impassable obstacle, is indestructible to any of the weapons the player character has at this time. If players miss viewing the wall opening up, they might try to fight the tank. Of course, the tank will win the fight every time. In this instance, the player does not know that the tank is an impassable obstacle. For a solution, an AI-controlled character might tell the player character that they have to retreat to escape the tank. Another solution might be to place the tank out of reach. It can destroy the wall and disappear.

Another danger of impassable obstacles is that they often aren't consistent. For example, if a player can climb one fence and not another, he will become confused. A solution for this would be to make only barbed-wire fences impassable.

Avoiding repetition

Another common problem in levels is a lack of gameplay variety. Variety in games takes several different forms; how the player character moves through the level is one example. While playing your level in template form, does the player character just run through the level from beginning to end or are they forced to run, jump, climb, crawl, and fall to get to the exit? The latter option provides a good amount of variety for the player.

Varying the sizes and shapes of the level spaces is another tool for keeping your players engaged. Long, narrow hallways offer the player no choices and no variation of space. Even rooms that are connected by doorways and are all approximately the same size and shape can become boring and confusing. If your level contains a hallway that seems too long, you might be able to shorten the connection or place an event at some point in the hallway to provide a different experience.

The 10-Second Rule

Although designing levels shouldn't really have rules or limitations, the "10-Second Rule" is a good one to know. If a player character travels through a level, and they experience over 10 seconds of just running, something is missing. Either the area needs to be more compressed so that the player can experience some change within 10 seconds or the level designer needs to add an event to the area. This event can be something very simple such as an item to pick up or a ledge to jump up to.

Levels should also use a variety of skills and obstacles. For example, if the player character has the ability to jump, the level should contain more than one kind of pit for the player character to jump over, as shown in **Figure 7.1**.

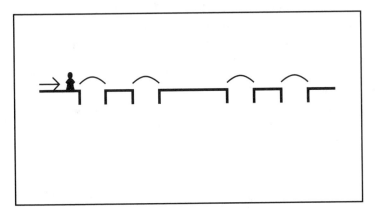

FIGURE 7.1 The pit obstacle requires a jump skill, but it is overused.

Figure 7.2 uses an electric fence to jump over, a raised platform to jump on top of, a trap to avoid by jumping, and a moving lift that allows the player to find a secret.

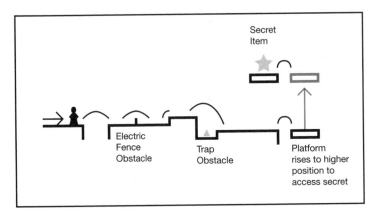

FIGURE 7.2 In this sequence, the player character still only uses the jump skill, but the obstacles vary and provide different experiences.

If the player character has more skills, then the level should mix up the obstacles so that different skills are used in different ways, as shown in **Figure 7.3**.

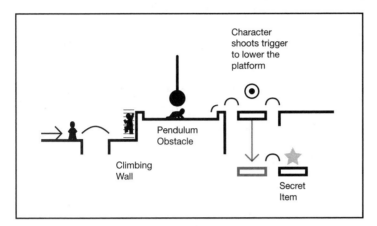

FIGURE 7.3 The player character can now use a few skills, and the jump skill is mixed with other skills to add variety.

Adding gameplay variety to a level keeps players interested in the game and allows them to have different experiences within the assets created for that setting.

Providing direction

When watching people play through your level, you might hear the question, "What am I supposed to do here?" quite a lot. Another popular one is, "I can't find the [insert location here]." When someone asks either of these questions, it means that they probably aren't being given enough direction in that particular part of the level.

As a level designer, one of your goals is to lead the player in the right direction. Of course, another goal is to give the player a sense of accomplishment. If you make the level wide open for the player to explore and you don't give any clues on how to solve a puzzle, the player will feel frustrated. If you completely hold the player's hand and show him or her where to go or how to solve a puzzle, the player won't experience that feeling of accomplishment. In **Figure 7.4**, the level designer wants the average player to find the "Item" before the "Exit," but it's still acceptable for a player not to find the Item until later in the game. The player has a higher chance of finding the Exit before the Item because the player is already traveling up in the same direction.

More players might find the Item first in **Figure 7.5**, which guides the player by simply aligning the Item room directly across from the Start.

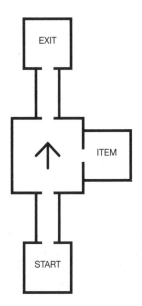

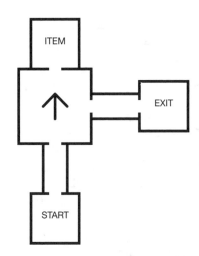

FIGURE 7.4 Most players would miss the Item simply because they are more inclined to continue in the same direction as the Exit.

FIGURE 7.5 A higher percentage of players will find the Item room in this arrangement because of its placement.

In some situations, such as large, open areas, the player can get lost without some kind of help. They may even completely miss a feature that the level designer wants them to find. In **Figure 7.6**, the large, open area that contains the Item forces a lot of players to "wall-hug," which means to follow the borders of the area and clear it from the outside to the inside. If players find the Exit by wall-hugging, they will miss finding the Item.

In **Figure 7.7**, a texture of a path leads to the area where the Item rests. This is a simple solution that gives the player some direction but still allows him or her to explore. This doesn't force the player along a restricted space, but it does make the position of the Item fairly obvious. A less obvious solution might be to place torches at intervals from the Start to the Item.

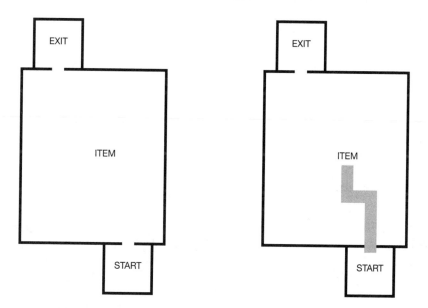

FIGURE 7.6 Using the border of the area as a guide, a player may "wall-hug" from the Start to the Exit without finding the Item.

FIGURE 7.7 The texture for a path has been added to Figure 7.6 to give the player direction.

Highlighting Puzzle Components

As a level designer, you can also give more direction within puzzles to help the player find a solution more efficiently. Adding direction in puzzles is similar to adding direction to the player's progression. Puzzles can consist of pieces or components that the player solves in a sequence. Highlighting these components, or making them more noticeable, can guide a player toward the solution without restricting possibilities.

You can highlight a puzzle component in a number of ways. Lighting a component so that it pops out visually is a simple fix. For example, if the player needs to hit a target with some kind of projectile to open a door, the target can be lit a special way so that the player can't miss it.

Another popular way of highlighting is with a consistent texture. Let's say that our target in the above example requires a certain skill and this target appears in other areas of the level and other areas of the game. All of the targets can have a similar texture that helps the player know that he can use the same skill on it. In Harry Potter and the Chamber of Secrets, Harry could use a spell called "Flipendo" that pushed objects. Any object that could be pushed with Flipendo had the same symbol on its texture.

You can also highlight puzzle components with a scripted sequence. For example, in a puzzle where the player character needs to turn a wheel to open a gate, a scripted sequence might show an AI-controlled character turning the wheel first while the player watches. The gate would close before the player character could get to the wheel, but they would have seen what the wheel does.

Don't be afraid or reluctant to completely change or redo puzzles. Of course, one comment in a play-test session isn't enough to warrant a complete redo, but if there isn't an "easy fix" for a puzzle to work, it might be time to start over—at least, for that particular space. For example, in the cookie factory level, I had to make several changes for the mixer puzzle to work. In fact, it wasn't really much of a mixer puzzle any more. **Figure 7.8** shows the new mixer puzzle in a diagram form. Notice the differences from Figure 4.11.

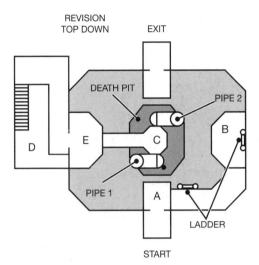

A. Part 1 - The player character's view straight ahead is blocked by Pipe 1 which is in a raised position. The only way to go is down the catwalk to the right.

B. The player character climbs up a ladder to find controls facing the center of the room. When activated, Pipe 1 lowers to dump ingredients into the pit.

A. Part 2 - The player character can now jump on top of the lowered Pipe 1 to get to the center platform.

C. The player character is blocked from the Exit by Pipe 2 which is in a raised position. The only way to go is down the catwalk into a room.

D. The player character fights enemy soldiers to work his way up the stairs and above the entrance of the room back to the mixer room.

E. The player character finds another set of controls that lower Pipe 2. He can jump off the platform to the catwalk directly below.

C. Part 2 - Pipe 2 is now positioned so the player character can walk onto it and jump to the Exit.

FIGURE 7.8 The mixer room puzzle from the cookie factory level gets a revision. Through play-test sessions, you'll find that you need to revise a lot of your designs.

In the original mixer puzzle, players wanted to immediately jump to the mixer bridge even though it seemed obvious that the jump was to too far. In addition, players missed the fact that the controls were adding ingredients to the main container. For a solution to both problems, I placed pipes that dump ingredients immediately in front of the player character to block them from attempting the jumps. The pipes are shown in a screenshot in **Figure 7.9**, on the next page. Then, lowering the pipes became the object of the puzzle. This was just one revision that I had to make for players to receive just enough direction.

FIGURE 7.9 The mixer room built in its revised state using the Half-Life 2 engine. The pipes shown are raised to block the player character from attempting to jump across to the middle section.

Making the level feel right

There's more to improving a level than adding consistency, direction, and variety. The level might require solutions for other issues, such as the level's overall size. A level might be too big or too small compared to other levels in the game, and you might have to add or cut areas accordingly. The level may also feel too long because the player doesn't receive that sense of accomplishment frequently enough. The level designer can remove sections of the level to give reinforcement to players that they are progressing.

Areas of the level can also be too challenging or not challenging enough for players to complete. You'll need to balance a level for difficulty to make it feel "just right." If players become frustrated trying to complete an area of the level, they might not continue with the level or the game. If they breeze through much of a level, they might become bored and stop playing.

Editing content

Like a film, the levels need to be edited. Some of the content in the level can be cut and some content needs to be added to make the level complete. These edits can take place less painfully if the level is in its earlier stages, such as the diagram or the template stages.

Why would you cut content out of a level? Well, if the content is too similar to other parts of the level, you can remove it to vary the gameplay experiences for the player. We've already discussed the common problem of repetition. Even if the level requires a variety of actions from the player, those actions might be too similar to another set of actions in another part of the level or in another part of the game. If players encounter a situation they are already too familiar with, it becomes predictable and tedious. In addition, if the content distracts players too much from the main focus of the level, you can remove it. For example, a section of a level that contains an unnecessary bonus item can lead players too far off the main path.

> **NOTE** Cutting content may also reduce the overall size of the level, which may be necessary due to time constraints. The size of a level could affect the schedules for a number of team members, not just the level designer.

Editing content may also mean cutting out a puzzle or a part of the gameplay that extends the level unnecessarily. For example, in the cookie factory, I originally planned a puzzle in the first area for how the player character enters the loading dock from the parking lot. After play-tests, I realized that players would struggle to solve the puzzle and would get frustrated from the very beginning. I simplified the area to allow players to start feeling good about themselves early on. In the template phase, the player character jumped into the open door on the right and had to press a switch that would open the door on the left. He would then have to run out of the loading dock and jump into the door on the left before it closed again. I changed this whole sequence so that the player could jump onto a vehicle, and then jump again into the open door on the left. The door on the right had some bonus items that players could find it they chose that path. **Figure 7.10**, on next page, shows the revised version of the parking lot.

You might need to add content to a level for other reasons than to add variation or provide direction. For example, a level might need more content to lengthen the gameplay in that particular area. Players purchase a game expecting a certain amount of gameplay; if they finish a game too soon, they might be unsatisfied with the product.

FIGURE 7.10 The entrance into the loading dock in the cookie factory level was reduced from an elaborate timing puzzle to a jumping maneuver. Removing puzzles is another way to edit content in a level.

Smooth Transitions

Just like a film or a book, video games need smooth transitions from one area to another. Jumping from one distinct section to another can be jarring. For example, you wouldn't want a character to walk a few steps to travel from a sandy beach to a town in the same level. You might consider adding a section of boardwalks and dunes between the two areas. Some games have large open worlds that contain many different kinds of areas. Blizzard Entertainment's World of Warcraft, for example, needs to transition between dense forests, rocky mountain passes, grassy plains, and even swamps. There are sections between these distinct areas that are devoted to smooth transitions.

Transitioning between exterior and interior spaces also needs to be seamless. Characters shouldn't go from a city street straight to a hotel room; they should enter the hotel from the street at some kind of façade, go into a lobby, climb a set of stairs, and go down a hallway to find the hotel room.

Balancing the level

If players think that the level is too easy or too difficult to complete, it needs to be balanced properly. A lot of game developers wait until the level is almost complete to balance it. Unfortunately, waiting this long does not allow the level to go through proper play-test sessions and restricts the feedback to fewer areas. While a lot of balancing can't possibly take place until later, you can start the process of balancing so that levels feel right before they are complete.

> **NOTE** ▸ It may not be possible to balance a level at the template stage. For example, if the game involves enemies that attack the player character, some enemies may not be created yet. Remember, the art team is just starting production at this time too. They may not have every character designed, modeled, and animated yet.

There are several steps you can take to start balancing the level. Based on the feedback from the play-test sessions, you may need to integrate some geometry changes to the level template. For example, if the player character needs to jump across a gap, and play-testers have trouble with the length of the gap, you can make the gap shorter. Or, if enemy soldiers are shooting at the player character in an open area and the player character gets hit in most play-test sessions, you might need to place geometry such as columns or crates for the character to hide behind. Hallways can be made wider to give the player character more room to avoid dangers. Since all of these solutions require geometry changes to the level, they should be implemented before the level goes through any art passes.

Another way to start balancing your level is by changing gameplay elements. Gameplay elements can involve the obstacles contained in the level, such as enemy soldiers or the speed of moving platforms. You can remove enemies to make an area easier or add them to make an area more difficult. You can work with programmers to edit the properties of enemies to give them more or less life. Some enemies can use different weapons against the player character. You can change the groupings of these enemies, or even the paths that the enemies patrol, to give the player an advantage or a disadvantage. These changes usually don't require the level to change in significant ways, so they can be continually revised and tweaked as the level progresses through its completion stages.

Once you've incorporated all of these revisions into your level, it's time to send it through another round of play-testing. It's kind of a never-ending process. Hopefully, though, you'll have made progress on some of the issues that players initially encountered in the level. Of course, you might have a new set of issues, but the level should start to feel better and better with each revision. The end result should also give you a level that you are confident in. You'll be able to start adding the layers of completion that make the level speak for itself.

> **NOTE** ▸ I believe that, in general, the more you play-test a level, the better it gets for the player. However, a side effect of numerous play-tests is that the team's morale might diminish. In other words, as a developer, you might start getting tired of working on a level after a certain point. If you're on a team of level designers, this might be the opportune time to rotate levels among the other level designers. This may give you a fresh jolt to continue on with the project. You can rotate levels back again at a later point.

Assignment 7

Revising Your Level

Part 1—Ask someone to play through your template. Take on the role of observer and document the issues that you see in your level while watching your play-tester.

Part 2—Focus on three major problems that are apparent in your level. Try to solve each of the problems and make the changes in your template.

CHAPTER 8
Taking It to 11

BY THIS POINT IN development, your level is progressing as a
compelling game experience. The spaces all connect and flow smoothly
between each other. Players are challenged by the obstacles placed in
the level, and they have enough direction to develop that feeling of
accomplishment without getting frustrated. However, the level isn't ready
to ship. It still needs a couple of passes or "layers" to meet requirements
set by the team—and a few more passes to push it to five-star quality.

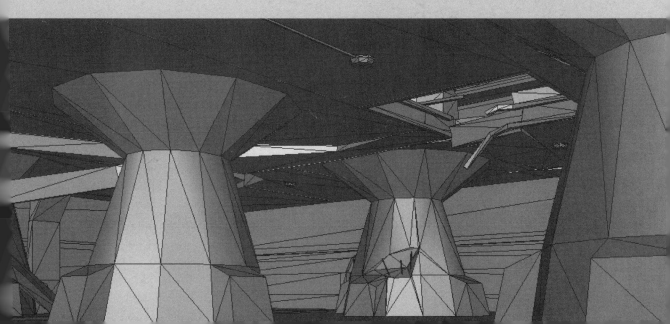

The Quality Curve

Given time constraints during game development, you'll probably have to cut down the amount of time and effort you can devote to your level. If you're working on multiple levels, you'll need to discuss with your lead which levels have the highest priority. And within any level, you'll also need to decide which areas you want to spend more time on.

Due to limited resources and time, game developers often must use the "quality curve," which basically dictates that the beginning and ending of a game should have the highest priority (**Figure 8.1**). The beginning section of the game must pull players in and get them hooked on the gameplay, the visuals, and the story. The ending section of the game is like the big finale, and should leave players with the best memories of the game. Generally, players will forgive the team a few flaws if they're contained in the middle of the game especially if their initial and final experiences in the game are outstanding.

The same curve holds true for a level. The beginning and ending sections in a level should have more details, more unique models and textures, more complex geometry, and more visual and audio effects.

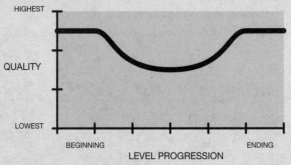

FIGURE 8.1 The quality curve showing the areas of a game and level that should have the highest priority for added layers.

First of all, your level probably doesn't look like a level you'd see in a completed game. It might have placeholder textures that need to be replaced. It might not have any details or props such as furniture or decorative pieces like statues. The level might still feel "boxy," which means that it uses all right angles. You might have simply copied and pasted the same light over and over and now the level looks a bit flat. All of these issues can be solved with an art pass.

During this phase of your level's development, you can replace simple template geometry with more complex geometry. Later in this chapter we present two Unreal tutorials that illustrate some techniques used by level designers to create geometry based on a texture and geometry with curves. These techniques show you how to start making the geometry in your level more visually appealing and less boxy.

As you saw in Chapter 1, art passes can involve a number of team members. At this stage, you can hand over your level to a background artist. Other times, you work with a background artist who can provide art assets, such as textures and models, for the level. In rare instances, you will have to create these assets yourself.

Second, your level still needs a functional layer that incorporates all of the elements necessary for the level to be called complete. Among these elements is the audio piece of the equation. Your level will need sound effects added to its moving parts, including doors, elevators, and buttons. You should also place ambient sounds like wind and machinery to provide atmosphere to your level. In addition, you can place triggers so that music begins playing during certain sections of a level. Music can be used to get the players' adrenaline pumping—or to calm them down.

An effects pass will add additional functionality. Effects are the visual components in a level that make it more realistic. Particle effects, such as steam coming from a vent or sparks coming from a broken circuit, make a level seem all the more real. And other effects, such as fog or a blinking light, might even change the gameplay slightly.

By adding layers to your level, you can bring the level to a shippable state and still continue to enhance the quality of the level without jeopardizing the overall experience.

Adding Visual Layers

In Chapter 4, we talked about gathering reference materials for the visual style of the level. These reference materials help you gain a better idea of the spaces contained in the level. Once the level has been created in template form and has gone through adequate play-testing, these reference materials will help you with the visual layer you need to add to your level. You can look at materials such as concept art to understand the architectural style you want to bring to life. Other materials, such as the photographs you might have taken or gathered, can provide ideas for the details that fill the level.

Following an architectural style

You don't need to know anything about architecture to follow an "architectural style." You simply translate the art direction of the project, and the materials approved by your art lead, into the level you're building. For example, if the art lead has approved materials that portray columns that are round in shape as opposed to square, you can replace the columns from the template phase with round columns.

During an art pass, some, if not most, of the geometry for the level will need to be changed or replaced. This includes adding detailed geometry such as trim for walls and floors and frames for windows and doors. As you might guess, this takes a lot of time and effort. However, the geometry changes you make during an art pass will be well appreciated by both players of the game, and by people looking at screenshots of your level. Some of the geometry can be created as smaller pieces that you can duplicate throughout the level for efficiency as well as consistency.

Once the geometry of an area is set, you can start to apply the proper textures. Textures, when used properly, can really make a level look complete. Special or unique textures can also make an area stand out to the player.

> **TIP** You should complete the geometry for an area before texturing it because the changes you make in the geometry will affect the textures applied to it. This does not mean that you should perform all of the geometry revisions for the entire level before you begin texturing. Instead, take one area at a time to revise geometry and then texture. This allows you to get areas complete for approval and provides some variety to your routine.

The art pass for a level includes lighting. Lighting is an art form all by itself. Lighting can make the difference between a flat, plain level and a completely immersive experience. It takes a lot of trial and error to get the lighting just right for an area. Some companies have dedicated "lighters" who are solely responsible for lighting a level.

The final element for an art pass is placing the props. Props are models, usually created by artists, that add complex details to a level. Props can be interactive or noninteractive. Interactive props are the models that affect gameplay. For example, if the player character collides with a prop such as a large rock or a pile of debris, then it is interactive. Interactive props can even affect gameplay by blocking projectiles. So, a sign on a post can be considered an interactive prop. Noninteractive props are the decorative elements that are added mainly for visual purposes. Level designers place noninteractive props in a level to make it look and feel more realistic. In Unreal, you can place both kinds of props as static meshes, such as the pipe that you placed in the static mesh tutorial in Chapter 6.

Using primitives for efficiency and consistency

Level designers can create "primitives" for architectural pieces that are repeated in several areas. A primitive is a piece of level geometry that can be copied and pasted throughout a level. The round column from our earlier example could be a primitive. As shown in **Figure 8.2,** the level designer can create one column that the art lead is happy with and then duplicate that column all around the level wherever columns are used.

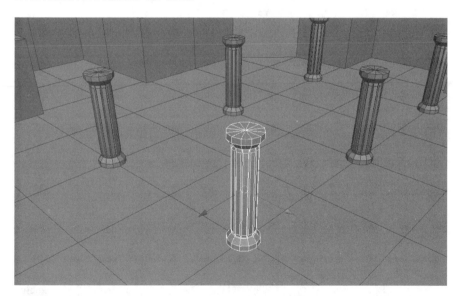

FIGURE 8.2 A column primitive created in Maya that has been duplicated and placed around a room.

Primitives can encompass much more than just one piece of geometry. A primitive intended to create a chunk of hallway could consist of the floor, the walls, the columns, the lights, and the ceiling. This chunk can be constructed so that it can connect any two rooms (as in **Figure 8.3**, on the next page) or combined with another chunk to make a longer hallway (**Figure 8.4**, on the next page).

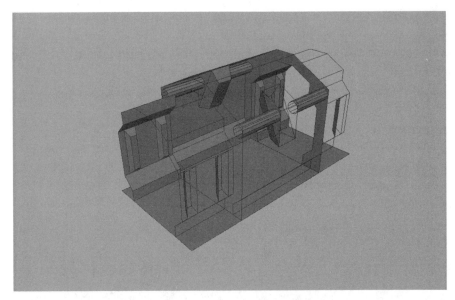

FIGURE 8.3 A hallway section created as a primitive to connect two rooms.

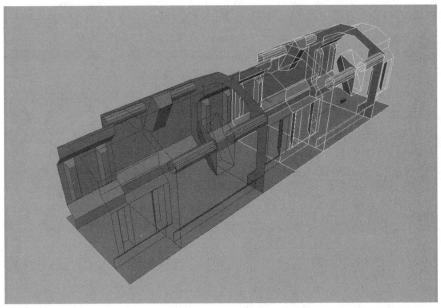

FIGURE 8.4 The same hallway section can be duplicated and connected to form a longer hallway.

You can use primitives to save a lot of time while replacing geometry in your level. Instead of creating geometry, applying textures, and tweaking lighting for several hallways, you can build just one complete hallway. Primitives can also ensure that geometry stays consistent throughout a level. Not only will it give the level a consistent look, it will also make the construction of the level cleaner, since creation of one small piece can be tested more easily than an entire level.

> **NOTE** Use primitives to reduce the amount of geometry-related bugs in your level. A problem found in one of the primitives can be corrected and replaced efficiently.

Using trim, borders, and frames

A vital part of adding detail to level geometry is using trim, borders, and frames. Most surfaces in the real world don't just end without some kind of edge. For example, walls don't just meet directly with floors or ceilings. Most of the time, there's a trim or border between the wall and the floor, the wall and the ceiling, and so forth. **Figure 8.5** shows the hallway primitives from Figure 8.4 and highlights the trim used between the walls and floor.

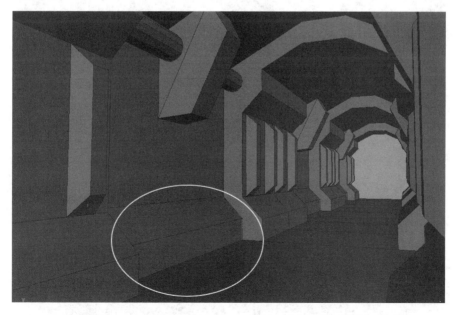

FIGURE 8.5 Wall trim makes the transition between a floor and a wall. Trim adds that extra detail that is simple to create but incredibly effective in conveying realism in a level.

Adding trim and borders is one of the first steps you can take toward a more detailed level. Simply add small brushes between surfaces in the level geometry and assign trim textures to the added faces. Whenever possible, you can use a texture with a trim or border painted into it instead of breaking up the geometry with more surfaces, as shown in **Figure 8.6**. This helps to keep the scene running efficiently and may save time during construction.

FIGURE 8.6 This wall trim was painted into the texture to help the performance of the area. Building a trim with polygons can add unnecessary geometry.

Surface openings, such as windows and doors, are also typically surrounded by frames. Adding these frames to your level will make a big difference in the visual appeal of a space. **Figure 8.7** shows the difference between a window with a frame and a window without a frame.

 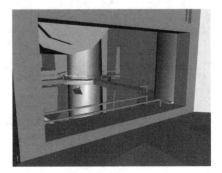

FIGURE 8.7 A frame is only appreciated when you see a window without one.

Frames can also hide the changes from one room to another. For example, if a character is walking through a hallway that has one set of textures, and he enters a room with another set of textures, the doorway between the hallway and the room can have a frame that breaks both of the texture sets. **Figure 8.8** illustrates how a door frame can hide an abrupt change.

FIGURE 8.8 A door frame can hide a change in texture sets.

Using textures to break up repetition

Applying textures is probably the easiest way to improve the visual quality for a level. However, you might still need to implement some geometry changes for textures to work the way you want. For example, if a high wall in Unreal has a top texture, a middle texture, and a bottom texture, you will need to divide the wall into three parts (**Figure 8.9**, on the next page). This can break up some of the repetition that large surfaces can appear to have in game levels.

Another option for breaking up textures, particularly on a large plane, is to add a solid brush within that plane. For example, if you have a large, flat wall that has the three vertical sections as in Figure 8.9, the wall still might look repetitive horizontally. By adding a section with a variation texture that works with the original texture, you can break up the space and add an amount of detail without changing the space. Examples of a variation texture for the middle and a variation texture for the bottom are shown in **Figure 8.10**.

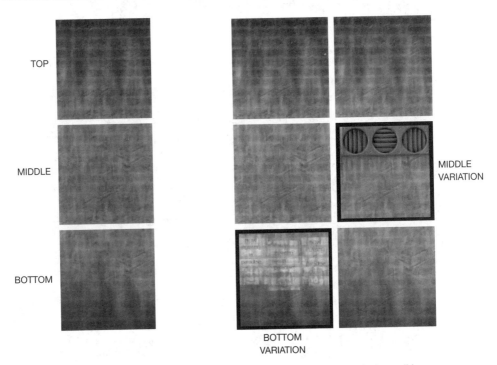

FIGURE 8.9 An exterior wall has three parts that require three textures to make the wall less repetitive. The three textures tile with each other to form a top, middle, and bottom.

FIGURE 8.10 The same exterior wall in Figure 8.9 can have variation textures to break up repetition even more. A background artist can create variation textures after creating the base textures for the level.

Decals

Hammer, the level-editing program for Valve Software games (including Half-Life 2 and Counterstrike), has a decal application tool that places decals directly onto any surface. A decal is a texture that has transparent portions that allow another texture to be seen behind it. Using decals, you don't have to break up your level geometry to allow for completely new textures. You can simply apply a decal on top of a wall to break up the repetition. Common decals include dirt and grime stains, floor details such as drains and grates, and wall details such as signs and graffiti (shown in **Figure 8.11**).

FIGURE 8.11 A photograph of a tunnel wall with graffiti spray painted on it. Decals can break up the repetition of a tiling texture.

Using lighting to give your level depth

Lighting is often an aspect of level design that is saved until the very end. Unfortunately, this can result in a level being poorly lit, because lighting is complex and involves many different factors. For example, an area can have one or a dozen lights that all affect a single surface. There are also different kinds of lights that you can use: point lights, which affect the area all around them; spotlights that have a direction; and even a sunlight that works like a real sun. These various kinds of lights can be combined to create the desired effect for any given surface.

> **NOTE** Some games today, such as Blizzard Entertainment's World of Warcraft, have day/night cycles that simulate how the light changes from day to night and back again. In this case, you might not have a lot of control over the way the lighting works with the level because all outdoor levels would use the same lighting.

Lights have several attributes or properties that change the way they affect surfaces. Brightness, as the name suggests, affects the light's intensity. Some games also have a light falloff setting. The falloff is the distance from the light to the furthest point it can affect. For example, a light with a high falloff distance might provide light for a large area like the lights in a stadium. A light with a low falloff distance, like a Christmas tree light, would not affect as many surfaces.

Colored Lighting

When colored lighting first became available in games, many developers went a little overboard. Levels often used purple and bright green even though these colors didn't make sense for the areas the levels took place in. If you're using colored lighting, it's best to start with some subtle color tones so that the color doesn't seem too intense.

Because there are so many kinds of lights and so many attributes that can affect the lighting of a surface, developers often create a test level with many different (and artist-approved) lighting examples. These lighting examples may consist of the light actors that are creating the light, the light fixture prop model, and the position of the lights relative to the affected surfaces (walls, ceilings, and floors). With this test level created, you could can copy and paste these exact lights into your level, at least for a start.

Filling your level with props

Props are the extra models and details that can fill the areas in levels without changing the shapes or sizes of the areas. Props can be large objects such as a spaceship seen outside a window of a space station. They can also be small objects such as cups that are sitting on a bar, as shown in **Figure 8.12**.

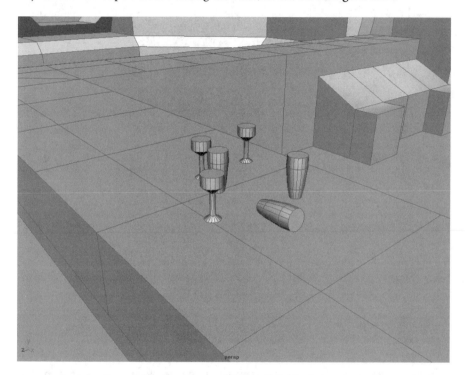

FIGURE 8.12 Small props like these cups add just a little bit of clutter to make a scene feel more realistic.

Levels would look quite bland without the use of props. In a lot of cases, the level geometry is really basic and functions as more of a base for the props to be placed inside. In **Figure 8.13**, on the next page, all of the pipes shown are considered props. This scene would not be the same without them.

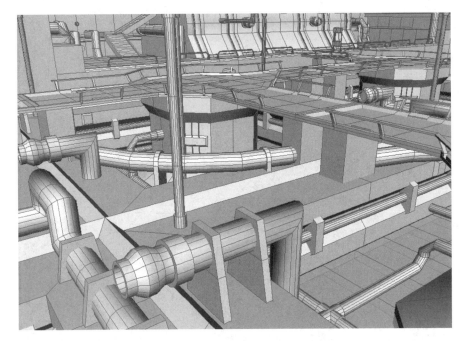

FIGURE 8.13 This scene is mostly constructed of simple level geometry (blocks and wedges). The pipes are placed around as props to give the level its actual visual appeal.

In Unreal, props are placed as static meshes or actors.

> **NOTE** Although it's possible for you to construct props out of brushes, smaller props that are made up of small polygons can cause errors in the BSP.

Common Props

For each theme, there is a set of common props you can always place to fill up a level. You might recognize some of these from your favorite games:

Fantasy: Chains, torches, candles, debris, grates, barrels, statues, paintings, carts, wagons, cages, furniture

Modern: Pipes, vents, grates, debris, crates, barrels, boxes, machinery, electronic equipment, consoles, monitors, books

Science Fiction: Pipes, vents, grates, crates, barrels, boxes, machinery, consoles, monitors, computer discs

There are technical limitations you should consider when adding props. When a level is built in Unreal, the level geometry is cut up so that the engine can display it properly, and too many cuts can slow down the frame rate. Props don't add any more cuts to the geometry, but they do affect the performance of the level. Props are fairly complex. They have a lot of polygons, and they might require a detailed texture. The more props you place in the player's view, the slower the performance of the level. Props are also lit in a different way than the geometry you create in the editor. You'll need to adjust your lighting to make the props blend into the environment smoothly.

The beauty of imperfection

Nothing in life is perfect. In fact, if something appears to be perfect, it isn't realistic or believable—even in real life. If you were to walk down the street and see nothing out of place, broken, or slightly askew, you'd feel like you were on a movie set. When adding visual layers to a level, adding certain imperfections can actually greatly enhance the appeal of an area. For example, a cathedral that has two perfect rows of columns along the aisle is not as visually interesting as a cathedral with a few columns that are cracked, damaged, or even crumbled. Similarly, a metal-plated floor that has been flawlessly installed might appear boring compared to a floor that has a few metal plates popped off, bent, or rotated, as shown in **Figure 8.14**.

FIGURE 8.14 A floor made up of metal plates can be made more interesting if one of the plates is off-kilter from the rest.

These elements of imperfection can even contribute to the progression of a level. For example, a player character might notice the metal plate in Figure 8.14 simply because it is not like all the others. The fact that the metal plate is out of place gives a clue to the player that there may be something below. Imperfections such as holes in the floor (**Figure 8.15**) or cracks in a wall can also be areas from which enemies can emerge.

FIGURE 8.15 This floor has been damaged to open up a hole for enemies to climb out of.

Imperfection isn't limited to level geometry. Textures can use the same principles. Sometimes, a dirt stain on the floor can add realism to the game world as well as break up the tiling of the base floor texture.

> **NOTE** Imperfections are dependent on the art direction for the project. It may be the lead artist's desire for some areas to appear "perfect."

UnrealEd Tutorials: Enhancing Visual Layers

The main goal of adding visual layers is to improve the artistic quality of the level. The artists on your team can be a big help in achieving this goal. They can provide you with textures, models for props, and even lighting examples. However, the level may require a lot of geometry changes to achieve the proper look.

The following tutorials are construction techniques that level designers use to create more interesting shapes in their spaces. These concepts can also be translated to other level editors and modeling tools. Personally, I have used similar techniques in several programs.

> **NOTE** ▸ These construction techniques are a bit complex. The tutorials are intended for people who are comfortable using UnrealEd and have successfully created a template for a level in the editor.

UnrealEd Construction Methods: Texture Templates

You can base level geometry on textures. Since a lot of the art direction comes from the artists on your team, you can take a texture that an artist creates and create a brush in your level that matches a shape in a texture perfectly. A texture like an archway may require the geometry of the brush to fit accurately so that elements in the texture, such as ornamentation, shadows, and highlights, appear properly. In this case, artists can provide you with either the final texture or a template of the texture that they want you to use. In UnrealEd, you can load this texture into the 2D Shape Editor (which was introduced in Chapter 6) and use the texture as a guide for the vertices you place and move. Think of it as connecting the dots in reverse. Once you have the 2D shape drawn from the texture, you can convert your active brush into a 3D volume based on the 2D shape. So, for an archway, you can create the subtractive brush you need that fits inside the arch.

For this tutorial, you're going to create two rooms connected by a hallway in a science fiction theme. The doorways to the rooms are going to be airlocks created from a special texture template.

Setting up the scene

First, you're going to create the two rooms and the hallway.

1. Run UnrealEd. For a refresher on how to do this, see the basic operations tutorial in Chapter 6.

2. Bring up the Texture Browser window. Choose Open from the File menu and then select SciFi.utx.

3. Click the Open button. Select the texture Texture Wall01.

4. Open the CubeBuilder dialog box by clicking the Cube icon in the toolbar.

5. Type a Height value of 256, a Width value of 1024, and a Depth value of 1024.

6. Click the Build button and close the dialog box. Subtract the brush.

7. Place a PlayerStart actor in the middle of the floor and a light on the middle of the ceiling.

8. In the Front or Side view, move the active brush up 256 units and subtract it again.

   This will be your first room. Texture the room with the textures you want.

9. Open the CubeBuilder dialog box again and build a cube with a Height value of 256, a Width value of 512, and a Depth value of 512.

10. In the Top view, move the active brush so that there is a 64-unit gap between the bottom edge of the active brush and the top edge of the first subtracted brush (**Figure 8.16**). In the Front or Side view, move the active brush down 256 units so that the bottom of the active brush is lined up with the floor of the first room. Subtract this new brush.

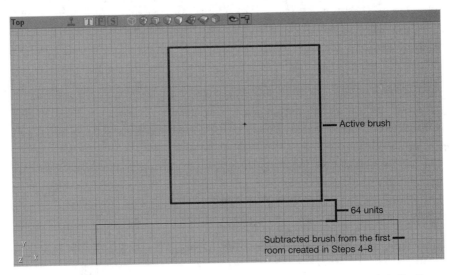

FIGURE 8.16 The active brush shown 64 units above the first subtracted brush in the Top view.

11. Open the CubeBuilder dialog box and, this time, change the Height value to 128 but keep the other values the same. Click the Build button and close the dialog box.

12. In the Front or Side view, move the active brush to rest on top of the last brush you subtracted. Subtract this new brush. This will be your hallway.

13. Place a light in the middle of the hallway and texture the walls, floor, and ceiling how you want.

14. Now, in the Front or Side view, select the subtracted brushes that make the first room and duplicate them.

15. In the Top view, move the duplicated brushes so that there is a 64-unit gap between the bottom edge and the top edge of the hallway brushes (**Figure 8.17**).

This will be your second room. You can duplicate the light from the first room too and move it to the second room. Build the map, but do not play it for now.

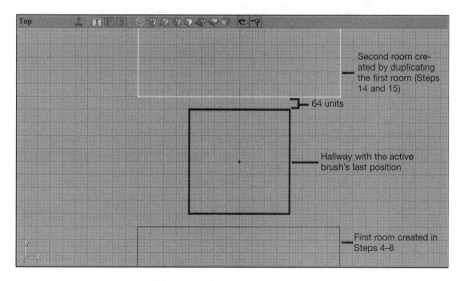

FIGURE 8.17 A 64-unit gap is left between the hallway brush and the room brushes.

16. Next, create an active brush with a Height value of 384, a Width value of 96, and a Depth value of 512.

17. In the Top view, move the active brush so that it overlaps into both the room and the hallway by 16 units (**Figure 8.18**).

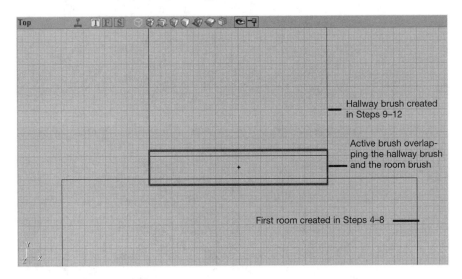

FIGURE 8.18 Place the active brush so that it overlaps the room and hallway brushes.

18. In the Front or Side view, line up the bottom of the active brush with the floors of the room and hallway. Add the brush.

19. Select the surfaces of the brush you just added. In the Texture Browser window, select Texture Arch01. You should see an airlock template shape projected onto the added brush between the room and hallway (**Figure 8.19**).

20. Duplicate this added brush and move it to connect the hallway with the other room. Build the map, but do not play it yet.

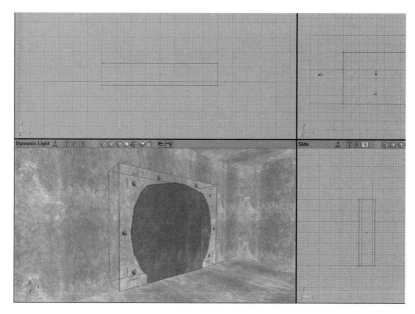

FIGURE 8.19 The airlock template shape shown on a face of a brush in the 3D view.

Creating the shape

Now it's time to create the subtractive brush for the inside of the airlock.

1. Click the 2D Shape Editor icon in the toolbar to open the 2D Shape Editor. Click File and scroll down to Image. You should see a drop-down menu with the choices Open From Disk, Get From Current Texture, and Delete (**Figure 8.20**).

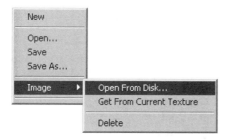

FIGURE 8.20 To open a texture template from a file, choose from the drop-down menu in the 2D Shape Editor.

2. Select Open From Disk. In the directory where you installed the UnrealEngine2Runtime demo, open the Textures directory; then open the Raw directory and select Arch01.bmp. Click the Open button. You should see a texture of an archway in the 2D Shape Editor.

3. Move the vertices already shown to the points of the archway in the texture. Add more vertices by clicking the Split Segment(s) icon. You may need to adjust the grid size using the Edit menu (**Figure 8.21**) to move the vertices exactly where you want them. Eventually, your 2D Shape Editor window should look like **Figure 8.22**.

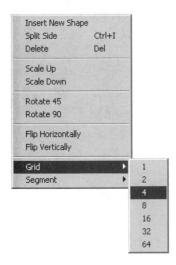

FIGURE 8.21 Adjusting the grid size in the 2D Shape Editor.

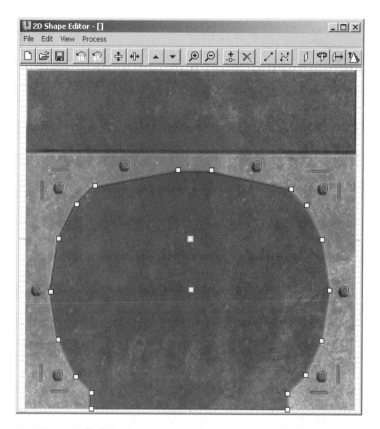

FIGURE 8.22 By following the shape of a texture in the 2D Shape Editor, you can create brushes that match.

4. Once your shape is complete, click the Extruded Shape icon to bring up the Extruded Shape dialog box.

5. Enter a value of 96 for the depth and click the OK button. Your active brush should now be in the shape of the archway and should be extruded at a depth of 96 units.

6. In the Top view, move the active brush so that its bottom edge matches the bottom edge of the brush you added to apply the archway texture. In the Front or Side view, line up the bottom of the active brush with the bottom of the room.

7. Subtract the brush. You should see the interior portion of the archway disappear in the 3D view (**Figure 8.23**).

8. Texture the brush in whatever way you wish. Build the level and run the map to test it.

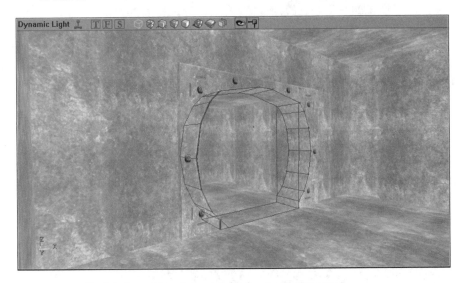

FIGURE 8.23 The interior portion of the archway has been subtracted.

NOTE You can compare your level to the level called Tutorial4.urt on the CD.

Using the texture template construction method, you can make interesting shapes that match the art style set by your art team. In this tutorial, an arch connects each of the rooms to the hallway. You can also use texture templates to create other geometry openings, such as windows, pits, and skylights.

So, how do you create interesting shapes on a larger scale? How would you create a curved hallway or a network of organic pipes? The next tutorial will demonstrate another construction technique that should do the trick. I call it the radial building technique.

UnrealEd Construction: The Radial Building Technique

An artist once told me that there's a reason why Times Square in New York City is shown so much on television shows, advertisements, and photographs: the unusual angles of the buildings make it a special place. You can make the areas of your level stand out in much the same way by giving them different angles. A common complaint about video game levels is that they appear "boxy." For many settings and locations, it may be more realistic to use only 90-degree angles. However, you may want to consider adding some different angles to your areas and levels to make them more unique.

You can change the angle on any brush in Unreal by using the vertex editing tool, which we learned about in Chapter 6. But, how do you make a smooth curve? There are a couple of different ways you can achieve curved geometry in Unreal. The standard way is to use the Cylinder tool, which changes the active brush from a box to a cylinder. This method might create simple round rooms, but it isn't very flexible and you can't create a curved hallway with it. The other method for creating curves is by using a radial building technique that is popular in brush-based level editors like Unreal as well as 3D modeling applications like 3D Studio Max and Maya. This radial building technique involves a bit of math and a bit of extra building, but as you'll see, the results are worth the effort.

Making a round room

The first thing we'll make is a curved room. Of course, you can make a simple round room with the Cylinder icon in the toolbar. However, it's not easy to add details like trim and borders using just the Cylinder brush. To illustrate the difference, we will first construct a round room with the Cylinder button before we start a radial-built room.

1. Start UnrealEd and bring up the Texture Browser window. Choose Open from the File menu and select Tutorial.utx. Click the Open button and select the texture Texture Wall01.

2. Right-click the Cylinder icon (**Figure 8.24**, on the next page) in the toolbar to open the CylinderBuilder dialog box. Type a Height value of 256, an OuterRadius value of 512, and an InnerRadius value of 384. Next, enter a Sides value of 8 and click the Build button.

    This should change your active brush to be an 8-sided cylinder with a height of 256 units and a radius of 512 units. Close the CylinderBuilder dialog box.

FIGURE 8.24 The Cylinder icon on the toolbar.

3. Subtract the cylinder by pressing Ctrl+S or clicking the Subtract icon on the toolbar.

4. In the Front or Side view, move the active brush up 256 units and subtract the brush again. This should double the height of your round room.

5. In the Texture Browser window, change the texture group to Details and select Texture Metal01. Texture the floor of the round room with this metal texture.

6. Now, open the CylinderBuilder dialog box again by right-clicking on the Cylinder icon in the toolbar. This time, change the Height value to 32 and the OuterRadius to 480. Click the Build Button and then close the dialog box.

   This should create an active brush that is a smaller cylinder than the one we used to create the room.

7. Position the active brush in the middle of the cylinder room in the Top view. In the Front or Side view, move the active brush down so that the top of it lines up with the floor of the round room (**Figure 8.25**).

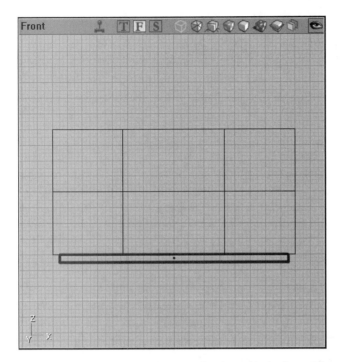

FIGURE 8.25 The active brush shown lined up with the floor of the round room.

8. Add the brush by pressing Ctrl+A or by clicking the Add icon on the toolbar.

9. In the Texture Browser window, select Texture Floor01 in the Floors texture group. Use this to texture the middle section of the floor in the round room. You should see a border around the floor texture of the metal.

10. Add a light to the middle of the room by right-clicking on a surface in the 3D view and selecting Add Light Here from the surface drop-down menu. Move it to the center of the room in the Top view and either the Front or Side view.

You have now created a round room using the Cylinder tool.

Now, we're going to create a round room using a radial building technique. Think of radial building in terms of a circular pie or pizza. You cut a pie or a pizza by crossing the center of it. Radial building is almost like forming a pie or a pizza by using the individual slices. This might seem weird right now, but it'll all make sense when we go through the steps to make a round room with the radial building technique.

> **NOTE** If you need help during this tutorial, open the Tutorial05.urt map from the CD.

First, we're going to make a section of the room. To show the difference between the two end results, let's continue using the same map from the previous tutorial.

1. Open the CubeBuilder dialog box and type a Height value of 256, a Width value of 512, and a Breadth value of 512. Click the Build button and close the dialog box.

2. In the Top view, move the active brush (which should look like a square) so that the left edge is at the middle of the round room you created with the Cylinder tool (**Figure 8.26**). In the Front or Side view, move the active brush down so that the top of the active brush is 512 units below the floor of the first round room you created with the Cylinder tool (**Figure 8.27**).

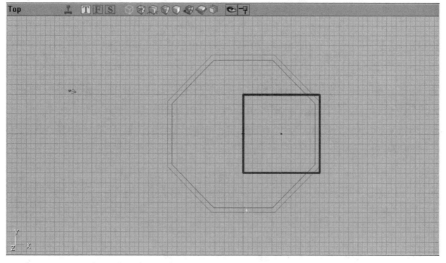

FIGURE 8.26 The active brush lined up in the Top view so that the left edge is at the middle of the round room.

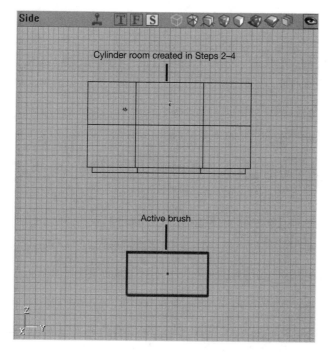

Cylinder room created in Steps 2–4

Active brush

FIGURE 8.27 The active brush shown 512 units below the first round room.

3. Subtract the brush.

4. While still in the Front or Side view, move the active brush up 256 units and subtract it again. This should double the height.

5. Open the CubeBuilder dialog box again and type a Height value of 32, a Width value of 512, and a Breadth value of 480. Click the Build button and close the dialog box.

6. In the Top view, move the active brush again so that the left edge is in the middle of the first round room. In the Front or Side view, move the active brush down so that the top of the active brush is lined up with the bottom of the subtracted cube from Step 3.

7. This time, add the brush.

8. Texture the larger floor piece with Texture Floor01 and the smaller border piece with Texture Metal01. Texture the walls and ceiling however you want. You now have a section of the round room.

   You'll notice that the room isn't round at all right now. So, you're going to cut the room to shape it into a pie slice.

9. Open the CubeBuilder dialog box and type a Height value of 640, a Width value of 640, and a Breadth value of 1280. Click the Build button and close the dialog box.

10. In the Top view, move the active brush so that bottom edge is at the center point of the first round room you created in the previous tutorial. In the Front view, move the active brush so that its center point is where the two subtracted brushes meet (**Figure 8.28**).

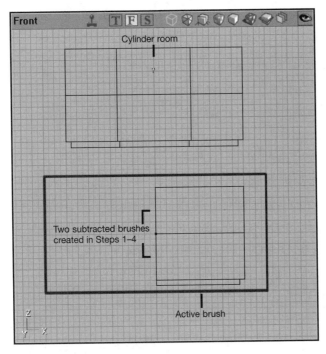

FIGURE 8.28 The active brush shown in the Front view with its center point where the two subtracted boxes meet.

11. Back in the Top view, hold down the Alt key and left-mouse-drag the pivot point of the active brush down to the center of the first round room (**Figure 8.29**).

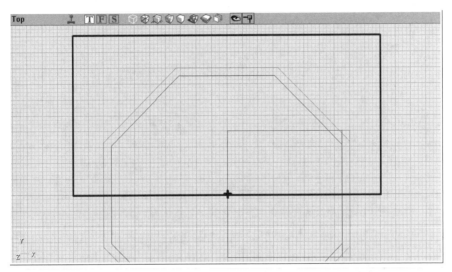

FIGURE 8.29 The pivot point has been moved to the center of the first round room.

12. Still in the Top view, hold down the Ctrl key and right-mouse-drag so that the active brush rotates counterclockwise four intervals (**Figure 8.30**). The brush will snap to a position at each interval.

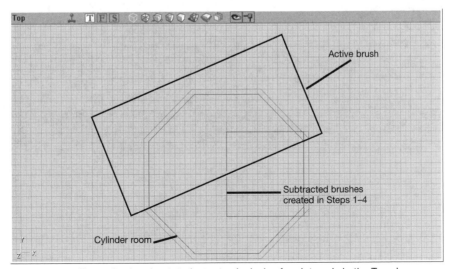

FIGURE 8.30 The active brush rotated counterclockwise four intervals in the Top view.

13. Add the brush.

14. Rotate the active brush back clockwise four intervals to bring it to its original rotation.

15. In the Top view, move the brush down so that its top edge is at the middle of the first round room.

16. Hold down the Alt key and left-mouse-drag the pivot point to the center of the first round room.

17. Hold down the Ctrl key and right-mouse-drag so that the active brush rotates clockwise four intervals.

18. Add the brush.

19. Rotate the active brush back counterclockwise four intervals to return it to its original rotation. In the 3D view, you should now see what looks like a slice of a round room (**Figure 8.31**).

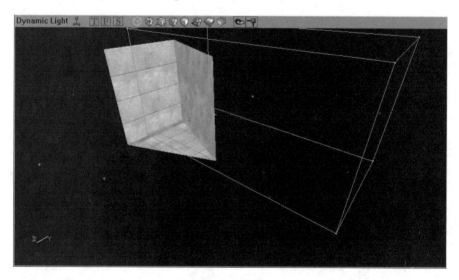

FIGURE 8.31 A slice of a round room shown in the 3D view.

It's time to use the slice you've just created to make a round room.

20. Move the same active brush so that its center point lines up with the center point of the first round room in the Top view.

21. Click the Deintersect icon in the toolbar to capture the slice into a new active brush.

22. Now, move this active brush 2048 units to the right in the Top view to avoid changing the existing geometry for the map (**Figure 8.32**).

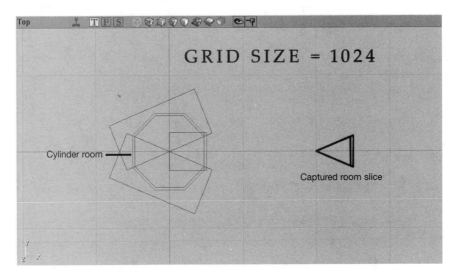

FIGURE 8.32 You have moved the captured room slice to make a scratch pad area.

23. Subtract the brush. You should see a slice of the room appear.

24. Hold down Ctrl and right-mouse-drag to rotate the active brush eight intervals (this rotation value is double the amount of intervals you used to create the slice).

25. Subtract the brush.

26. Repeat this action of rotating eight intervals and subtracting the brush (Steps 24 and 25) until you go all the way around in a circle (**Figure 8.33**, on the next page). You now have a new round room using the radial building technique.

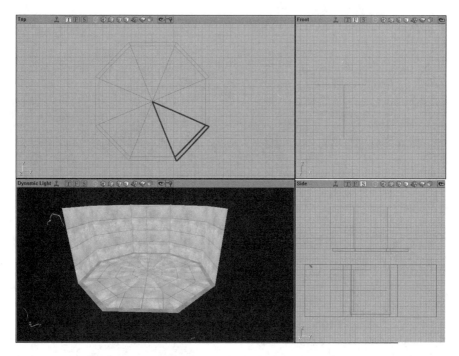

FIGURE 8.33 Creating a round room by rotating and subtracting a room slice around in a circle.

So, why is this fairly complicated radial building technique better than using the Cylinder tool? It definitely seems to have more steps. While the radial building technique is certainly more time consuming, you can see that the textures on the floor and ceiling rotate in a circular pattern with the room slices. In other words, they align to each other and they match the room's shape. In the first round room you created using the Cylinder tool, the floor and ceiling textures don't match the shape of the room. Also, it's easier to add different angles to the round room using the radial building technique.

To illustrate this, let's add some angles to the ceiling.

1. Go back to the room slice you created underneath the first round room (Steps 1–18 of the previous tutorial). Delete the large box brushes we added to create the angles of the slice (**Figure 8.34**). Rebuild the level to bring back the room half.

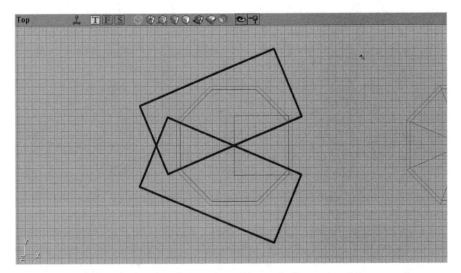

FIGURE 8.34 Delete the brushes that were used to create the angles of the room slice.

2. Open the CubeBuilder dialog box and type a Height value of 128, a Width value of 512, and a Breadth value of 128. Click the Build button and close the dialog box.

3. In the Top view, move the active brush so that its right edge lines up with the right edge of your subtracted boxes (**Figure 8.35**, on the next page). In the Front view, move the active brush up and to the right to line up the top and right edges of the active brush with the upper-right corner of the subtracted boxes (**Figure 8.36**, on the next page).

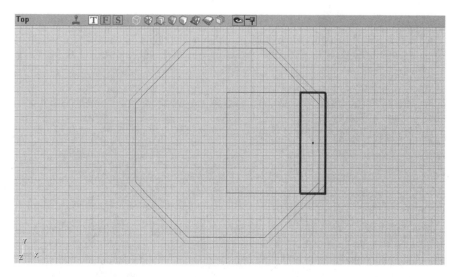

FIGURE 8.35 Line up the active brush in the Top view so that its right edge is on the same plane as the right edge of the subtracted boxes.

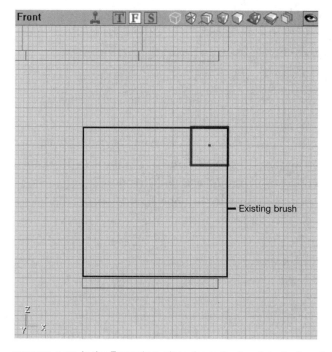

FIGURE 8.36 In the Front view, place the active brush in the top-right corner.

4. Click the Vertex Editing icon in the toolbar to switch to vertex edit mode. In the Front view, select the bottom-left vertices of the active brush by holding down Ctrl and Alt and left-mouse-dragging over the bottom-left corner. Hold down the Ctrl key and left-mouse-drag the vertices to the right 96 units (**Figure 8.37**).

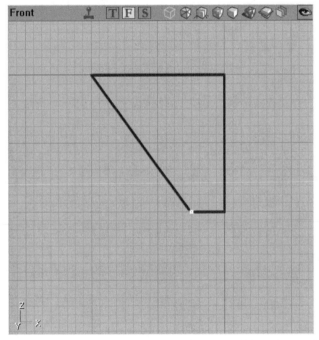

FIGURE 8.37 In the Front view, move the bottom-left vertices to the right 96 units.

5. Switch back to the selection tool and add the brush.

6. Open the 2D Shape Editor tool by clicking the 2D Shape Editor icon on the menu bar. Select the bottom-left vertex and press the Delete key.

7. Click the Extruded Shape icon and enter a Depth value of 512. Click the OK button.

8. In the Front view, move the active brush so that its top is lined up with the bottom of the brush we just added (**Figure 8.38**). Still in the Front view, switch to vertex editing mode and move the upper-left vertices to the right so that they line up with the bottom-left corner of your added brush (**Figure 8.39**).

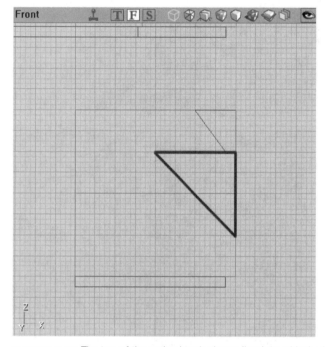

FIGURE 8.38 The top of the active brush shown lined up with the bottom of the last brush added.

9. Add the brush.

You've now created a curved transition from wall to ceiling in your room half. Now, perform the same operations to create your room slice and rotate the slice around to form a new round room (Steps 9–26 in this section). This new round room now has a dome-like ceiling, and all of its textures seam together (**Figure 8.40**).

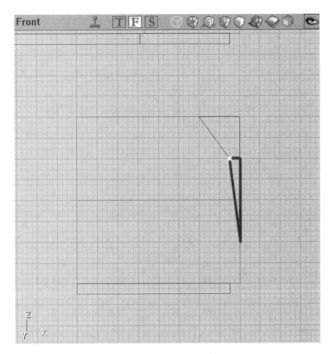

FIGURE 8.39 Move the top-left vertices to the right to line up with the brush above it.

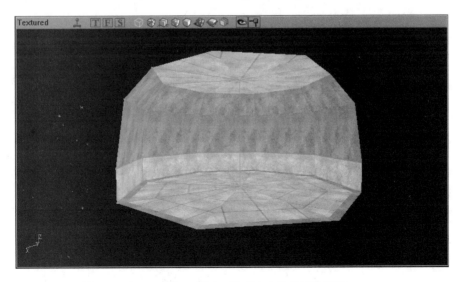

FIGURE 8.40 The round room with angled walls shown in the 3D view.

Making a curved hallway

Making a curved hallway follows the same principles as making a round room using the radial building technique. The difference is that instead of starting out with a room half, you're starting out with a section of the hallway that is straight.

> **NOTE** ▶ If you need help during this tutorial, open the Tutorial06.urt map from the CD.

First, you're going to make a simple hallway. You can continue to use the same file in the previous tutorial.

1. Open the CubeBuilder dialog box and type a Height value of 256, a Width value of 1024, and a Breadth value of 384. Click the Build button and close the dialog box.

2. In the Top view, move the active brush somewhere far from your existing geometry (about 3072 units should be fine—that's 3 grid squares using a grid of 1024 units). In the Front or Side view, move the active brush so that the bottom of the active brush is lined up with the floor of the first round room.

3. Select the Texture Wall01 texture from the Texture Browser window and subtract the brush.

4. In the Front view, move the active brush up so that the bottom of the active brush is lined up with the top of the brush you just subtracted.

5. Switch to vertex editing mode. Still in the Front view, select the top-left vertices and drag them to the right 128 units. Then, select the top-right vertices and drag them to the left 128 units (**Figure 8.41**).

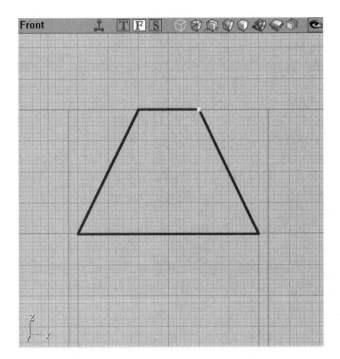

FIGURE 8.41 To make an arched ceiling for the hallway, move the top vertices in.

6. Subtract the brush. You should now see a hallway with an angled ceiling. You can texture the hallway however you like, but it's best to line up the textures now before you slice and rotate the hallway.

> **TIP** ▶ You might want to duplicate your hallway and set one off to the side where it won't be affected by other brushes. That way, you'll have a version of the hallway that is straight.

Next, you're going to slice the hallway.

1. Open the CubeBuilder dialog box and type a Height value of 640, a Width Value of 1024, and a Breadth value of 2048. Click the Build button and close the dialog box.

2. In the Top view, move the active brush so that its bottom edge is at the center of your hallway subtracted brushes, and the center of the active brush is 640 units to the right of the hallway. In the Front or Side view, line up the center point of the active brush with where the two subtracted brushes that made the hallway meet (**Figure 8.42**, on the next page).

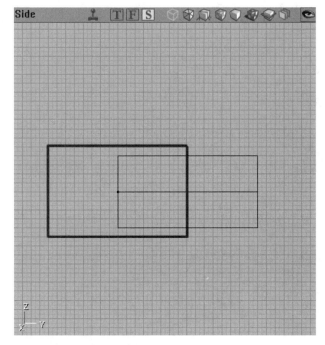

FIGURE 8.42 The active brush shown in the Front view lined up where the two subtracted brushes meet.

3. Hold down the Alt key and left-mouse-drag the pivot point to the bottom edge of the active brush in the Top view.

4. Hold down the Ctrl key and right-mouse-drag to rotate the brush four intervals clockwise.

5. Add the brush.

6. Rotate the active brush back to its original rotation.

7. Still in the Top view, move the active brush down so that its top edge is lined with the middle of the hallway.

8. Hold down the Alt key and left-mouse-drag the pivot point to the top edge of the active brush.

9. Hold down the Ctrl key and right-mouse-drag to rotate the active brush counterclockwise four intervals (**Figure 8.43**).

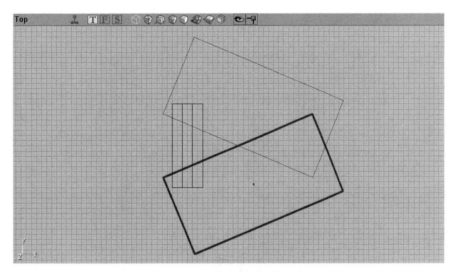

FIGURE 8.43 The active brush has been rotated in the Top view.

10. Add the brush.

11. Rotate the active brush to its original rotation. You now have a hallway slice.

Next, you're going to capture the hallway slice using the Deintersect tool and subtract and rotate the captured hallway around in a curve.

1. Keep the same active brush from before and move it in the Top view so that its center point is where the two angled brushes meet.

2. Click the Deintersect icon to capture the hallway slice into a new active brush.

3. Move the new active brush somewhere far from the existing brushes and subtract it.

4. Hold down the Ctrl key and right-mouse-drag to rotate the active brush clockwise eight intervals.

5. Subtract the brush.

6. Hold the Ctrl key down and right-mouse-drag to rotate the active brush clockwise another eight intervals.

7. Subtract the brush again. You'll see that you now have a hallway that curves 45 degrees and then another 45 degrees (**Figure 8.44**).

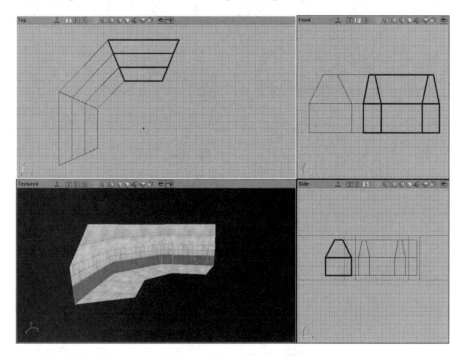

FIGURE 8.44 A hallway that turns 90 degrees using two 45-degree angles.

If you look at your hallway now, though, it doesn't end at either side with an orthogonal edge. The next step is to slice the ends so that they can match up to existing geometry cleanly.

1. If you left-click the Cube icon in the toolbar, you'll bring your active brush back to the shape of a large box.

2. In the Top view, move the active brush so that its top edge is at the midpoint of the bottom end of the curved hallway (**Figure 8.45**).

3. Add the brush.

4. Move the same active brush in the Top view so that its left edge is at the midpoint of the right end of the curved hallway (**Figure 8.46**).

5. Add the brush.

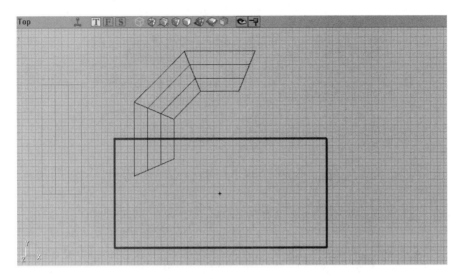

FIGURE 8.45 Cut off the bottom side of the hallway with an active brush placed so that its top edge is at the midpoint of the bottom end.

6. Then, open the CubeBuilder dialog box and type a Height value of 640, a Width value of 2048, and a Breadth value of 2048. Click the Build button and close the dialog box.

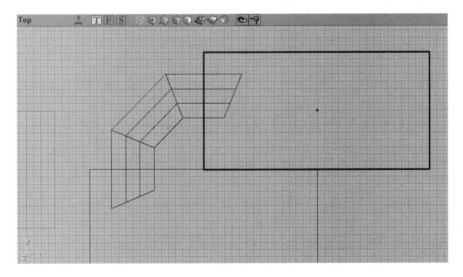

FIGURE 8.46 Cut off the right side of the hallway with an active brush placed so that its left edge is at the midpoint of the right end.

7. Position the active brush in the Top view so that the center is at the exact point where the last two brushes you added meet (**Figure 8.47**).

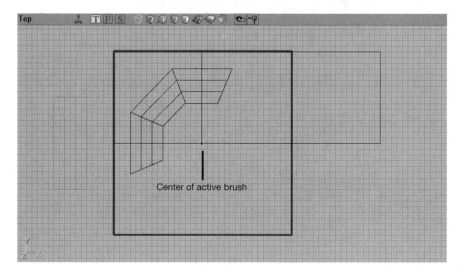

FIGURE 8.47 Make sure to Deintersect the curved hallway with the center of the active brush at the midpoint of the hallway "pie."

8. Click the Deintersect icon in the toolbar to capture the entire hallway in a new active brush.

9. In the Top view, move the active brush somewhere away from existing geometry and subtract it. You now have your curved hallway.

You can use these curved hallways and round rooms as primitives for your level. Add different angles to the ceilings and floors and add other structures like columns for variation.

Adding Functional Layers

In addition to the visual layers, you can add functional layers to make your level feel more complete. This layer consists of audio effects such as sound and music, special effects such as particles and ambient animated objects, and scripted sequences.

The audio component is the most notable functional layer for your level. Audio components include sound effects that are associated with movers and animated objects, and they are also ambient sounds that can be placed throughout the level to liven up the atmosphere.

Special effects comprise another functional layer. Although special effects are visual, they are more a part of the atmosphere of the level than the art style. For example, steam coming out of a vent, or water dripping from a pipe, is called a particle effect. These effects enhance the experience for the player, and are often directly connected to specific sound effects. Other special effects can include a ship flying on the outside of a window on a space station or even rats scurrying across the floor in a dungeon.

The last functional layer is adding the scripted sequences for actors. In the template stage, you may have placed enemies that stayed in one place until the player character arrived. Their AI kicked in at that point, causing them to realize the character's presence and attack accordingly. Until this point, these characters may not have acted realistically, which can detract from the overall experience of playing through the level. In Chapter 4, you brainstormed a list of scripted sequences that you wanted to see in your level. Now is the time to start working with a programmer or scripter to get those scripted sequences in place.

> **NOTE** As I've mentioned, level designers are not usually responsible for the scripted sequences contained in their levels. A scripter or programmer may be dedicated to create this content for you.

All of these functional layers combine to make the level, and the game's world, more believable and more exciting.

Hearing what you see

Placing audio components in a level makes a huge difference in the player's experience. A sound effect that plays at the right time can have players jumping out of their skins in fear. Music that triggers when you receive a cool weapon can excite players enough to cause goose bumps.

You can place three types of audio components in a level. First are sound effects that are attached to moving or animated objects. These are the sounds that play when something in the level moves, such as a door or an elevator. Next are ambient sounds, which the players hear as they progress through the level. Unlike sound effects, these sounds are not necessarily attached to specific objects. Ambient sounds, like gusts of wind or water dripping, help to create the atmosphere of a level. And finally, you can place music in a level to add the final piece to the audio experience.

Attaching sound effects

Sound effects are the audio components that are associated with moving or animated objects in a level. A door that opens can have a sound effect for its "opening" animation and another sound effect when it completes the animation and is in its "opened" state.

In UnrealEd, sounds can be attached to movers in the Mover Properties dialog box. Expand the MoverSounds list and you'll see several entries to add sound effects.

Nearly every moving object in your level should have a sound effect associated with it. In real life, you may not think about the sound of a leaf blowing through the air, or the sound of a river as it runs gently downstream. But if no sound effects are attached to these same movements in your game, the lack of sound will be very noticeable.

Surface Properties: Footsteps

In many game engines, you can change the surface properties of a brush face to alter the way the surface sounds. When the player character walks from a concrete landing to a metal catwalk, the footstep sounds can reflect that change. Surface properties can also change other sounds such as projectiles that collide with the surface.

Placing ambient sounds

Right now, as you're reading this book, you can probably hear a few different ambient sounds constantly in the background. You might hear some cars drive by on the road outside or a construction crew hard at work down the street. You might hear water running or a computer hard drive spinning. All of these are known as ambient sounds in games.

Ambient sounds don't have to be associated with a moving or animated object. They might be more related to the setting of the level. For example, a level that takes place in a canyon might have a gusty wind ambient sound; a level that takes place in a sewer might have the constant swishing and splashing of water. These ambient sounds can be placed in specific areas in a level and can even be located outside the boundaries of the level for the desired effect.

Ambient sounds can also be related to props. A generator prop might have a constant drone or winding sound. A car engine might be in an idle state. These sounds should be placed spatially at the point where the props are located so that the player can walk around the prop and have the sound emanate appropriately.

There are two types of ambient sounds: loops and stingers. Ambient loops can be repeated continuously to sound like a really long sound effect. Ambient loops can be played beginning when the level starts and they can end when the player leaves the level. Ambient sounds such as wind, engine drones, birds chirping, and water splashing are examples of ambient loops. Ambient stingers are played just once at key moments based on the actions of the player character. For example, when the player walks past a doorway in a haunted house, an ambient stinger can play the sound of a woman screaming inside the room. Similarly, if the player character is walking through a trench on a battlefield, an explosion sound effect can play in the distance to give the illusion of ongoing battle.

Placing an Ambient Sound in UnrealEd

Run UnrealEd and open a level in which you've already created a room. In the Actor Browser window, expand the Actor list by clicking on the + sign next to Actor. Expand the *Keypoint list and select *AmbientSound (**Figure 8.48**). In the 3D view, right-click on the floor of the room and select Add AmbientSound Here from the contextual menu. You have just placed an ambient sound keypoint into your room.

Double-click the AmbientSound Keypoint to open up its properties. Move the properties box off to the side and go back to the Browser window. Click the Sounds tab. From the File menu choose Open, and a window will appear allowing you to browse to find a sound package. Under the Sounds directory, open the file EM_Runtime_A.uax. Back in the Sounds Browser window, select wind04. Now, return to the AmbientSound properties window and expand the Sound list. Click on the AmbientSound value and then click the Use button that appears to the right of the value box. The wind04 sound should appear in the value box. This assigns the sound file to the AmbientSound.

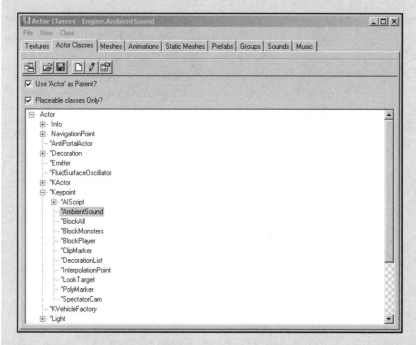

FIGURE 8.48 The AmbientSound actor can be selected from the Actor Browser window.

Starting the music

For most projects, the level designer plays a minimal role in choosing the music for a level. That decision is usually left up to the team lead, the producer, and the sound department. What you can participate in, however, is how the music is triggered, or started. You can trigger a music track based on the player character's location or you can trigger a music track based on the player character's actions. A character can simply cross a threshold of some kind, such as a doorway to a room or a hallway, to start a music track. The threshold can also be the very start of the level so that the music can start right away. Alternately, the character can perform an action, such as pulling a lever or picking up an item, to start a music track.

> **TIP** One thing to watch out for is overlapping music tracks. You probably don't want more than one music track playing at the same time. If you're triggering a music track based on the player character's actions, then it should be impossible for another track to be playing already.

You might need to fade music out for track changes or to allow other sound effects, such as dialogue, to be heard. You can place triggers to accomplish this.

Sprinkling special effects

Even after all of these layers have been added to your level, the level can still feel lifeless. As a level designer, you not only strive to make every frame displayed on a player's screen a wonderful picture, you also strive to make that picture come alive. So, you need to think about all the extra elements that can push the spaces in your level over the edge. Those extra elements can be special effects. Special effects are usually not just visual; they have both visual and audio parts to them that make up the overall effect. For example, steam coming out of a vent has both the graphical representation of the steam coming out and an ambient sound that loops.

Creating special effects through particle systems

A lot of game engines use particle systems to create special effects. A particle system is like a generator. It churns out little images, known as particles, in different ways. The particles can be tiny specs that have a color assigned to them and that color can even change over the course of time. A smoke particle system generates tiny black particles that change gradually to white and then fade away. Other particles can actually be an image created by an artist for the desired effect.

Leaves that fall from a tree can be a particle system that uses the image of a leaf instead of the solid color particles used to make smoke.

Not only do particles provide visual movement in a level, but they also make the game world more believable. Particles in a particle system can be affected by other systems in the world. For example, steam coming out of a vent can be affected by wind so that the steam particles can blow in different directions or dissolve with more variation. Other world systems that affect particles include gravity, temperature, and forces, such as explosions.

Using area effects

To make an area come alive, you can add area effects. Weather effects, which serve to make outdoor areas more realistic, fit in this category. If a player character walked from the inside of a building to an outdoor courtyard and the outdoor area was wet and rainy, the difference between the indoor and outdoor areas would be more dramatic.

Weather effects are subtle changes that provide the variety players need to stay engaged. For example, if it takes your player ten minutes to cross a grassy field, you might consider adding a weather effect, such as rain, to start about halfway across the field.

At this point, your level should be looking, sounding, and feeling like a complete product. There are still a few loose ends to tie up, but you're almost there. You now have to go through the vicious cycle of optimizing, balancing, testing, and fixing that is sometimes called "crunch mode" in the game industry. Don't worry, though. You've made it this far, so you'll be ready.

Fog

Fog can serve two purposes in games. It can hide things from the player and it can add atmosphere. You can add fog to a large open space so that the player can never see what's beyond a certain distance. The level geometry gradually fades out into the fog. This is sometimes used as a performance enhancement. Some engines use what is called as a "clipping plane," which is the farthest distance the player can see. The game engine does not need to display anything beyond the clipping plane. Fog as an atmospheric effect can also hide things like enemies lurking around.

Assignment 8

Enhancing Your Experience

Use Unreal or the level editor of your choosing to complete this assignment.

Part 1—Add the geometry changes you'll need to visually improve your level. Add trim, borders, and frames. Break surfaces up to add variation and imperfection.

Part 2—Apply the proper textures to your level using a texture package. Choose textures that work together as a set, like a wall that has top, middle, and bottom sections.

Part 3—Fill your level with props: actors and static meshes. Try to make each area look realistic, but avoid changing the way each area functions.

Part 4—Add the audio components to your level. Attach sound effects to movers and place ambient sounds and music at key points.

Part 5—Add the special effects to your level. Make your level really come alive in various places by adding particle effects, weather effects, and fog.

CHAPTER 9
Ship It!

CONGRATULATIONS! YOU'VE JUST hit the alpha stage of development. As you know, this means that your level has all of the features it needs to be complete. You can play through your level from beginning to end and experience everything you've planned for, and more. So, how come you're not done yet? Well, there's still a lot to do and not a lot of time to do it (if you're working toward a deadline).

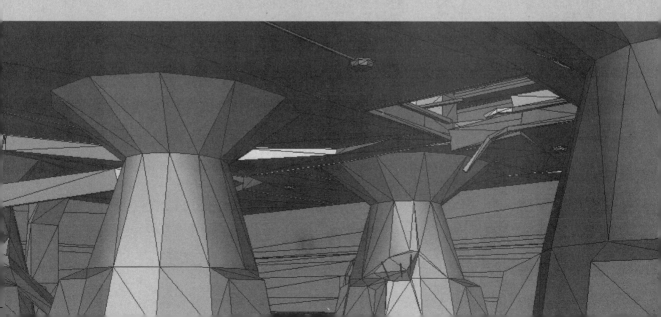

During the alpha stage, you'll need to get your level player-ready, and each team on the project will have different requests for the level to be complete. The art team will probably want you to replace some placeholder textures and props in your level with final art. The programming team will probably want to help you "optimize" your level for increased performance. The design team will ask you to make changes to the balance of the game, making levels easier or harder to please players of all experience types.

Once the alpha stage is complete, it's just a brief period until the game gets shipped out to store shelves. In just a few short weeks, the game will go from beta to final candidate to gold master. This period is often referred to as "crunch" time for development teams. The entire development team switches into tester mode, spending every spare moment playing through the game to check for any bugs. Fixing bugs takes top priority for all developers, but the bugs are ranked according to importance. At a certain point, the minor bugs get ignored. If no major bugs surface or re-surface from past revisions, the game is done.

Even when the finished version of the game gets shipped to store shelves (or made available for download), there are still a few loose ends to tend to. These days, many games are "ported" to different platforms, which means that the same gameplay and content are transferred over to another game system. The development team—including the level design team—archives their data in case they need it later. It's also a good idea to archive data for personal reasons. You might need to update your portfolio if you wish to apply to a different company or even a different team at the same company. The team may also participate in a postmortem, which is a documentation of the project's development: what went right and what went wrong. This exercise can help evaluate the methods for the next project and can remind the developers of the lessons they've learned.

So, you can see that you have your work cut out for you. Finishing a level, and a game, is often the most difficult—but the most rewarding—thing you can do in your career. Once you see your name scrolling by in the credits or see your game in a store window, you'll know that it was all worth it.

Tasks During Alpha

The alpha stage is the beginning of the end. The good news is that most of the creative process is over at this point, so you won't need to think too hard about design decisions and revisions. Another bit of good news is that you should feel confident about your level or levels and the progress you've made throughout the process. The bad news is that this is usually the time when things start to move really quickly. Before you know it, the testing department will be assigning you dozens of bugs they've found in your level (or levels), and the producer might be assigning you bugs from other level designers' levels to even out the workload. Every day, you'll have a new long list of tasks that need your immediate attention.

Also, at about this time, the rest of the team will realize that the game is going to be seen by thousands and thousands of players. The programming team will want you to change your level to make the game perform better. This will require you to make optimizations to your level, such as cutting down polygons in scenes or reducing texture sizes or uses. You might even need to remove some props or even some enemies to improve performance.

During alpha, the art team may want you to replace some artwork in your level, like a texture or a prop. As we mentioned in earlier chapters, level designers sometimes use placeholder textures and props to get across the full idea for play-test sessions. Alpha is the art team's last chance to get those final pieces of art into the level.

The design team may push you to improve the balance in your level. The balance refers to making the game challenging enough for experienced players yet easy enough for beginners. Balancing the game may require you to get involved in the numbers behind the game. This means that you might need to change the amount of damage certain player weapons do to the enemies in the level or the amount of damage certain traps or enemy weapons do to the player character. You can even change the amount of health enemies have, and the amount of helpful items, such as med kits and armor, that you place in your level.

The alpha stage ranges from a few weeks to several months depending on the project and the company. Some projects, such as Blizzard Entertainment's Warcraft III, tend to take a long time to fine-tune, tweak, and balance. Getting the game to be feature complete, which is the definition of alpha, can only be half the work required to ship a quality title. So, let's start getting your level through the alpha stage by pleasing the art team first.

Replacing art

Now, I know what you're thinking: "Didn't I just spend half of the last chapter adding visual layers to bring the level up to five-star quality?" That's exactly true. But, it's also true that making quality art takes a lot of time. The art team may need time during the alpha stage to replace some of the placeholder art still contained in the game. And as I mentioned earlier, alpha is the last chance to replace this content before a "content freeze." During a content freeze, no one can change any of the content contained in the game except to fix a bug. At the end of the alpha stage, the development team will set a date for a content freeze so that they can kick off the beta stage. Beta stage is when things go into hyper-drive.

Level designers place textures and props to fill out their levels during production. The artists may have provided these textures and props with specific areas in mind only to find that the level designers have used them throughout a level. For example, let's say that a level contains an area with power generators and an area with furnaces. An artist may provide a prop for the generator first. You may take the generator prop and use it as both a generator and a furnace. This fills the furnace area for gameplay reasons, but now the landmark of the "generator room" may refer to two different places. Also, the level might not make sense as a functional setting. The artists, who are tied up creating other art assets during production, may not get to create a furnace prop until during alpha.

Optimizing your level

The experience that a player has while playing a game greatly depends on the game's performance. The game's performance is how well the game runs, which is often measured in frames per second, or fps (which is, unfortunately the same abbreviation for first-person shooter). The ideal fps for a game is anything above

30. This means that 30 frames of the game are drawn every second. The human mind cannot perceive any change higher than 30 fps. Once the fps starts to drop below 30, then you may need to start thinking about optimizations.

Minimum Spec Machine

For PC game development, there are different configurations that players can have for their game system. PCs can have a different speed processor, a different amount of memory, and a different video card. During preproduction, the development team determines the minimum specifications that the game will run on when it ships. Most of the time, the minimum specifications are set once the programming team has started work on the engine. Of course, if the team is licensing an existing engine, the minimum specifications might exist from the moment the team decides which engine to use. The level design team should have a designated machine with these specifications called the "minimum spec machine." Continually playing your level on the minimum spec machine throughout production will help you keep your level within the performance boundaries set by the team.

You can optimize your level in one of several ways. Of course, some of the optimizations can alter the gameplay for an area. For example, if you have a scene where a dozen enemy zombies emerge from the ground and start to chase the player character, you could cut down the number of zombies to six. This would make the area play differently. You might be able to make up for the difficulty by giving each zombie a larger amount of health or by making each zombie faster. Still, the experience would change, and that might not be something you want.

Another way to optimize your level is to keep the gameplay the same but change the actual scene so that it runs faster. This might require you to remove any extra details in the area, such as props that are strictly decoration or wall trim and borders. However, this solution can detract from the visual quality of the game. In some game engines, like Unreal, you can "help" the game to perform better by adding special brushes to divide the level into smaller sections so that the engine can ignore other sections that the player isn't involved with at the time. This method is sometimes called *zoning*.

Zones and portals

Most game engines don't display everything contained in a level all the time. The game's performance would suffer. Instead, game engines use different methods to choose what to display and when to display it. Of course, the engine doesn't always have the best judgment of how to display sections of levels because every level is unique. Here's where you come in. As the level designer, you can help the game engine by dividing the level into smaller portions called *zones*. The game engine connects all the zones together to form the entire level and also determines what needs to be displayed based on the player character's location. Zones are connected together to form the entire level. The doorways or openings where zones meet are called *portals*. Using zones and portals gives you greater control over how a level performs.

So, how do zones work? Basically, the engine doesn't care about the contents contained in a zone that the player can't see. That means the engine doesn't display any geometry, textures, lighting information, objects, props, or actors in that zone. When the engine displays less, it performs better. Let's use our cookie factory level again to show how zones can optimize performance. **Figure 9.1** shows the outline for the ground floor of the cookie factory level.

If we don't add any portals to the level, the engine will consider it one large zone, as shown in **Figure 9.2**.

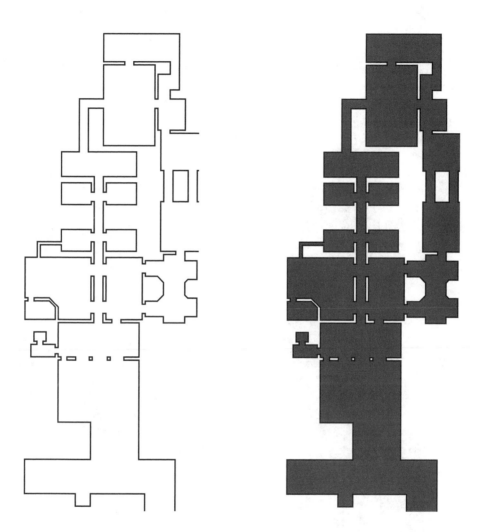

FIGURE 9.1 The outline for the ground floor of the cookie factory level.

FIGURE 9.2 The entire level is considered one zone and the engine can't disregard information about any part of the level based on the player character's location.

Adding portals to the level, we make decisions for the engine about how to divide the level into sections. **Figure 9.3** shows the placement for the portals.

When we build the level in the editor (using the Build Options dialog box), the engine creates separate zones for each of our areas, as **Figure 9.4** illustrates. The letters label each zone.

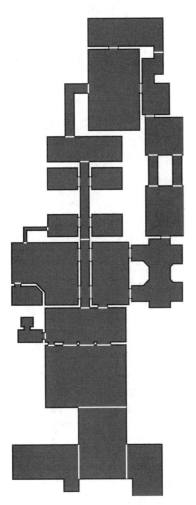

FIGURE 9.3 Different layouts call for different placements for portals. In this example, the doorways were primarily used as portals.

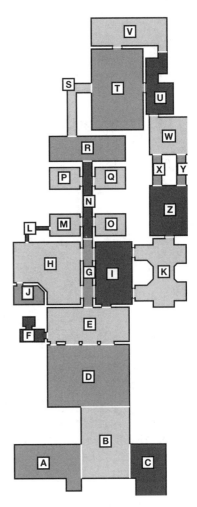

FIGURE 9.4 Any area separated from another area by a portal is considered a different zone. Each zone has been labeled a unique letter for descriptive purposes.

The engine now calculates what it should "care about" when the player character is in a specific zone. If the player can't see any part of a zone from another zone, then the engine ignores it. In our illustrations, if you can't draw a straight line from any part of one zone to any part of another zone, then that zone is ignored. For example, let's say that the player character is in Zone P. The only other zones that the engine needs to be concerned about are Zones N, O, Q, and R; the other zones in the level can be dropped temporarily. **Figure 9.5** shows the appropriate zones.

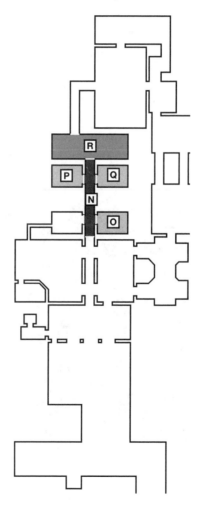

FIGURE 9.5 When the player character is in Zone P, the engine displays information only to Zones N, O, P, Q, and R. Other zones are ignored temporarily.

Unreal tutorial: zoning your level

Using UnrealEd, you can zone your level with special sheet brushes. These sheet brushes act as portals between zones. In Unreal, zones can control a number of different functions in addition to optimizing performance. You can create a zone for the player to swim in or a zone that has less gravity so characters can jump great distances. You can even create zones, such as death pits and lava pools, that cause harm to player characters if they enter them.

Typically, you can start zoning your level in the template phase. You'll continue to edit the portals to rearrange your zones as you revise your level. By alpha, you'll be testing with the zones in different configurations to see which gives your level the best performance.

We're going to take a small, simple level that hasn't been zoned yet and add portals to divide the level into zones. We're also going to place ZoneInfo actors into each zone to define them. Start UnrealEd, and open the level Tutorial07.urt. When the level loads, click on the Zone/Portal icon on the 3D view menu bar (**Figure 9.6**).

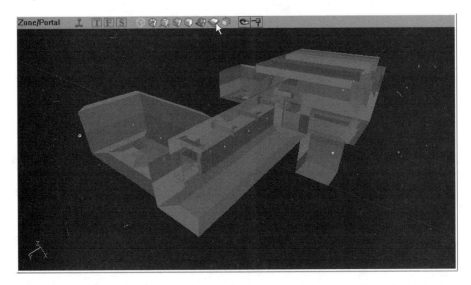

FIGURE 9.6 The Zone/Portal icon on the 3D view menu bar will switch to Zone/Portal viewing mode.

You'll see the level turn into different shades of a single color. In this case, the level should turn blue. This tells us that the level is one single zone. First, we're going to add portals between each room to divide the level into four unique zones.

1. Right-click the Sheet icon (**Figure 9.7**) on the toolbar to bring up the SheetBuilder dialog box.

FIGURE 9.7 The Sheet icon on the toolbar.

2. Enter a Height value of 256 and a Width value of 384 and click the Build button. Close the dialog box. Your active brush should become an active sheet with the dimensions you entered. A sheet is a plane, not a box.

3. In the Front view, rotate the active sheet clockwise 90 degrees. In the Top view, move the active sheet so that it covers the doorway between the hallway with the PlayerStart actor and the first room on the left (**Figure 9.8**, on the next page). Line up the active sheet so that it covers the doorway in either the Front or Side view as well.

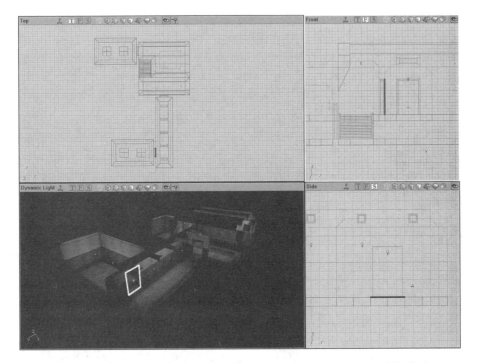

FIGURE 9.8 The active sheet should cover the doorway between the room and the hallway completely.

4. Now, click the Add Special Brush icon in the toolbar (**Figure 9.9**) to bring up the Add Special dialog box.

FIGURE 9.9 The Add Special Brush icon in the toolbar.

5. Select Zone Portal from the Prefabs drop-down menu (**Figure 9.10**). This will automatically select the right options in the dialog box to place a zone portal. Click the OK button. This will create a zone portal between the hallway and the first room on the left. Rebuild and save the map.

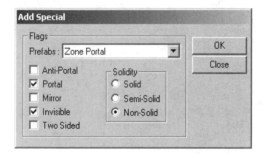

FIGURE 9.10 The Add Special Brush dialog box. Selecting a Prefab will select the right options for common special brushes.

6. In the 3D view, click the Zone/Portal icon on the 3D view menu bar and observe how the room on the left of the hallway is now a different color than the rest of the level. This means that it is a separate zone.

Let's add zone portals at all of the doorways in the level.

1. Move the active sheet to cover the doorway between the hallway and the big room with the stairs in it. You'll need to rotate it 90 degrees to cover the doorway properly.

2. Add a zone portal using the Add Special Brush procedure we went through earlier.

3. Move the same active sheet to cover the doorway between the big room with the stairs and the room to the left of the stairs in the Top view (**Figure 9.11**). Rotate it back 90 degrees to completely cover the doorway.

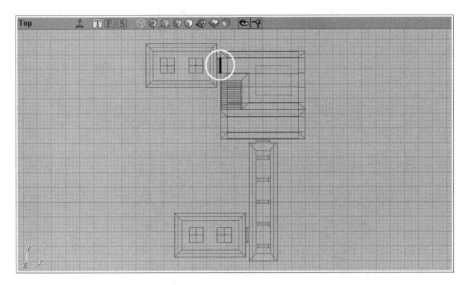

FIGURE 9.11 The placement for the active sheet in the Top view.

4. Add another zone portal to create four divisions in this level. Rebuild the map and save it.

   You should see that the level is split into four zones in the 3D view when you click the Zone/Portal icon.

   > **NOTE** You may notice that when you move around in the 3D view, you can see the zone portals but not what lies behind them. To see what the area will look like in the game engine, you can click the Realtime Preview icon on the Perspective view menu bar.

Now that the level has been sectioned, we can place ZoneInfo actors in each zone and give them different settings to see how each zone can be unique. In the following exercise, we'll create fog in the hallway. You'll be able to move your character in and out of fog by entering and exiting the hallway.

1. In the Actor browser window, expand the Actor group and then expand the Info group below it. You should see a group labeled *ZoneInfo (**Figure 9.12**).

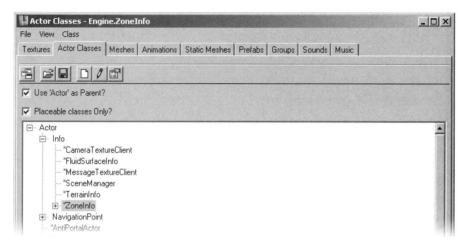

FIGURE 9.12 The ZoneInfo actor can be found in the Actor browser window.

2. Click on this group to select it.

3. Back in the 3D view, right-click on the middle of the floor in the hallway and select Add ZoneInfo Here to place a ZoneInfo actor (**Figure 9.13**).

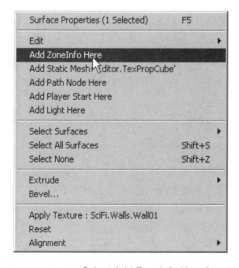

FIGURE 9.13 Select Add ZoneInfo Here from the contextual menu that appears when you right-click on a surface.

4. Double-click on the ZoneInfo actor to bring up its properties.

5. Click on the plus sign next to ZoneInfo to expand the ZoneInfo list. Click in the value box next to bDistanceFog and you should see an arrow next to the word False.

6. Click this arrow to bring up the drop-down menu and change the value to True (**Figure 9.14**). You can also double-click on the value box to automatically switch back and forth from one to the other.

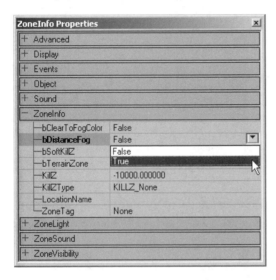

FIGURE 9.14 The value for bDistanceFog changed from False to True.

Switching the value to True in this field makes this zone have a distance fog. You'll see the result shortly.

7. Next, click on the plus sign next to ZoneLight to expand its list. Click on the plus sign next to DistanceFogColor to expand its list.

8. Let's give the distance fog, the solid color that the fog will fade to in the distance, a colder feeling by making it slightly blue. Leave the values for A (Alpha) and B (Blue) the same. Enter a value of 32 for G (Green) and R (Red).

9. Below R, you should see an entry for DistanceFogEnd. This is the distance from the player camera where the fog becomes the solid color of the distance.

10. Finally, enter a value of 1 for DistanceFogStart, which is the distance from the player camera that the fog starts to appear. This means that we'll be able to start seeing the fog right in front of the camera and it will transition gradually to the solid color of the distance fog out to 4000 units.

Figure 9.15 shows the completed properties for this ZoneInfo actor. This will blend the fog from a distance of 1 (where the fog is barely noticeable) to 4000 (where the fog will be a solid color). Rebuild and save your map. Play the level to check out the fog effects in this hallway, as shown in Figure 9.16, on the next page. You'll notice that the distance fog does not appear in the other zones in the level.

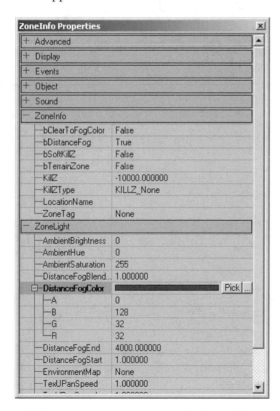

FIGURE 9.15 The completed version of the ZoneInfo properties that create a blue distance fog in a zone.

FIGURE 9.16 A screenshot of the hallway with fog. The room behind the far doorway is obscured by the fog.

In addition to visual effects, zones can affect the gameplay of your level. You can use a variety of different types of ZoneInfo actors to add water zones, death zones, and teleport zones. You've already used a type of ZoneInfo actor called the SkyZoneInfo to create a skybox in Chapter 6.

A lot of procedures in games are done best through trial and error. Optimizations are no different. You may want to continually test your level as you create new zones to check the performance.

Balancing the game

When you turn on a faucet, the water temperature is never quite what you intended, is it? When you turn the temperature knob just slightly colder, it gets way too cold, and if you turn it just slightly hotter, it gets way too hot, right? Well, video games have a similar problem. The developers want the game to be just right: not too easy for experienced players and not too difficult for beginners. Unfortunately, there is no one knob that you can turn slightly to find the right balance. Several factors contribute to the difficulty setting. For example, in Requiem: Avenging Angel, a level designer could alter the following conditions:

▶ The number of health kits

The health kit item could be picked up by the player character to give him more life points. If a level contained several health kits, it would be easier to survive. If a level contained fewer kealth kits, it would more difficult to survive.

▶ The number of ammunition items

The player character had weapons in his inventory that required ammunition. If the weapon was more powerful, we would place less ammunition in the level for the player to find. To make a level easier, you could place more ammunition, and you could even place more ammunition for the more powerful weapons. To make the level more difficult, you would place fewer ammunition items.

▶ The types of enemies

Of course, the game had design goals that required certain types of enemies to be placed in certain levels, but we left some room for tweaking. You could hold back a more effective enemy for a later level or you could introduce it in an earlier level.

▶ The number of enemies

Instead of the player character fighting 12 enemies in the area, reduce the number to 6 to make it easier. Increase the number to 15 to make it more difficult.

▶ The ways an enemy could attack

Soldiers in the game could use different weapons that we, as level designers, could assign. Giving a soldier a less powerful weapon, like a pistol or a shotgun, would make him easier to compete against. Giving him a more powerful weapon, such as an assault rifle or a laser rifle, would make him a tougher foe.

▶ The life amount of an enemy

Each enemy had properties that the level designer could change. The amount of life for an enemy meant how much damage he could take from your attacks before dying. Increasing the number made the enemy more powerful and decreasing the number would produce the opposite effect.

Almost every game has conditions that the level designer or game designer can tweak to change the difficulty of levels and areas within levels. Unfortunately, there isn't some magic equation you can use to come up with all the numbers you need to balance a game. Like optimizations, this procedure takes a lot of trial and error. The trial part can't even be done by you, the level designer, in most cases. As discussed in Chapter 7, you'll need to continue the play-testing system with fresh play-testers in order to put your balancing solutions to the real test.

Beta and Final Bug-Testing

Welcome to crunch time! The period of game development after the alpha phase has been completed is technically called beta, but a lot of game developers will say that they are "crunching." The bug list has shrunk considerably since alpha, so during beta the development team is able to fix bugs as they're found. A testing team is now dedicated to the project and is testing the game nonstop.

> **NOTE** Actually, developers often use the term "crunch" to refer to any time they are trying to meet a deadline. The deadline doesn't have to be the ship date although "crunch time" is traditionally the period between alpha and gold master. Deadlines can be a milestone such as a press demo, which will be shown to members of the press. Each phase itself, like alpha or beta, might also be a milestone that developers "crunch" for.

The QA department and the producer assign bugs to the appropriate team member. Every day, the producer, the team lead, and the lead tester start meeting to prioritize bugs. Bugs with the highest priority need to be fixed and bugs with the lowest priority are documented, but only fixed if there is time.

At the end of beta, the team doesn't care about any bug that's not a "showstopper" or an "A bug." The entire development team converts to testing, and they work with the QA department to put enough testing hours on every portion of the game. Members of the team and QA department are assigned certain sections of the game that may include a few levels. When enough hours are played throughout the game without any showstoppers, the game can be moved into the final candidate stage.

During the final candidate stage, new builds of the game are created at a rapid pace. Each build must go through a number of bug-free hours to be considered gold master, the version that is copied and distributed to the public. Bug-free, in this case, doesn't mean that no bugs exist; it means that no bugs are found in the version to require a fix before shipping.

Builds and the bug database

During the beta stage, everyone on the development team becomes both a tester and a developer. Every game needs to be as clean (bug-free) as possible, and the best way to make sure this happens is for more people to test every part of the game. Even if the company has a dedicated quality assurance group to test the game, you can never have too many hands on deck for this final push.

In this end phase, the development team puts together a version of the game, called a build, at an increasingly rapid pace. At the beginning of beta, a new build might be created every few days. At the end of beta, a new build can replace the old one in a couple of hours. A new build is created to fix bugs found in the last build. For a beta build to move on to final candidate and then to gold master, it needs to have a certain amount of bug-free hours played. Any major, or showstopper, bug found will cause a new build to be created to fix the bug. This new build will need to start the cycle over. So, for example, if there was a major bug in a level that caused the player character to become stuck, that level would need to be fixed and submitted with a new build of the game. The new build starts the process over again, and the team jumps on it and reports any defects to the bug database.

As we discussed in Chapter 1, the bug database becomes the task list for developers throughout the latter part of production (from the alpha phase on). You might have a notebook during the play-testing and revision period to list all of the tasks you need to do. Now that the tasks for revision have become less of an issue, the bugs found by the testing team take the highest priority. Bugs are constantly entered into the bug database and assigned by your producer according to importance. Developers rely on the bug database to keep track of the numerous actions they need to complete.

Different companies use different ways to track bugs. Some companies even develop their own "bug tracker" database to customize it to their projects. Typically, entries in the bug database contain as much information as possible to help developers reproduce the bug in the game and figure out how to fix it.

Developer Cheats

All games have cheat codes that allow players various advantages while playing the game. The main reason that cheat codes exist is so that developers can test the game more easily. There are cheat codes that don't let your character die, don't let enemies attack your character, and even teleport your character to different areas in a level. PC games occasionally have a "developer console" that can be brought up in the game. This is an interface which lets the user type in specific commands that alter the game in various ways. For example, you might be able to display the coordinates for where the player character is located in a level, as shown in **Figure 9.17**. This feature is especially helpful when a bug is written with the exact coordinates enclosed. You can teleport your player to this location and try to reproduce the bug to figure out why it is happening.

FIGURE 9.17 In New Legends, we could display the coordinates for the location of the player character and teleport to a specific location according to its coordinates. So, if a tester found a collision bug, where the player character got stuck or encountered an invisible barrier, a developer could find the problem efficiently.

What makes a good bug entry?

In my opinion, every developer should know how to write a bug correctly. Not only will you be writing bugs that you find, you'll also be reading bugs that other people find. After reading them, you'll need to understand the bugs and be able to come up with a solution (if you are responsible for fixing the bug). Here is a list of information that should be contained in a bug entry:

1. Severity/Priority: How severe or important is the bug?

    We discussed this category in Chapter 1 illustrating the difference between an A bug, which is the highest, to a D bug, which is the lowest. The severity of the bug should be the first thing developers see in the bug entry, so that they can skip to the most important bug entries first.

2. Location: Where in the game did the tester find the bug?

    You should describe the bug according to its location from the broadest category to the most specific. For example, some databases have drop-down menus that contain the various levels in the game. The writer may then add in text to get more specific such as "In the library…" or "On the second tightrope…" It is also extremely helpful to include a screenshot of where the bug took place or even the bug in action. There can be little confusion concerning the location with a screenshot. Most bug databases have a separate field for an attachment.

3. Frequency: How often does this bug occur?

    Some bugs happen every time the player performs a certain action or sequence of actions. Other bugs happen less frequently. It's important to note whether the bug happens once, twice, frequently, or occasionally. If the bug happens consistently, then the frequency might have a unique term used by the company. When I worked for Sega, the term "Binary" meant that the bug happened consistently.

4. Description: What is the step-by-step process to reproduce the bug?

    Developers need to know exactly how to re-create or reproduce a bug. Once they have those specifics, they can run the game with a debugger like Microsoft Developer Studio and find the offending code. When a developer reproduces a bug while debugging, the bug can be fixed faster. Programmers can step through the code line by line to find the location of the problem.

Descriptions tell the developers what the player did and in what sequence. For example, a good bug description might read, "If the player character activates the button in the elevator, exits the elevator, waits until the elevator rises, and runs under the elevator, the game freezes."

5. Owner: Who is the best team member to fix this bug?

    The owner is usually the team member who has been responsible for the portion of the game most directly related to the bug. In some cases, level designers are considered the owner of a bug that occurs in their level. In some cases, the bug is more related to the programming or even the art. Most of the time, the lead tester, the producer, or the team lead will know best who to assign a bug to and, therefore, a lot of bugs get initially assigned to one of them.

After alpha, each member of the development team goes "on-call"—like a doctor monitoring several patients. Any time a bug is found that requires your attention, it is added to the bug database, which gets checked by your producer, your lead, and members of the team constantly. If you don't check the database in time, someone else will. They may let you know about the bug in person, through email, or by phone (if you can't be found in person). The fix needs to take place as soon as possible for a new build to be created and tested. This cycle continues over and over until the game is bug-free for its designated period.

The Finish Line—Almost

You now deserve a much-needed rest. Completing a level or a group of levels and shipping a game is a huge accomplishment. You, and your whole team, should be very proud (and tired!). Most team members take this time to go on vacation and spend time outside of work. Some team members take this time to look for another job. An unfortunate side effect of the video game industry is that developers frequently move on to other companies after a product ships. In some cases, the company realizes that they don't need the whole team anymore, or they may not need everyone until the next project goes into production. Team members can also become frustrated working on a project and look for greener pastures. In any case, after shipping a game, there's an opportune time to archive the work that you've done on a title and keep it for personal reasons.

Archiving data also serves another purpose. Some titles get *ported*, which means they are developed for different platforms or game systems. Porting a game typically means that the same content, including the levels, is used but the game might need to be reengineered to work with different hardware. So, you may need your level files if you are asked to work on the port.

The development team might get together one last time as a whole and evaluate the methods used to create the product. This evaluation is called the *postmortem*. The team can change a lot for the next project. Some members will leave, some will be moved to other roles, and some will be new. The postmortem can help remind the team of the lessons learned from the previous project.

Archiving data

When I went to high school, a bunch of my friends would gather all of their notes they'd taken throughout the semester and burn them after the final exam. In college, a lot of students, including myself, would sell our books back to the bookstore for some cash when the course was over. After your game has shipped, you probably won't want to delete your files that you used to create your levels. You may need them in the future.

A lot of game titles these days get ported to different platforms. They may start on the PC and get ported to a console, or vice versa. They might even be ported from one console to another. Ports of games tend to use the same content as the original, but some of the content needs to be tweaked for technical reasons. For levels, this usually entails optimizations for performance and for technical limitations. Some platforms don't have the capacity to load a large level. Levels may need to be cut down or split up.

The downside of the game industry is the turnover rate. Developers frequently change teams, change companies, or even leave the industry altogether. Of course, new developers are constantly entering the job market as well. Archiving the data created during development helps to promote yourself as a level designer to those who don't know about you. The assignment at the end of Chapter 5 can be coupled with screenshots that you take from your level when it's done and sent to companies looking for good people. You can also include descriptions of revisions that you made to the level during the process that will show how well you can adapt as a designer and how well you handle criticism and feedback. If the level you are creating is from a common game, such as one from the Unreal, Quake, or Half-Life series, you can even submit the level itself for developers to play through firsthand.

Becoming a photographer

One way to document the work that you've done is through screenshots. Most PC games allow you to take screenshots from within the game program. Find out the key or command to take a screenshot so you can take some of your level. In Unreal, the F9 key is used to take a screenshot and save it in your Unreal\System directory.

The level diagram, paired with screenshots taken of each area, tell developers the story of your design process. These elements demonstrate your methods for designing and your ability to execute a design into a complete product. Your goal in presenting these pieces is to spark the interest of a company that is hiring. Unfortunately, level design is a popular position and companies receive a lot of materials every day. The people in charge of hiring might not get to thoroughly inspect every candidate's work. Therefore, the diagram and the screenshots should work well both individually and collaboratively so that they can catch the eye of prospective employers and still demonstrate your design abilities. Here is a checklist for taking highly visual and informative screenshots:

▶ Use actual game camera angles.

   You might be tempted to take screenshots of your level using cheat codes to fly around to different viewpoints that you would never ordinarily witness while playing the game. While these screenshots might be visually appealing, they don't represent the actual game camera and they may not show the attention you have paid to the game camera while designing your level. Of course, if you are strictly trying to demonstrate your building skills, these screenshots are acceptable.

▶ Capture actual gameplay.

   Whether the screenshot shows the player character in battle with enemies or jumping over a gorge, it should display actual gameplay contained in the level. Is there ever really a moment when you can get face to face with an enemy and take a picture of him standing in his idle pose? If there is a moment like that, then go ahead and document it, but it might seem a little odd.

▶ Capture unique and interesting areas.

If you have a hallway in your level that looks like hallways in other games, don't take a screenshot of it. Again, your goal is to stand out. Concentrate on the areas in your level that only you have thought to build.

▶ Capture various areas.

As we've discussed throughout this book, people like variety. Your level should contain a variety of different kinds of spaces. Take screenshots to illustrate that point and let your audience know that you're flexible.

▶ Discard less-than-stellar screenshots.

Just as editing can be more important than filming in the movie industry, editing out bad to average screenshots will greatly increase your chances of getting noticed. All it takes is one bad screenshot for a development team to get a negative impression of you.

▶ Include editor screenshots.

Sometimes, developers want to see your construction process. It might help to take screenshots of the level in the editor to show how the level is organized.

The postmortem: learning from mistakes

No development project is perfect. Even if you think that a game itself is the greatest creation of all time, I can pretty much guarantee that the process for developing that game had its fair share of problems. A way to analyze the life of a project is through a postmortem. The postmortem, which is usually a document created by one or two team members after the project has ended, is a good opportunity for the team to learn from its successes and shortcomings. The writer or writers of the postmortem can meet with the team (both individually and in a group) to understand everything that went on during development. Occasionally, a postmortem is released to the public, via a game developer publication or through an Internet site, to help other developers share insights.

You are your own worst critic. It's a common phrase, but it's also very true. Creating your own postmortem to analyze your process is just as important as a team postmortem. A "personal" postmortem allows you to reflect on the areas you need to improve. Developers will also appreciate your commitment to correcting your shortcomings. Here is a checklist of what any postmortem should include:

▶ The good news: What went right during the project?

There are surely parts of the development that went smoothly. It's important to find those parts and figure out why they were so successful. In your level design process, think about the steps you took to create your level. What steps did you make efficiently and successfully? To gauge efficiency, estimate if any task took a relatively short amount of time and if any tasks were successful on the first attempt. To gauge success, ask yourself if you had fun during any step. Having fun often means that you were succeeding with the task. This is about video games, after all.

▶ The bad news: What went wrong during the project?

Even if the entire development process went smoothly, there are undoubtedly a few aspects that could have been better. What part of the process was particularly inefficient? Did any process take too long to complete? In your level design process, what step did you find to be the least fun? Was there any task that you had to repeat so many times that you settled for something less than satisfactory?

▶ Action items: What can we do to make the process better?

This is the most important step. How can you get better at a stage of the process so that you become more efficient or more successful? For example, you can pick a different setting for a level in the game you defined in Chapter 2, but keep the skills and obstacles from Chapter 3 so that you can practice the brainstorming process from Chapter 4.

This last assignment will put you in a category that isn't easy to get into. Anyone can start designing a level. Anyone can start constructing a level. It takes real dedication and determination to complete a level that you're truly proud of.

Assignment 9

Your final assignment is the culmination of all of your efforts so far:

Part 1—Balance your level for difficulty.

Part 2—Optimize your level for maximum performance.

Part 3—"Ship" your level. Ask your friends to play test your level, and document any bugs that come up. Go through the same "build-and-fix" process that a professional level designer would. Imagine that this level is going to be played by many people, including developers who are looking for level designers.

Part 4—Put together a presentation for the level. Take screenshots of your level to accompany your level diagram. Include your level description and a description of the revisions you made to your level after receiving feedback. Also, write a brief postmortem document explaining the lessons you learned while designing and building your level.

Epilogue

Level Exit

The game development process is quite intense and demanding. As you've seen over the last nine chapters, every aspect of the game requires a lot of thought, as well as a lot of work. However, developing games is also incredibly rewarding. You can take great pride in the product you've contributed to.

Not every project ships. Projects can get canceled or "shelved," which means they are put away for an indefinite period. Even in these cases, you'll learn much throughout the process that you might not have learned in any other way.

You might work with a combination of modeling and editing tools that you never used before, or you might work with a team member who approaches design problems in an unusual way. So, I wouldn't consider an unfinished project to be a complete waste of time. Quite the contrary: it's a learning experience, and it happens to most of us in the game industry.

Level design is just one part of game development. As you have seen in this book, it takes several people working together to carry a game from an idea in someone's head to a box on a store shelf. A ton of information about game development is out there waiting for you. You can find several sites online dedicated to game development in general as well as to specific titles and franchises. Books are available that tackle game development from the perspective of every position on the team. Coupled with what you've learned in this book, you will be armed with more knowledge than most aspiring game developers, which will give you an edge. As for tools, many level editors are available for free to download. However, you may need to purchase the title that the editor refers to in order to test your levels. For example, Radiant allows you to create levels for the Quake series of titles from Id Software. Online tutorials teach you how to use the editors, and some companies, like Epic Games and Valve Software, offer sites of their own that developers can turn to for guidance.

In this book, I've taken you through the design and creation process for a single level, from beginning to end, emulating what the process would be like if you were on an actual development team. Although I've tried to stay as true as possible to a real-world setting, your experiences in the game industry may vary from what I've described. For starters, you would probably receive more day-to-day direction from fellow team members, such as the other level designers, the lead designer, and the team lead. You would probably also have the support of other team members: artists who could create custom models and textures for you, and programmers who could create custom tools and functionality in the game and editor.

Of course, the biggest difference between what you've experienced in this book and what transpires on an actual team is the deadlines. Most projects have ship dates and dates set for alpha and beta. You may be forced to cut out parts of your level just to adhere to the schedule.

In addition, some companies don't follow the process as I've described. For example, at Blizzard we never had a design document, and at Valve we have no distinction between preproduction and production. However, I feel that these are exceptions to the rule, and most game developers are not as free-form as Blizzard and Valve. In many ways, this book is an accumulation of the process that I have learned in all of the companies I have worked for, not one in particular.

I hope you have enjoyed reading this book as much as I have enjoyed writing it, and I look forward to playing your levels in the future.

Index